TOWN AND CITY H.

Belfast

TOWN AND CITY HISTORIES

Titles in print or forthcoming include

Bath by Graham Davis and Penny Bonsall
Blackburn by Derek Beattie
Blackpool by John Walton
Bradford by David James
Halifax by John Hargreaves
Manchester by Alan Kidd
Nelson by Jeffrey Hill
Stoke-on-Trent by John Briggs

Titles of related interest from Ryburn include

A History of Lancaster 1193–1993
Edited by Andrew White

Managing Divided Cities
Edited by Seamus Dunn

TOWN AND CITY HISTORIES
HISTORICAL EDITOR: STEPHEN CONSTANTINE

BELFAST

W. A. Maguire

Ryburn Publishing
KEELE UNIVERSITY PRESS

First published in 1993
by Ryburn Publishing
an imprint of
Keele University Press
Keele, Staffordshire

Text © W. A. Maguire
Composed and originated by
Ryburn Publishing Services
Printed in Bodmin by Hartnolls
for Ryburn Book Production
Keele University, England

Town and City Histories
ISSN 0952-6153

Belfast
Paperback ISBN 1-85331-060-3
Limited edition of 200 copies in cloth
ISBN 1-85331-071-9

Contents

To the memory of

Reginald and Sarah Maguire

Historical Editor's Foreword

The books in this series are designed and written with a broad readership in mind: local people interested to know how the character of their town has been shaped by major historical forces and the energies of their predecessors; newcomers and visitors curious to acquire a historical introduction to their new surroundings; general readers wishing to see how the sweeps of national and international history have manifested themselves in particular urban communities; and the scholar seeking to understand urbanisation by comparing and contrasting local experiences.

We live, most of us, in intensely urban environments. These are the products largely of the last two centuries of historical development, although the roots of many towns, of course, go back deep into the past. In recent years there has been considerable historical research of a high standard into this urban history. Narrative and descriptive accounts of the history of towns and cities can now be replaced by studies such as the TOWN AND CITY HISTORIES which investigate, analyse and, above all, explain the economic, political, social and cultural processes and consequences of urbanisation.

Writers for this series consider the changing economic foundations of their town or city and the way change has affected its physical shape, built environment, employment opportunities and urban character. The nature and interests of those who wielded power locally and the structure and functions of local government in different periods are also examined, since locally exercised authority could determine much about the fortunes and quality of urban life. Particular emphasis is placed on the changing life experiences of ordinary men, women and children – their homes, education, occupations, social relations, living standards and leisure activities. Towns and cities control and respond to the values, aspirations and actions of their residents. The books in this series therefore explore social behaviour as well as the economic and political history of those who lived in and helped make the towns and cities of today.

Stephen Constantine
University of Lancaster

Location of Belfast (1)

Preface and Acknowledgements

The history of Belfast during the past two hundred years is something of a paradox. On the one hand, in economic matters the city developed rapidly by being as modern and progressive as any other of the great industrial centres in the United Kingdom (and unlike anywhere else in Ireland). Belfast had much the same urban social problems too, and its municipal government expanded in a similar way to tackle them. On the other hand, it developed patterns of community division and conflict, based upon religion, which in their severity and permanence have rendered it unique among the cities of the British Isles. Any history of the place must acknowledge the one and try to account for the other. I hope that in trying to explain matters to myself I may also have produced a coherent explanation for those who read this book.

* * * * * * *

I am grateful for the help I have received from a number of people. They include David Johnson and the Rev. Dr Ambrose Macaulay, both of whom generously let me have copies of unpublished papers and permission to make use of them; Edwin Finlay (for statistics on the port and harbour); Sir Peter Froggatt (for help in pursuing lunatics); Professor David Harkness (for assistance with sources); the Librarians of the Linen Hall Library and the Queen's University Library and their staff; and my wife Joan (for much practical assistance). I owe a particular debt to Dr G. J. Slater, for the generous loan of his as yet unpublished thesis, to the usefulness of which the footnotes for Chapter 2 bear ample witness. Dr W. H. Crawford obliged me greatly by reading the entire text with the eye of a benign eagle. Most of the illustrations come from the collections of the Ulster Museum and are used by kind permission of the Trustees; for the remainder I have to thank the *Belfast Telegraph*, the Northern Ireland Housing Executive, Queen's University and Short Brothers plc. The Belfast Natural History and Philosophical Society has generously made a grant towards the cost of illustrations. Sir Charles Brett kindly gave leave to adapt the map of Belfast in 1985 from his book *Housing a Divided Community*; I am indebted to Deirdre Crone for drawing both maps. Lastly, I have to say that any virtue the book may have owes much to the scrutiny of the editor of the series, Dr Stephen Constantine, whose comments and suggestions were invariably helpful and to the point. Any remaining shortcomings are my own.

W. A. Maguire

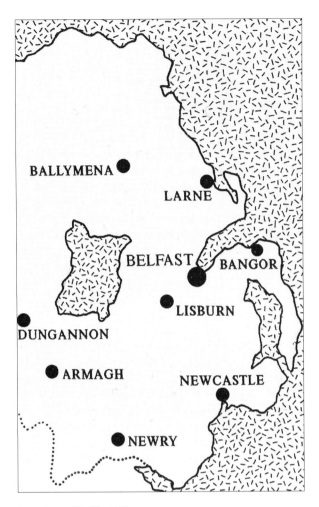

Location of Belfast (2)

10

Chapter 1

Plantation Town, 1603–1800

Belfast was a comparative latecomer among the great Victorian cities. It became a major manufacturing centre and international port only in the later nineteenth century, and officially a city only in 1888. This book is mainly about Belfast during the last two hundred years – its growth from small town into large city, its heyday and its later decline. Its history as a place of some importance in the north of Ireland, however, goes back a good deal farther than 1800.

Site and First Settlement

Belfast lies at the mouth of the River Lagan where it flows into Belfast Lough, overlooked from the County Antrim side by steep hills which form an escarpment in the Cave Hill (the dominant feature in most views) and from the eastern, County Down, side by the gentler Holywood and Castlereagh hills. Between them lay a flat alluvial site where the meandering Lagan flowed out into extensive tidal mudflats or sloblands.[1] From early times this low-lying and swampy place was strategically important because it controlled a ford where the river could be crossed at low tide; the name Belfast, indeed, in Irish Béal Feirste, means 'the approach to the sandbank' which led to the crossing place.[2]

The first settlers of a permanent kind (some earlier mesolithic hunters have left traces of their camps along the river bank) were neolithic farmers who with their stone tools cleared some of the forest, cultivated the slopes of the valley above the marshy bottom and built the great earthwork enclosure to the south known as the Giant's Ring. Weapons used by the Bronze Age settlers who followed them have been found near the Cave Hill, and a few of the 'raths' or earthen ring forts of later, Iron Age farmers still survive on the rising ground on the outskirts of the modern city. The early presence of Christianity in the area, perhaps as early as the seventh century, is indicated by the original attachment of St Columkille's name to the old graveyard at Knock. There was also an ecclesiastical settlement at Shankill ('the old church'), the name by which the parish of Belfast was formerly known; some fragments of a ninth-century bronze crozier have been found nearby. Though none of these people saw the site by the ford as a suitable place on which to build their dwellings, they fought to control it; for example, the annals record a battle there in the year 668.

The first builders were the Anglo-Normans, who arrived in Ulster in the 1170s and erected a castle at the ford sometime in the late twelfth century to safeguard communications with their great stronghold at Carrickfergus, a few miles along the coast to the north. The Ford (as the English called it) with its castle, chapel and cluster of small houses could be regarded as the aboriginal Belfast, though the settlement subsequently declined rather than developed as English power in Ulster shrank in the fourteenth century. The castle then passed into the hands of a branch of the O'Neills, whose Gaelic kingdom of Clandeboye, stretching from Lough Neagh in the west to Strangford Lough in the east, was linked by the ford at the sandbank. The sway of the O'Neills was not unchallenged, however: there are a number of references in the Irish annals to the capture and demolition of the castle. One such entry, dated 1476, is the first to name the place Béal Feirste or Belfast.[3]

Plantation

A hundred years later, in the reign of Queen Elizabeth I, Ulster was still the most Gaelic, least known and least developed part of Ireland. True, an English garrison always held the castle and walled town of Carrickfergus, but most of Antrim and Down, as well as central and western Ulster, was under the control of Irish chiefs, and Brian MacPhelim O'Neill ruled Clandeboye. As English interest in establishing settlements or 'plantations' in Ulster began to grow, the Belfast area with its oak woods and undeveloped land became increasingly attractive to 'adventurers' – private citizens such as the courtier Sir Thomas Smith, who in 1571 was granted lands in Clandeboye by Elizabeth. O'Neill easily thwarted this adventurer's hopes, however, which ended for good in 1573, when Smith's son was killed by some of his own followers.[4] In the same year, however, Walter Devereux, first earl of Essex (1541–76), was given a much larger grant, which included 'the river of Belfast'. Essex soon arrived with a formidable force and defeated O'Neill's men when they tried to hold the ford. He planned to establish an English-style settlement at Belfast, a place he described as 'meet for a corporate town, armed with all commodities [such] as a principal haven, wood and good ground', and to construct a bridge across the Lagan. Despite removing O'Neill by treachery (he and his family were seized after a banquet, then sent to Dublin to be executed), Essex was driven out. When he died in Dublin in 1576 his plans for a town at Belfast died with him, though the castle there remained in English hands.[5]

The downfall of the Gaelic chiefs in Ulster came at the end of Elizabeth's reign, when Hugh O'Neill, earl of Tyrone (c. 1540–1616) and his allies were defeated in a war that lasted on and off for nine years. Thereafter their lands, which 'before these last wars, like the kingdom of China, were inaccessible to strangers', were laid open to exploitation. The author of those words was Arthur Chichester (1563–1625), one of the most successful of the many landless younger sons of West Country families (he himself came from Devon) who sought their fortunes in Ireland. As a soldier and governor of Carrickfergus, Chichester played a prominent part in the defeat of O'Neill, and an even more prominent part afterwards in the division of the spoils. In 1603 he was given a large grant of land in south Antrim, including the castle of Belfast, by then a ruin. In 1605 King James I appointed him lord deputy (chief governor) of Ireland, and he was subsequently one of the main organisers – and the greatest individual beneficiary – of the Plantation of Ulster which followed the flight of O'Neill and his friends in 1607.

Arthur Chichester, Baron Chichester of Belfast (1563–1625): the effigy on his tomb in St Nicholas's Church, Carrickfergus.
Ulster Museum

Chichester was an enthusiastic coloniser, declaring he 'had rather labour with my hands in the plantation of Ulster than dance or play in that of Virginia'. He soon set about rebuilding the castle at Belfast and attracting Protestant settlers to the town he established beside it. In 1611 the plantation commissioners reported: 'The Towne of Belfast is plotted out in a good forme, wherein are many fameleys of English, Scotish, and some Manksmen already inhabitinge, of which some are artificers who have buylte good tymber houses with chimneys …'.[7] There was also a good inn. Two years later in 1613 the little town was made into a corporate borough by royal charter and its founder was created Baron Chichester of Belfast. For the next two centuries or so the fortunes of the town were to be closely bound up with those of the Chichester family, earls (from 1647) and marquesses (from 1791) of Donegall.

In addition to the usual powers of landownership, the Chichesters were given a controlling position as lords of the castle. Under the terms of its charter the town was administered by a corporation made up of the lord of the castle, his deputy the constable, a sovereign (mayor) elected each year at the Feast of the Nativity of St John the Baptist (24 June), and twelve free burgesses appointed for life.[8] Any vacancies that occurred were filled by the sovereign and remaining burgesses; the corporation alone elected the two members who represented Belfast in the Irish parliament. Under this system the power of the Chichesters was supreme. Each year the lord of the castle made the short list of three from which the sovereign was chosen; and no statutes or by-laws could be made without his advice and consent. In practice, therefore, the corporation came to consist largely of the friends and supporters of the Chichester family, and the MPs elected were always its members or nominees. So Belfast became, and for well over two hundred years remained, the closest of close boroughs and under the control of a single family.[9]

Seventeenth-Century Town

The early town lay entirely on the County Antrim bank of the Lagan. Its main street developed on either side of the little river Farset, which flowed into the Lagan just below the ford. High Street still follows the course of the Farset, which was crossed by several small bridges in the seventeenth century but was later covered over and now flows under the roadway; the last part of its length was the site of the first quay. Unlike the much older town of Carrickfergus, Belfast never had stone walls, but an earth rampart was built in the early 1640s to protect this largely English settlement against the Irish, who nearly captured it in a surprise attack in 1641. During the disturbed years of the Civil War that followed, the town was occupied in turn by the troops of English royalists and their local supporters (who included the Chichester family), an army of Scots under

Monro and English parliamentarians under Monck. Fortunately for the inhabitants these changes were effected without bloodshed. If anything the town prospered by the increased business the soldiers brought. The draconian peace established in Ireland by Cromwell encouraged an expansion of civilian commerce. By the end of the 1650s Belfast's trade far outstripped that of Carrickfergus and included some direct commerce with the continent as well as cross-channel trade with England and Scotland. This economic activity attracted new settlers with capital, such as George Macartney who came from Scotland in the 1640s. In the 1660s he was exporting large quantities of fish, hides and butter to France and importing wine and sugar (he started a sugar refinery in 1666).

Though still a small place even by seventeenth-century standards, Belfast in the 1660s was already on the way to becoming one of the principal ports of Ireland. Much of its trade was carried in English ships, but some of its merchants were also shipowners, and over a dozen of their small vessels had been built at Belfast. Trade expanded greatly during the next twenty years: by 1682 the number of locally-owned ships had risen to sixty-seven. Small quantities of manufactured goods were exported – some linen yarn, linen and woollen cloth, hats, stockings, shoes – but the town was then and for long after remained primarily a trading centre rather than a place of manufacture. Most of its exports were cattle products (beef, butter, hides, tallow) and corn; the largest single customer was France. Imports included coal and cloth from Great Britain (large quantities of linen cloth came from Scotland); wine, brandy, canvas, paper and playing cards from France; wine and fruit from Spain; spices from the Netherlands; timber from the Baltic, and extraordinarily large amounts of tobacco from the American colonies.[10] Of course, these products were not consumed by the inhabitants of Belfast alone; the port served a well-populated hinterland, from which it drew its agricultural exports. In the 1680s communications between the two were greatly improved by the building of a bridge across the Lagan, at the site of the ford. This Long Bridge of twenty-one arches was paid for jointly by the counties of Down and Antrim, since it lay beyond the town boundary.

The old corporation of Belfast seems to have contributed little to the town's development. The Town Book, which is the meagre record of its activities, refers to the election of sovereigns, the replacement of burgesses, the making of by-laws to prohibit or control public nuisances and so on. But the corporation never had enough money to maintain a permanent town hall (from 1663 it rented a building from the then sovereign, George Macartney, at £5 a year); and the lack of any corporate property or common purse meant that even trifling sums had to be raised by assessments on the grudging inhabitants. In 1671 it tried, without success, to increase its powers by having the charter amended. Apart from administering whatever small sums were bequeathed for charity (a total capital amount of £320 by 1690), the provision of a water supply in 1678 was its biggest

15

venture, at a cost of £250. Even here nothing would have been done without private initiative: it was the ubiquitous Macartney, sovereign once again, who proposed to bring the water in wooden pipes from his mill-dam and who subsequently supervised the work and paid the bills (he had to wait some years to be repaid).

However, the Chichester family became increasingly conspicuous during the course of the century. Arthur Chichester, the town's founder, had seldom lived in the castle, preferring Joymount, his great mansion at Carrickfergus; and he was buried at Carrickfergus in 1625. Since he had no surviving children, all his property went to his brother Edward (c. 1568–1648), who was created Viscount Chichester. Edward's son Arthur (1606–75), who was made earl of Donegall in his father's lifetime for his services to the cause of King Charles I, lived after the Restoration mainly in Belfast, where he enlarged the castle and laid out 'dainty orchards, gardens and walks planted' which were admired by King William III when he stayed at the castle in 1690 on his way to the battle of the Boyne. The first earl was succeeded in 1675 by a nephew who held the title for only three years before being followed in turn by his son in 1678. The third earl (1666–1706) is credited with making the first reclamation works along the Lagan. They can be seen on a map of 1685 which marks a 'sea banke', a 'New Cutt River' and 'improvements made out upon the strand'. Incidentally the purpose of the map, which was drawn by a military engineer, was to survey the defences of the town and outline proposed fortifications (never built).

During the reign of James II the charter was revoked, as were many in Great Britain, and replaced by one under which approximately equal numbers of Protestants and Catholics were appointed to the hitherto exclusively Protestant corporation. Most if not all of the Protestant appointees were Presbyterians, as was the new sovereign, Thomas Pottinger, a wealthy merchant. Pottinger and the rest were at least residents, but there were few local Catholics of any kind and none of any substance in the plantation town. When William of Orange took over the English throne in 1689, many northern Protestants, including Lord Donegall and the Presbyterian minister in Belfast, sent to assure him of their support against King James II. For this, Donegall was attainted and his property declared forfeit by James's Irish parliament, and a Jacobite garrison occupied Belfast. These troops withdrew in the summer of 1689, however, when the Williamite general Schomberg landed nearby with a large army, for the crumbling ramparts were in no state to withstand a siege. Schomberg at once restored the former charter and corporation. Donegall went on to become a general in the British army, dying in 1706 in Spain. His widow and children continued living in Belfast until 1708, when the Castle was completely destroyed in an accidental fire in which three of the children perished. When attempts to obtain government assistance with rebuilding failed, Lady Donegall and her remaining family went off to live in England, where they and their descendants were to remain for almost a century.[11]

As the presence of a number of substantial Presbyterian merchants in James II's remodelled corporation indicates, the religious structure of Belfast changed in the course of the seventeenth century. Though it had started as an English and episcopalian settlement, it later acquired a substantial Scottish and therefore largely Presbyterian element, which was excluded by the charter from participation in the corporation. Before 1691 burgesses were required to take the oath of supremacy, which was obnoxious to Presbyterians. However, this was no longer required after William's victory. In consequence, Presbyterians soon outnumbered Churchmen on the corporation and for the next ten years or so dominated the public life of the town. Their meeting house in Rosemary Lane was so well attended that a second congregation was formed in 1708. Catholics, on the other hand, who became the chief target of discriminatory legislation in the country as a whole, were almost invisible in Belfast. In 1708, when a Jacobite invasion of Ireland was feared, the sovereign was ordered by the authorities in Dublin to make a return of all the Catholics in the town. His reply was: 'We have not amongst us within the town above seven Papists, and by the return made by the High Constable there is not above 150 Papists in the whole Barony'.[12] It is no wonder that the Church of Ireland in the north feared the numerous and well-organised Presbyterians much more than the Catholics. With the accession of Queen Anne in 1702 the dominant High Church party launched an attack on the Presbyterians, applying to them as well as to Catholics the religious test which required all holders of civil and military positions to receive the sacrament according to the usage of the Church of Ireland. The Presbyterian sovereign of Belfast resigned, along with one of the town's MPs. The new sovereign then removed from office all who refused the test and replaced them by Churchmen. The Presbyterian minister was even denounced by the vicar as a Jacobite and had to flee to Scotland for a time. There was bitter pamphlet warfare between the two sides.[13] The accession of George I in 1714, which brought the Whigs to power, eased the plight of the Presbyterians somewhat, but the test remained on the statute book until 1780. Throughout the eighteenth century the religious divide in Belfast was between Episcopalians and Dissenters, rather than between Protestants and Catholics.

The Donegalls and Eighteenth-Century Development

The first part of the eighteenth century was a time of difficulty for the Chichester family and in some respects for the citizens of Belfast also. The third Lord Donegall was succeeded in 1706 by a son aged eleven, the fourth earl (1695–1757), whose affairs were administered by trustees. The absence of a strong hand encouraged the corporation to challenge the lord of the castle for once, over the right to levy and collect tolls from shipping

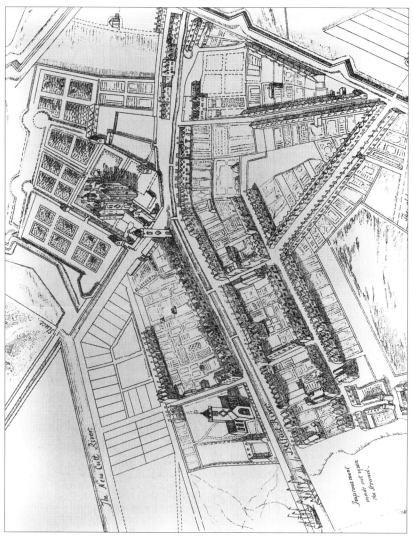

Plan of Belfast, c.1685, after the map of the fortifications by Thomas Phillips (detail). Note the 'Belfast River' (the Farset) flowing down the middle of High Street into the Lagan, which it joined just below the ford; the Castle in its walled gardens; the tower of the Market House nearby; and the Church – all within the rampart built in 1641 (the 'old works'). *Ulster Museum*

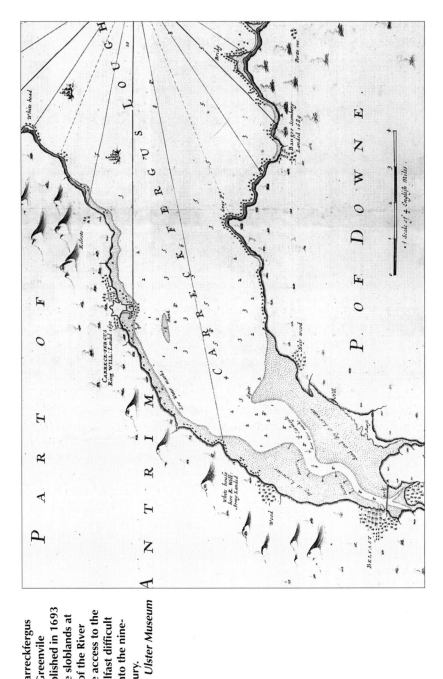

Chart of 'Carreckfergus Lough' by Greenvile Collins, published in 1693 (detail). The sloblands at the mouth of the River Lagan made access to the quays at Belfast difficult until well into the nineteenth century.

Ulster Museum

19

to keep the quay in repair and the channel clear. In 1709 the corporation promoted a parliamentary bill to further its interest in the matter. The Donegall trustees' response was to suggest that the corporation should draw up a short list of three from which the lord of the castle would select a collector of 'keyage'. The corporation's reply reveals the tensions which existed but did not often find expression in the official records: 'The naming of three to be collectors will be like the naming of three to be Sovereign. The Lord of the Castle puts a mark upon the one he would have chosen Sovereign and whoever votes for any other is ill-looked upon by the Castle. This we have found by experience'. Furthermore, it went on to say, 'The cause of the present misunderstanding between the Castle and the Town is because the Town would not consent to give up the entire manage-ment of the Corporation in making burgesses, choosing a Sovereign and electing such persons to parliament as were recommended to them by the Castle'.[14] The trustees managed to have the bill withdrawn. Private enter-prise in the shape of a leading merchant, Isaac Macartney, later provided two new quays and persuaded the revenue authorities to move the Custom House to the same quarter.

The coming of age of the fourth earl did not improve matters. Unfor-tunately he was a simpleton, incapable of running his own affairs and potentially a prey to any swindler who could get his confidence.[15] His mother, the dowager countess, married him off to an amenable girl, ensuring in the marriage settlement that her son was deprived of power to sell any property or to grant long leases. The Donegalls lived with her in England for some years before setting up there on their own, but when his wife died in 1732 Donegall returned to live with his mother until her death in 1743. Thereafter he lodged with his brother and finally, when the brother too died, with a trustee. Attempts by his loving relatives to have him declared a lunatic failed (at one hearing the lord chancellor apparently refused the application on the grounds that the examinee could answer some simple questions in arithmetic), but the property was taken over by trustees amid much family squabbling. Donegall died at last in 1757.

The effect of the fourth earl's incapacity was serious for the Donegall estate in general but particularly for Belfast. No other Irish town of similar importance was owned and controlled by a single landowner. Its popu-lation and trade grew, albeit slowly, during the early eighteenth century despite the lack of leadership from the castle; a market in brown linen developed from 1720, foreign trade grew in volume, the first bank was established in the 1750s. As time went on, however, the citizens became increasingly reluctant to invest capital in building or repairing without the security of long leases. By 1752 Donegall's kinsman Lord Massereene was claiming that Belfast was 'in a ruinous condition' and would 'lose both its Trade and Inhabitants if it is not speedily supported by proper tenures'. Merchants indeed threatened to settle in Newry or Lisburn if they could not get favourable leases. It was stated that as most of the existing leases were near expiring the houses had been allowed to go out of repair and were 'so very old, ruinous, and unfit for habitation that it is become necessary for the Preservation and Support of the Trade of the Town and for preventing the Inhabitants from quitting and deserting the same, that the said Houses should be rebuilt'.[16] Such was the state of affairs in 1757 when the fifth earl (1739–99), a youth of seventeen, succeeded his unfortunate uncle as owner of Belfast, at that date a town of 8,500 people.

Like his uncle, the new owner was an absentee. Indeed he was a spectacular absentee, who deliberately built a splendid house in Staffordshire rather than live on his Irish estates. As the most prominent of the species of absentee Irish proprietors, he got a very bad press and was publicly accused of 'draining a manufacturing country of £36,000 a year' in order to 'build palaces in another land'. Unlike the fourth earl, however, he was an active, intelligent and cultivated man who was determined to exploit the potential of his inheritance to the full and to make Belfast a fitting reflection of his own wealth and status. In sheer size, in fact, his estates were the greatest in Ireland, amounting to not less than a quarter of a million acres and yielding (after he had raised the rents) an income of £30,000 a year. His first marriage, to the daughter of a duke, reflected his social standing and ambitions. After he came of age in 1761 he commissioned a complete survey of his inheritance and proceeded to re-let the entire property. In rural areas his policy of taking part of the increased letting value in 'fines' (lump sums in cash) enabled some Belfast merchants to acquire leases over the heads of existing tenants and sparked off a serious outbreak by agrarian agitators calling themselves the Hearts of Steel. The rioters were bold enough at one point to invade Belfast and – despite the presence of a garrison – force the authorities to release one of their leaders by threatening to burn down the town.[17]

The new leases for Belfast itself, most of them for rebuilding, were granted in 1767. Those for houses in the main streets prescribed the height and minimum thickness of walls, the quality of materials to be used, and details such as slate roofs and sash windows to ensure a fashionable 'Georgian' appearance.[18] To mark the birth of his first son in 1769 Donegall built the Exchange, an arcaded market-house, to which he later added magnificent Assembly Rooms designed by Sir Robert Taylor, Architect of the King's Works. He also erected at his own expense a new parish church, and gave the land for the Poor House (1774) and the White Linen Hall (1783), though these buildings were paid for by public subscription. From the 1780s fine terrace houses were built in Linen Hall Street (now Donegall Place), which was laid out in the former gardens of the old castle; a more ambitious scheme, to include an ornamental canal in front of the Linen Hall, never materialised. Donegall did, however, complete at his own expense a real canal, the last part of the Lagan Navigation which ran from Belfast to Lough Neagh. Its construction facilitated the transport of linen from the bleach greens of the Lagan valley and Lough Neagh basin

The White Linen Hall (1785), photographed just over a century later, before it was demolished to make way for the present City Hall. Its erection was an important step towards establishing Belfast as the centre of the linen trade in the north of Ireland.
Ulster Museum

to Belfast, and thus helped to make the town the centre of the northern trade in fine linen. Donegall's purchase, in 1787, of the townland of Ballymacarrett, across the Lagan at the other end of the Long Bridge, was prompted at the time by his determination to prevent the development of a rival town. Thereafter Ballymacarrett became an industrial suburb – with glassworks, a foundry, vitriol works, ropeworks, weaving sheds – economically part of Belfast but outside the town boundary until the 1850s. In 1799 it ceased to be part of the main Chichester estate, however, passing on Donegall's death to his younger son.

The Lagan Canal apart, the fifth earl's interest in Belfast did not extend much beyond improving the appearance and amenities of his town, a larger version of the urge many great landowners exhibited in making their estate villages a credit to the taste of the proprietor. A stronger and more representative corporation might have undertaken necessary public projects, but in this respect things had got worse rather than better since the early years of the century. In the 1740s the election of non-resident burgesses in Irish boroughs was sanctioned by an Act of Parliament which settled a dispute in the borough of Newtownards; by the end of the century half of the members of Belfast corporation were non-resident. The vacuum left by the corporation was increasingly filled by self-help committees of citizens, a typically Presbyterian way of doing things. It was such groups, composed largely of the same people, which built and ran the Poor House, started a dispensary for the sick poor and a lying-in hospital, undertook to supply the town with water, founded the Chamber of Commerce, built the White Linen Hall and established the Belfast Academy (which was intended to be a college of higher education as well as a school). The Chamber of Commerce in turn took the initiative in trying to improve the harbour facilities, petitioning the Irish parliament for £2,000 towards the cost of cutting a straight channel from the quays (at low tide these dried up completely, and even in mid-channel the Lagan had only two feet of water) to deep water in the Lough, 'by means of which Vessels of a large Burthen would be enabled to pass up or down at high water in common tides'. Parliament gave no money but did transfer responsibility from the useless corporation to the merchant community which had a direct interest in the matter. A 'Corporation for Preserving and Improving the Port of Belfast' – commonly known as the Ballast Board because it provided dredged material as ships' ballast – was established which removed some of the worst shoals, made pilotage compulsory and constructed the first dry dock on part of the foreshore leased from Lord Donegall (he had at first said he would build the docks himself but decided to invest in the Lagan Canal instead).[19]

During the last two decades of the century this economically successful class of merchants and traders was joined by a number of cotton manufacturers. Protected with tariffs by the Irish parliament, cotton was originally introduced into Belfast as a way of employing and training children in the Poor House. Manufacturing of any kind had hitherto been very modest in scale. Cotton spinning by power, introduced by Nicholas Grimshaw, a

View of Belfast from the south, c.1772, by Jonathan Fisher. In the foreground the meandering Blackstaff makes its way into the Lagan upstream from the Long Bridge; to the left are the Cromac Woods and, in the background, the Cave Hill.

Ulster Museum

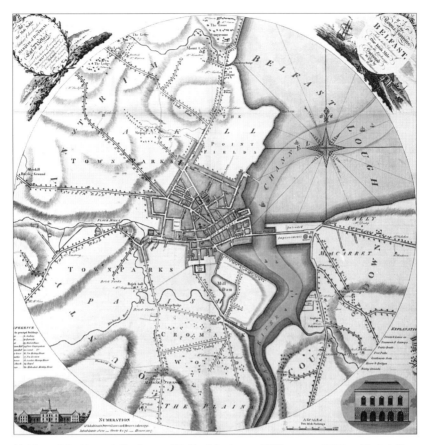

'A Map of the Town & Environs of Belfast' by James Williamson, 1791, with detail on facing page. Dedicated to the marquess of Donegall and embellished with pictures of the Poor House (bottom left) and the Exchange and Assembly Rooms (bottom right), the map shows a small place of some 18,000 inhabitants on the County Antrim side of the River Lagan. Across the Long Bridge in Ballymacarrett (acquired by Donegall only in 1787) are the beginnings of an industrial suburb, with glass kilns and pottery works. Excavations recently begun suggest that the latter were extensive, on a scale to rival major centres in Staffordshire. *Ulster Museum*

textile printer from Lancashire, when he built the first spinning mill in Ireland at Whitehouse near Belfast in 1784, was something quite new. Thereafter the manufacture of cotton largely replaced that of linen in the economy of Belfast, though the first mills, driven by water power, were to be found on the swift-running streams outside the town rather than on the flat site by the river. The number of handloom weavers grew: by 1791 there were nearly 700, of whom three-quarters were producing cotton cloth. Political disturbances and economic depression halted new investment during the next decade, but the establishment of cotton was to turn out to be the initial stimulus to Belfast's later industrialisation.[20]

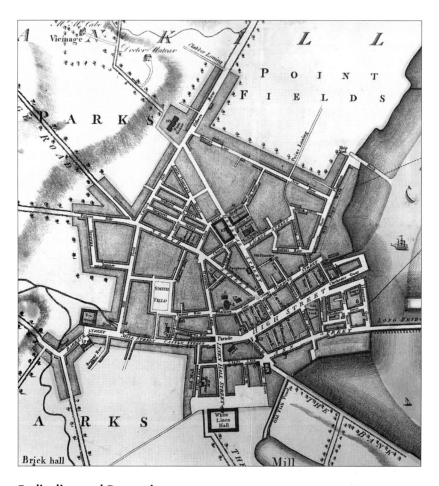

Radicalism and Repression

The fifth earl of Donegall, as his obituary in the *Belfast News Letter* claimed, may indeed have 'laid out above £60,000 in the Lagan Navigation and the Public Buildings in the Town', but the aristocratic and episcopalian monopoly in church and state that he represented was increasingly irksome to the prosperous Presbyterians who owned most of the town's wealth. This critical attitude to the established order was accompanied by a latitudinarianism in religion that favoured enlightenment and toleration. External events were to encourage such sentiments and give the citizens the opportunity to express them. The revolt of the American colonies, with which Belfast had close trading and ethnic links, was viewed with much sympathy. Then the Volunteer movement in Ireland, which arose originally to meet the threat of French invasion when most of the military garrison was removed to serve against the rebellious colonists, was adopted with enthusiasm in Belfast. Volunteer parades and manoeuvres offered all the colour and pageantry of war without any of the risks. The French, fortunately, never appeared. Instead, the Volunteer corps became middle-class political clubs, in which role they demanded first that the Irish parliament should have the right to make laws for Ireland without requiring English scrutiny and approval; then, when legislative independence was conceded in 1782, they went on to demand a reform of the Irish parliament itself. Liberal opinion in Belfast, a place whose MPs represented Lord Donegall rather than the citizens, was enthusiastic in its support for reform. A direct challenge to Donegall was impossible in Belfast itself, but in 1784 Waddell Cunningham – a leading Presbyterian merchant, a Volunteer captain and president of the Chamber of Commerce – stood against the Donegall candidate in Carrickfergus and was actually elected, only to be disqualified on a technicality.[21]

The reform movement was supported by the great majority of Presbyterians in Belfast up to 1785, but subsequently petered out without achieving its objective, even though only the episcopalians and a small group of conservative dissenters were opposed. Initially, the outbreak of the French Revolution in 1789 inspired a renewed agitation. The liberals soon divided, however, on the issue of whether – and if so when – the Catholics of Ireland should be emancipated from their disabilities. The Northern Whig club, founded in 1790, supported only a cautious degree of parliamentary reform. More radical spirits formed the Belfast Society of United Irishmen in 1791 to agitate for equal and democratic rights for all, propounding their views in a successful newspaper, the *Northern Star*. The outbreak of war between Britain and France in 1793, however, and the excesses of the Revolution, dampened the enthusiasm of the more cautious among the reformers and hardened the resolve of an alarmed Irish government, which presently forbade reform meetings and Volunteer parades and then proscribed the United Irishmen.[22]

Many of the radicals drew back at this point, but others organized in secret and plotted rebellion, looking with undue confidence to the arrival of armed assistance from France. In 1796 a number of leading radicals, including the manager of the *Northern Star*, were arrested and imprisoned, and the paper itself ceased publication the following year after its presses had been smashed by the military. The presence of a large garrison, even the failure of a French expedition in 1797, did not entirely deter the hopes of the most determined plotters, but when rebellion broke out in Ireland in 1798 they could attempt nothing in Belfast itself. A prominent inhabitant later recalled 'the death-like silence which pervaded the streets when the counties of Down and Antrim resounded with the noise and tumult of battle'.[23] Instead, Henry Joy McCracken, a scion of two prominent Presbyterian families in the town, led his rural followers to defeat in a skirmish at Antrim and was afterwards tried by court martial in Belfast and hanged outside the Market House. While McCracken and his friends plotted insurrection, many of the leading citizens volunteered to form a yeomanry

Waddell Cunningham (1727–97) in Volunteer uniform, by Robert Home. Cunningham made a fortune in the American colonies as a young man, before returning home to become one of the leading figures in late-eighteenth century Belfast. A Presbyterian, like most of the town's leading citizens, he challenged the Anglican establishment in the 1780s by standing for the Irish parliament against the candidate of his landlord, Lord Donegall.

Ulster Museum

corps to defend the town. The complete failure of the rebellion in Ulster, and the news that in southern Ireland the rebels had massacred Protestants, was a profound and bitter disappointment to the radical Presbyterians of Belfast. It was reported that one of the insurgent leaders said shortly before his execution that 'the Presbyterians of the North perceived too late that if they had succeeded in their designs, they would ultimately have had to contend with the Roman Catholics'.[24] Some of those arrested before the outbreak of the rebellion would see out the delusive decade of the 1790s in a Scottish prison. By the time they returned home to take up their lives again, the Act of Union of 1800 had put an end to the parliament they had set out to reform.

Belfast had changed a good deal in the previous half-century, during which its population had increased from 8,000 to 20,000. Thanks to its aristocratic owner it had acquired a modestly imposing appearance and one or two fine buildings, and thanks to the efforts of its citizens it had become a more important port and commercial centre, the hub of the northern linen trade and the location of a small cotton-manufacturing industry. Though never perhaps the 'Athens of the north' that a local poet claimed in 1793 (he was really talking about its devotion to political liberty rather than its cultural pretensions), it had a sizeable reading public served by a good library (still in existence as the Linen Hall Library), several news-papers and a well-patronised theatre. It was still, nevertheless, essentially a

Protestant plantation town, however fierce the political disagreements among its Protestant inhabitants, and it was still entirely owned by the family which had established it nearly two centuries earlier. As yet there was little to suggest the rapid economic, social and political changes by which it would be transformed in the coming century.

References

1. See E. E. Evans, 'Belfast: the site and the city', *Ulster Journal of Archaeology*, third series, 7 (1944), pp. 5–14; and 'The geographical setting', in J. C. Beckett and R. E. Glasscock (eds), *Belfast: The Origin and Growth of an Industrial City*, BBC, London (1967), pp. 1–13.
2. The derivation and meaning of place names in the Belfast area have been authoritatively discussed by Deirdre Flanagan, whose article on the subject, written in Irish, has been published in translation by A. J. Hughes as 'Belfast and the place-names therein', *Ulster Folklife*, 38 (1992), pp. 79–97.
3. B. C. S. Wilson, 'The birth of Belfast', in Beckett and Glasscock (eds), *Belfast*, pp. 16–17; J. O'Donovan (ed.), *Annals of the Four Masters*, 2nd edn, 7 vols, Dublin (1857), 4, p. 1101.
4. G. Benn, *History of the Town of Belfast, from the Earliest Times to the Close of the Eighteenth Century*, Marcus Ward & Co., London & Belfast (1877), pp. 24–36.
5. See Benn, *Belfast*, pp. 37–54.
6. Wilson, 'Birth of Belfast', in Beckett and Glasscock (eds), *Belfast*, p. 21; P. Roebuck, 'The making of an Ulster great estate', *Proceedings of the Royal Irish Academy*, 79, C, no.1 (1979), pp. 3–12.
7. Benn, *Belfast*, p. 86.
8. Benn, *Belfast*, p. 89.
9. J. C. Beckett, 'The seventeenth century', in Beckett and Glasscock (eds), *Belfast*, p. 27.
10. Benn, *Belfast*, pp. 310–12, 316–9; Beckett, 'The seventeenth century', in Beckett and Glasscock (eds), *Belfast*, pp. 34–5.
11. See W. A. Maguire, 'Lords and landlords – the Donegall family', in J. C. Beckett *et al.*, *Belfast: The Making of the City, 1800–1914*, Appletree Press, Belfast (1983), pp. 27–39.
12. Benn, *Belfast*, pp. 416–7. When the nearest Catholic priest surrendered himself and was lodged in jail, the sovereign reported, 'I had offered me the best Bail the Protestants of this Country affords.' Apparently this was because the priest had protected their property during the Jacobite occupation of Belfast.
13. Benn, *Belfast*, pp. 565–8; D. Kennedy, 'The early eighteenth century', in Beckett and Glasscock (eds), *Belfast*, pp. 41–2.
14. Kennedy, 'Early eighteenth century', in Beckett and Glasscock (eds), *Belfast*, pp. 45–6.
15. Donegall was apparently swindled (by a bishop) out of a valuable estate in the south of Ireland belonging to his wife. The attempts of the family to recover it went on intermittently for fifty years, before failing eventually in the House of Lords in 1769.

16. Benn, *Belfast*, p. 535.
17. See W. A. Maguire, 'Absentees, architects and agitators', *Proceedings of the Belfast Natural History and Philosophical Society*, second series, 10, (1981), pp. 5–21; and 'Lord Donegall and the Hearts of Steel', *Irish Historical Studies*, 21, no. 84 (1981), pp. 351–76.
18. See C. E. B. Brett, *Buildings of Belfast, 1700–1914*, revised edn, Friar's Bush Press, Belfast (1985), p. 2 ff, for the redevelopment of the town after 1760.
19. D. J. Owen, *A Short History of the Port of Belfast*, Mayne, Boyd & Son, Belfast (1917), pp. 19–20; R. Sweetnam, 'The development of the port', in Beckett *et al.*, *Belfast*, pp. 57–9.
20. E. R. R. Green, 'Early industrial Belfast', in Beckett and Glasscock (eds), *Belfast*, pp. 80–2.
21. G. Chambers, *Faces of Change: The Belfast and Northern Ireland Chambers of Commerce and Industry, 1783–1983*, Northern Ireland Chamber of Commerce and Industry, Belfast (1983), p. 43.
22. R. B. McDowell, 'The late eighteenth century', in Beckett and Glasscock (eds), *Belfast*, pp. 57–65.
23. [H. Joy], *Historical Collections relative to the Town of Belfast*, Belfast (1817), preface, p. x.
24. [Joy], *Historical Collections*, preface, p. xi.

Chapter 2

Industry, Trade and Politics, 1800–1860

The outstanding economic development in Belfast in the early nineteenth century was its rise as a centre of power-driven textile manufacture, first of cotton and then of linen. This was accompanied by, or led to, other economic changes which were to transform the Georgian town into a Victorian city – notably the creation of a superb port and the development of commercial and financial facilities. Such changes, and their social results, and the kind of municipal self-government that grew up to deal with the problems of urban expansion, were not dissimilar to those experienced by other British cities of the time. Indeed, even the tensions created by the sudden influx of large numbers of Irish Catholics into a hitherto Protestant town were not untypical. But only up to a point: in the case of Belfast these tensions were to prove in every way sharper, more persistent and more divisive than anywhere else.

Industrial Revolution

Though there were ten or eleven cotton spinning mills in the Belfast area by the end of the eighteenth century, the industrialisation of the town did not begin in a substantial way until after 1800. By 1820 more than 2,000 people were employed in some fifteen mills in or near Belfast. The Smithfield area of the town then became the main centre of new steam-powered enterprises. McCracken's mill there had 14,000 spindles and employed 200 hands. McCrum, Lepper & Co.'s five-storey mill behind the artillery barracks employed 300. Another five-storey mill in Winetavern Street was bought in 1815 by Thomas Mulholland, who later bought a second in Francis Street and in 1822 built a third in Henry Street.[1] By 1824, when tariff protection for Irish cotton ended, there were twenty mills employing 3,500 people, and though its prosperity depended largely on home demand the industry in Belfast was a very successful one. Even compared with Lancashire, it was neither particularly small in scale nor lacking in capital. The cost of raw material was the same everywhere, and while Belfast millowners had to import their coal they offset this additional cost by paying their workers less. So it was not, as used to be thought, an inability to compete with British producers after the removal of protection that led to the decline of cotton in the 1830s.[2]

What happened during the next ten or fifteen years was not so much the decline of cotton as its replacement by a more profitable, because modernised, linen industry. (The manufacture of linen, as distinct from the

31

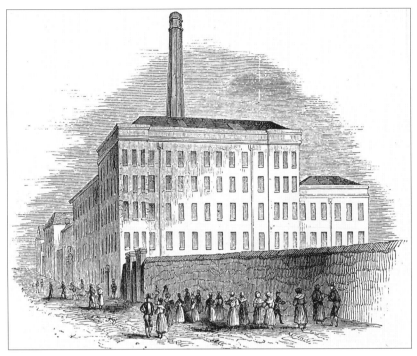

Mulholland's flaxspinning mill, c.1840, and (below) spinning room in Chartres's mill on the Falls Road, c.1840, both illustrations drawn from Hall's *Ireland*.

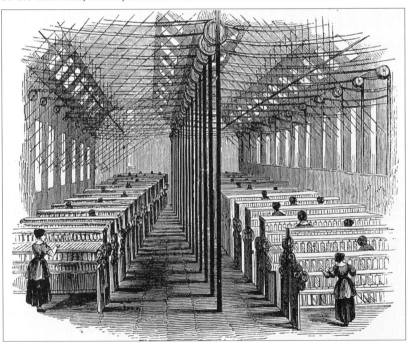

linen trade, had hitherto been largely a rural domestic industry.) The basis of this change was a technological invention, James Kay's discovery of how to produce fine linen yarn by the wet spinning process, and its adaptation for commercial purposes by Marshall's of Leeds. These developments were observed with great interest by cotton manufacturers in Ulster. When Thomas Mulholland's new mill in Henry Street accidentally burned down one Sunday morning in 1828 he rebuilt it to house 8,000 flaxspinning spindles, after a successful trial of 1,000 in his Francis Street mill. In 1830 there were two linen mills, in 1834 ten (nearly as many linen as cotton); by 1850 only four cotton mills remained, and by the end of that decade only two. By that time there were thirty-two linen mills with over half a million spindles. Apart from slumps in 1854–5 (the Crimean War) and 1857–8 (a financial crisis), linen enjoyed a prosperous period in the 1850s. This textile transfer was to prove enormously important for Belfast. By the early 1860s Belfast was taking over the lead in linen manufacture from Leeds and Dundee and was thus well placed to make the most of the opportunity created by the outbreak of the American Civil War, which caused a cotton famine.[3]

The spread of mechanised flaxspinning ruined not only handspinners but also handloom weavers, since many of the former turned to weaving and thus drove wages down. With weavers plentiful and cheap, factory owners had little incentive at first to introduce power looms, which in any case could weave only the coarser types of linen. One effect of the Irish potato famine of the 1840s and subsequent emigration was to force up the wages of the skilled weavers and encourage employers to look for an alternative. In response to this demand power looms were modified to make them more suitable for finer work. By 1850 two Belfast firms had begun powerloom weaving. By 1862 there were nearly 3,000 powerlooms operating in the Belfast area and the production of linen was becoming largely mechanised.[4] Visitors were increasingly struck by the resemblance between Belfast and industrial towns in the north of England – 'a clean Manchester' or 'the Irish Liverpool' – and by an impression of industriousness as well as industry which was thought to be un-Irish. 'The spirit of commercial enterprise that pervades the merchants of this prosperous place', wrote one visitor in 1834, 'appears to be reflected from the opposite shores.'[5] The Halls, who came to Belfast in 1843, found the place full of English virtues – 'so much bustle, such an aspect of business, a total absence of all suspicion of idleness'.[6] Such views were shared by the inhabitants themselves. The anonymous local patriot who wrote the entry for Belfast in the *Parliamentary Gazetteer of Ireland*, published in 1844, summarised its standing as

> the fourth town of the kingdom in amount of population; the third in extent of edificed area, and in aggregate value of general trade; the second in comparative regularity and beauty; the first in proportionate spirit, though only the second in actual appliances, of literature and science; and incomparably the first in enterprise, intelligence, and general prosperity.[7]

Apart from important developments in textiles, the basis was laid during this period of the two other industries that were to sustain the expansion of Victorian Belfast: shipbuilding and engineering. The building of wooden ships other than very small ones dated from the 1790s, when William Ritchie from Saltcoats in Ayrshire had established a successful yard on the Antrim side of the Lagan. There was a modest expansion of this and other yards during the early nineteenth century, but the crucial development came later, in the 1850s, and in a different place, across the river on the County Down side where improvements to Belfast harbour had created an artificial island. The Harbour Commissioners laid out part of the Queen's Island as a shipyard, with a patent slip and a timber pond, attracting in 1851 one of the builders of wooden ships. Two years later Robert Hickson, proprietor of an ironworks with plating to dispose of, took over a site there to build iron ships. In 1854 Hickson appointed Edward Harland, then only twenty-three, as manager. Harland bought the yard five years later for £5,000 with the help of G. C. Schwabe of Liverpool, whose nephew Gustav Wolff became the other half of Harland & Wolff in 1861.[8]

Industrial growth stimulated a demand for foundry products. Two new firms appeared in the early years of the century, Coates's Lagan Foundry and the Belfast Foundry. Both began to build steam engines. The engine for the first steamboat in Ireland, a wooden vessel, was made by the Lagan Foundry in 1820, and the same firm built the first iron steamship in 1838. The growth of textile factories produced a demand for spinning machinery.[9] The great expansion of heavy engineering, however, was to come later in the century, when both linen and shipbuilding really took off.

Trade, Finance and Communications

In commerce too the early nineteenth century was a time of remarkable growth. By the mid-1830s Belfast was the first among Irish ports in value of trade, £7.9 million compared with Dublin's £6.9. By far its biggest export at that time was linen, with provisions a long way behind; the town had become the centre of the Irish linen trade long before it became the chief centre of its manufacture. Most of the finance for this expansion came from local sources, through the medium of the banks which had developed since the early years of the century. From 1797 till 1808 there were no note-issuing institutions in Belfast, only a Discount Company, founded in 1793, which discounted bills of exchange and took deposits on interest. The business of the company expanded significantly after 1800, as Irish trade benefited from the Union and wartime demand, rising from £94,000 in discounted bills in 1800 to over £300,000 in 1806, with a matching rise in deposits. The monopoly of the Bank of Ireland at that time prevented the establishment of banks except as private partnerships, so the first developments were on that basis: the Belfast Bank in 1808, followed by the

Northern and the Commercial in 1809. Each of the partners in these ventures subscribed £10,000. All three banks survived the crisis of 1820, when most Irish private banks went under. When legislation in 1824 and 1825 ended the Bank of Ireland's monopoly, first the Northern and then a union of the Belfast Bank and the Commercial (as the Belfast Banking Company) formed joint stock banks on the Scottish model, each with a capital of half a million pounds.[10] These two were joined in 1836 by a third, the Ulster Bank. By the mid-thirties, then, Belfast had the head offices of three banks drawing funds from substantial depositors throughout the north of Ireland, as well as branches of the Provincial Bank and the Bank of Ireland. A flourishing Savings Bank served the interests of smaller investors who could not afford to buy £50 or £100 shares. That some of these humbler capitalists accumulated surprisingly large sums of money was revealed when they were tempted to buy the £1 shares of a disreputable bank which collapsed in the 1830s: a coach porter lost 150 guineas, a street constable £300.[11] The author of the *Parliamentary Gazetteer* entry loyally noted that the failure of the Belfast branch of the Agricultural and Commercial Bank was no exception to the soundness of the Belfast banks, 'for the affair was wholly a Dublin bubble'.

Industrial and commercial growth could not have continued much beyond the 1830s without the transformation of the port and harbour, since the textile industry (linen no less than cotton) depended on imports of raw material and all the essentials for shipbuilding, engineering and power generation – coal, iron and timber – were imported. The Ballast Board, the body established in 1785, had carried out some useful maintenance work on the channel and had opened a second graving dock in 1826, but despite consulting several eminent engineers (including Telford and Rennie) it was unable until 1831 to fix on a feasible way of tackling the main problem. This was that the Lagan, instead of running straight into the Lough, meandered across shallows and mud flats in two great bends before reaching deep water at the Pool of Garmoyle. Here large ships had to anchor and transfer their cargoes into smaller vessels for the last three miles of the journey to the quays.[12] Human cargo fared no better, according to the recollections of one traveller:

> It was usually the fate of the old *Eclipse*, the *Rob Roy*, the *Fingal* or the *Chieftain* steamers to miss the tide and stop between Whitehouse and Holywood. Then an open boat would come alongside, and any passenger anxious to get up to town had the offer of being rowed up in no time for a shilling. After the wearying journey of twenty-two hours from Glasgow or Liverpool, many of the passengers were glad to leave the steamer. When the boatmen had secured as many passengers as the boat could carry without the certainty of drowning them, they began their journey, the pleasures of which on a cold wintry morning were not much relished.[13]

In 1831 the Ballast Board accepted a plan by the engineers Walker and Burgess to make the first of two cuts, across one of the bends of the river; a second cut, to carry the deep channel all the way out to Garmoyle, was to be made later if necessary. It took six years, however, to obtain an Act of Parliament which conferred powers on the reconstructed Board 'for the formation of a new cut or channel and for otherwise more effectually improving the Port and Harbour of Belfast'. The £200,000 needed to begin the work was raised remarkably quickly by an issue of bonds. Work started in April 1839 and was completed in January 1841. At the same time the last part of the Lagan's course, below the Long Bridge, was deepened to link the town quays with the new channel. Some of the material excavated in the process was used to form an artificial island, at first called Dargan's Island after the contractor but later renamed Queen's Island in honour of Victoria's visit to Belfast in 1849. The private quays and docks downriver from the Long Bridge (which was taken down in 1841 and replaced by the Queen's Bridge) were all purchased by the Ballast Board, which was thus in a position to control the future development of the harbour. Charges for quayage and pilotage were reduced to encourage trade, so successfully that the Board's successors, the Harbour Commissioners (established under the Belfast Harbour Act of 1847), immediately made the second navigation cut. The resulting Victoria Channel, which carried the deep water all the way out to Garmoyle, was opened in 1849.[14] Thereafter even the largest vessels could come right up into the town and Belfast had one of the finest ports in the world.

During the same period the old docks were filled in, to be developed presently as Queen's Square (formerly Town Dock), Albert Square (Lime Kiln Dock) and Corporation Square (Ritchie's Dock). The transformation of the port's already considerable trade was one of many indications that Belfast was growing into a city. In 1837 the number of ships cleared was 2,724, with a total tonnage of 288,143; ten years later 4,213 ships and over half a million tons; 7,817 ships and 1,372,326 tons by 1867.[15] No wonder the Harbour Commissioners moved from the cramped quarters of the old Ballast Board to splendid new offices (built on the site of William Ritchie's shipyard) in 1854 and the revenue authorities to a palatial new Custom House in 1857.

At the same time as harbour developments were transforming the approach to Belfast by sea, the town's hinterland was being enlarged by the construction of railways. The first line, the Ulster Railway between Belfast and Lisburn with its terminus in Great Victoria Street, opened in 1839 and soon extended to Lurgan and Portadown. Sabbatarians immediately denounced the running of Sunday trains. One clergyman told his flock he would rather join a company for theft and murder than the Ulster Railway Company, whose business was sending souls to the devil at sixpence apiece. 'Every sound of the railway whistle', he thundered, 'is answered by a shout in hell.'[16] After the Railway Act of 1847 made public money available for

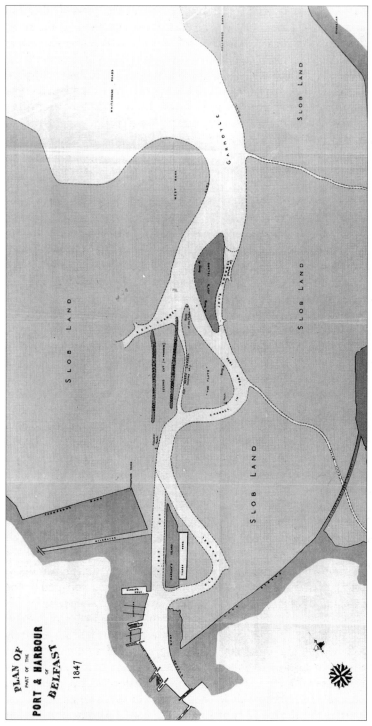

Plan of the port and harbour of Belfast in 1847 showing the first cut made by the harbour authorities – which straightened the channel of the River Lagan and created the Queen's Island (here called Dargan's Island) – and the line of the second cut, where work was in progress. These developments transformed Belfast into a first-rate port.

Ulster Museum

railway promotion, the network developed rapidly. Lines to Ballymena and Holywood opened the following year; Coleraine and Dublin were linked to Belfast in 1855, Londonderry in 1860. Communications in the town itself changed little until horse omnibuses began to appear in the 1850s; they scarcely needed to, since most people lived within easy reach of their work. Before that there was scarcely anything in the way of public transport: an old man looking back in the 1870s recalled that 'In addition to the expensiveness of public conveyances in those days, there were very few of them. I remember when Belfast could boast of only four outside cars'.[17]

Population Growth and Urban Problems

Industrial and commercial expansion attracted large numbers of immigrants into Belfast, first as labour for the cotton spinning mills and as handloom weavers of cotton, then to the linen mills and later the weaving factories. The large majority were from Ulster, and most of the rest from other parts of Ireland, but there were also a few Europeans – notably some Italian craftsmen associated in one way or another with the arts (drawing masters, carvers, gilders and so on). The population rose from about 20,000 in 1800 to 30,000 in 1815, to over 53,000 in 1831, to over 70,000 in 1841

Dr Andrew Malcolm (1818–56), a pioneer campaigner for improved public health in early Victorian Belfast. *Ulster Museum*

(when in addition to the 70,747 in the town itself the census-takers felt that another 4,861 living outside the boundary should be added). The rate of growth declined in the next decade, reflecting slower industrial growth and the effects of the great potato famine. Even so, the census figure for 1851 was 87,000. So far, this quadrupling of the population had taken place within the old boundary of the town, which enclosed an area of one and a half square miles. In 1853 the boundary was greatly extended to increase the area to ten square miles. By 1861 the population of this larger Belfast had reached 121,000.[18] This phenomenal rate of growth was to be exceeded in the second half of the century, but it was nevertheless already very striking and put Belfast among the major cities and towns of the United Kingdom; in Ireland only Dublin was larger by the middle of the century.

Urban growth created urban problems, especially when expansion was so rapid. Typhus fever, carried by body lice, was endemic but reached epidemic proportions in the famine year of 1847, when the hordes of starving poor who poured into the town from the stricken countryside were easy victims to it. The Poor Law Guardians, who controlled the Workhouse (built in 1841 with accommodation for a thousand inmates) and its infirmary, were warned by the fever hospital to expect a plague. In the event, the 1847 outbreak was, in the words of Dr Andrew Malcolm, a plague 'in comparison with which all previous epidemics were trivial and insignificant'. The Workhouse infirmary was enlarged and temporary hospitals were provided in huts and tents in several other places. The number of recorded admissions during the year was nearly 14,000. 'Yet hundreds', the *Belfast News Letter* reported on 20 July, 'for whom there remains no provision – are daily exposed in the delirium of this frightful malady, on the streets, or left to die in their filthy and ill-ventilated hovels …'. Malcolm reckoned that 'one out of every five persons in Belfast was attacked during this year'. The problem for the Poor Law Guardians was made worse by the arrival of several shiploads of Irish emigrants repatriated by the Poor Law authorities of Glasgow and other British cities, for whom Belfast was the most convenient port, regardless of their place of origin in Ireland.

The cholera outbreaks which ravaged the town in 1831–2 and 1848–9 were sadly inevitable in any large port in the early Victorian period and were experienced also in Glasgow and Liverpool. The epidemic of 1848–9, which followed hard on the heels of the typhus, was expected and prepared for. Even so it took a heavy toll in the poorer quarters of the town, killing nearly a thousand people in 1849. The death rate among patients, one-third, was twice that of the earlier outbreak in 1831–2; living conditions for the poor had evidently worsened in the meantime. A Sanitary Committee, with the reforming Dr Malcolm as its moving spirit, produced a damning report in 1849 on the unhealthy condition of working-class districts, in particular the absence of any proper drainage and sewerage; and Malcolm himself in 1852 (in an address to the British Association, meeting in Belfast for the first time) showed conclusively that disease caused far more deaths in houses without proper sewerage than in the better-drained parts of the town. Only 3,000 of the 10,000 houses, he estimated, had piped water, and few of these had cisterns; 3,000 had no yard of any kind; 1,800 were accessible only by covered archways into enclosed courts; 25,000 people had no privies. Though the science of statistics was in its infancy, it is certain that at this period Belfast had the highest death rate in Ireland and possibly the worst in the United Kingdom. Malcolm produced the extra-ordinary statistic that, due to the 'absolutely excessive' infant mortality, the average life expectancy in Belfast was no more than nine years.[19] Malcolm's figures confirmed the eyewitness accounts of a Congregational minister named O'Hanlon, who in a series of letters to the Liberal newspaper the *Northern Whig* (subsequently published in book form) revealed horrors that most citizens never saw for themselves.[20]

The presence of vice in the poorest quarters of the town caused more concern than the absence of privies. The extent of prostitution in early Victorian Belfast is impossible to establish with any accuracy in the absence of statistics, but in a garrison town and port it was inevitably considerable. O'Hanlon did not attempt an estimate but noted that it was rife and listed the areas where he came across it in his 'walks among the poor'. One entry contained 'five notorious brothels', another had nine, while Hudson's Entry near Smithfield was 'A complete den of vice and uncleanness, probably unsurpassed in what is called the civilised world', being filled with 'imbruted, guilty, shameless women' who 'breakfasted upon whiskey'. The fact that half of all the surgical cases in the General Hospital were syphilitic supports O'Hanlon's impression. To their credit, many concerned citizens felt that something must be done. While action at an official level was inevitably slow to materialise, a large number of charitable bodies did what they could to alleviate the situation.

No amount of private charity, however, could deal with such problems adequately. Housing, water, drainage and public health needed laws and regulations for the common good which would override the selfish interests of property owners. In the absence of an effective corporation, the Police Act of 1800 (40 Geo.III.c.37), one of the last Acts of the Irish Parliament, had established in Belfast two elected bodies, the Commissioners of Police (elected for life) and the Police Committee – the first supervisory, the second executive – to be responsible for paving, lighting and cleansing the town and providing it with a fire service and a night watch. A second Act, passed through the Parliament at Westminster in 1816, expanded the powers of the commissioners. Though never very satisfactory – the arrangement was a cumbersome one, with overlapping jurisdictions and frequent complaints from ratepayers about high valuations – this first essay in elected local government was by no means altogether ineffective, and would have been more effective still if its borrowing power had not been limited to £2,000. Within a year of its inception a visitor was praising the labelling of streets and the numbering of houses which 'gave a neatness and city-like appearance' to the town. Thirty years later another tourist remarked approvingly that the streets were 'marked by great regularity, having very good footways, and being, in general, well cleansed and lighted'.[21] By that time gaslight (supplied by the new Gaslight Company, a private concern which opened in 1823) had replaced the four hundred oil lamps purchased earlier.

Political Change and Political Power

Enlightenment soon extended to politics. But whereas the economic developments so far described, and their social consequences, broadly conformed to the experience of other industrialising British cities, their political consequences were rather more special to Belfast, if not unique. In 1832, by the Irish Reform Act, the Corporation was deprived of its monopoly in the election of the town's Members of Parliament, now increased to two. Under the new franchise of £10 householders (the same as in Britain) the electorate immediately rose from thirteen to over 1,600. A year later, the Corporation was comprehensively damned in the report of the Select Committee appointed to investigate the municipal corporations of England, Wales and Ireland, which concluded: '...now that the Sovereign and his colleagues have ceased to choose the Representative to Parliament of the Town, they do not appear to exist for any public or useful purpose'.[22] This judgement was echoed by the commissioners who investigated the Irish municipal corporations in 1835. The Irish Municipal Corporations Act of 1840 replaced the sovereign and burgesses by a Town Council of ten aldermen and thirty councillors, representing five wards, to be elected, like MPs, by male householders owning property valued at £10 or more. This franchise, it should be noted, was narrower than the one adopted in England, where after 1835 all ratepayers had the vote in local elections. The Council met for the first time in November 1842 and elected a mayor. The last sovereign, Thomas Verner, failed even to get a seat – an outcome that caused his patron and kinsman, George Augustus Chichester, the elderly marquess of Donegall, to burst into tears at a public meeting.[23]

This humiliation in fact virtually marked the end of the Chichester family's long domination of Belfast. The loss of political control, or at any rate the complete control formerly exercised through the old Corporation, was inevitable in an age of reform. The simultaneous decline in economic power, however, was a direct result of the second marquess's astonishing career first as a prodigal son and then as a prodigal father. Forced as a young man to flee from his English creditors, he came to live in Belfast in 1802 and never managed to escape from his exile. After surviving (by means of a retrospective Act of Parliament) the revelation that his marriage a quarter of a century earlier had been technically illegal, he and his eldest

41

Ormeau House, seat of the second marquess of Donegall, c.1830. This view shows one end of the rambling mansion, which had been extended and remodelled in the Tudor style a few years earlier by the fashionable young Irish architect William Vitruvius Morrison. The building was not inhabited after the mid-1850s, and what remained of it was demolished in 1870 when the demesne became Belfast's first public park. *Ulster Museum*

son, the earl of Belfast, made an arrangement in 1822 to raise more than £200,000 to pay off his debts. The money, which in the end amounted to more like £300,000, was raised by granting leases for ever at low rents but for large sums in cash. These perpetuities affected almost all the ground of Belfast, as well as thousands of acres in Antrim and Donegal. Paradoxically, whereas his father, the great absentee, had closely influenced the development of the town, the resident second marquess lost control of it.[24] The process was completed after his death in 1844, when his son discovered to his dismay that most of the old debts supposed to have been paid were still owing and, together with his own borrowings, now made up the immense sum of £400,000. Eventually, under the Encumbered Estates Act of 1849, the whole property was put in the hands of a receiver and as much of it sold outright as was needed to wipe the slate clean. Among the property disposed of was the freehold of Belfast.[25]

The new Town Council was a very different body from the old corporation, not least in its social composition. Of the forty councillors first elected in 1842, twenty-five were listed as 'merchants', eight as 'Esq.' or 'gentleman', three as 'manufacturers' (two of linen, one of cotton) and one as 'medical doctor'. Three of the 'gentlemen' probably had commercial interests or connections. Commerce, not industry, was still clearly in the ascendant, one might conclude, though at least one 'merchant', Andrew Mulholland, was also a manufacturer. The really extraordinary thing about the Council, though, was that all forty of its members were Conservatives, despite the fact that a substantial and influential section of the town's middle class was Liberal. Even more extraordinary, not a single Liberal (much less a Catholic) was elected until 1855; of the six then elected, Bernard Hughes, owner of a large bakery and flour mill, was also the first Catholic.

The virtual absence of manufacturers from the council in the 1840s and early 1850s can be explained by the fact that the old-established textile families, such as the Grimshaws, were Liberals – and Liberals, as we shall see presently, were excluded from the council by chicanery. Party organisation in Belfast dated from about 1830, when liberal Presbyterians began to agitate for a radical reform of Parliament. These men were the political heirs of the radicals of the 1790s, and had recently, like their forebears, demonstrated strong support for Catholic emancipation, but there was one crucial difference between them and the United Irishmen of a generation earlier: nationalism had ceased to be an essential element of their creed.

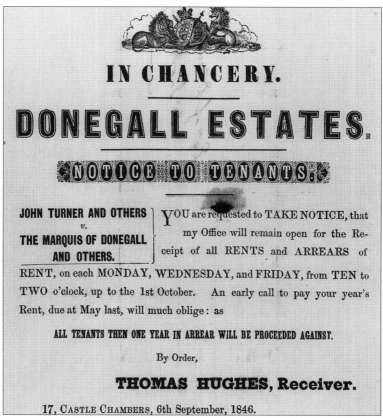

The Donegall estate in chancery, 1846. The spendthrift second marquess left enormous debts when he died in 1844, despite having raised the money to settle them. The creditors got a receiver appointed by the court of chancery and eventually forced the third marquess to part with the freehold of most of Belfast.   *Ulster Museum*

This came about because Irish nationalism after 1800 was, politically speaking, a protest against the union with Britain, yet the union had brought a period of great and growing prosperity for Belfast.[26] These Presbyterian Liberals formed an uneasy alliance with the Catholics, based on a common dislike of the Tory party and the established church with which it was so closely identified.

The Conservatives on the other hand were 'a defensive union of Protestants against the forces of Liberalism and Roman Catholicism', first organised to oppose the radical supporters of political change and thereafter, when the Reform Act became law, to secure the election of candidates to the House of Commons. The alliance consisted of traditional Tories (Churchmen), supporters of the Donegall interest in the corporation and moderate Whigs (Presbyterians). From the start they were more united than their Liberal opponents, who were increasingly divided in particular over the question of the repeal of the union, which Catholics supported and Protestants opposed.

Nevertheless, for the first twenty years Belfast was a keenly contested marginal constituency. The Conservatives won both seats in 1832, largely because the very radical programme of the Liberals did not appeal to the new electorate. Soundly defeated, the Liberals then abandoned radicalism and became a party of amelioration, supporting such local issues as municipal reform. This strategy worked so well that they took one seat in 1835, both in 1837 (when, however, they put up candidates without consulting the Catholics and on a platform which was distinctly Protestant and anti-repeal) and shared the representation again in 1842 and 1847. By 1852,

John Bates (d.1855), for many years Town Clerk, Town Solicitor and Conservative 'boss' of Belfast, from a posthumous sketch.
Ulster Museum

however, the constituency had become a safe Tory one. The Conservatives won both seats in a landslide that year and the local Liberals thereafter disintegrated, being crushed in 1857 and unwilling to make any challenge again until 1865.[27]

The adherence of a substantial number of Presbyterians to the Conservative cause came about despite a history of antipathy between Presbyterians and the established church. A crucial role in this development was played by Dr Henry Cooke, minister of May Street Church (which was built for him) from 1829 till his death in 1868. In October 1834 Cooke took part in a great Protestant meeting at Hillsborough in County Down called by Lord Downshire and other leading Anglicans. In a stirring address, he presented himself as a 'sample' of the Presbyterians of Ulster and advocated the coming together of Presbyterians and Episcopalians, as in 1688, in defence of civil and religious liberty against Catholicism and arbitrary government. He concluded with a rhetorical flourish in which he published 'the banns of marriage' between the two churches. Cooke himself admitted that he was not typical of his brethren in championing the Conservative cause – indeed many of them were scandalised by his action – but beyond a statement from the Moderator saying that Cooke had not been representing the views of the church there was no official repudiation of his performance.[28] Cooke became increasingly influential as the scourge of Liberals and Repealers. When O'Connell paid his only visit to Belfast in 1841, to propagate the cause of repeal, Cooke challenged him to a public debate, which was declined; and riotous mobs disrupted O'Connell's meetings till the police escorted him out of town. The identification of repeal with Catholicism and Catholicism with intolerance and lack of liberty which Cooke expounded struck a chord in many Presbyterian hearts and minds, and weakened the Liberal cause. Relations between Presbyterians and Episcopalians were soured in the 1840s by disagreements over education and the validity of 'mixed marriages' between members of the two churches performed by Presbyterian clergy, as well as by the conciliatory policies of Peel's Conservative government towards Irish Catholicism, but on the whole the marriage of interests heralded by Cooke in 1834 increasingly became a reality, in political terms at least.

The failure of the Liberals to gain any seats at all on the Town Council in 1842 was directly attributable to the local party's carelessness and the astuteness of John Bates, the Tory election agent from 1832 onward. Energetic, determined and unscrupulous – in 1835 he managed to have eighty Liberal voters disqualified because they had described their premises as 'house and shop' instead of 'house, shop' – Bates made himself expert in how to manipulate the voting register in both parliamentary and local elections. Under the terms of the Municipal Corporations Act of 1840, the register of local voters was based upon published lists, drawn up by the churchwardens of the parish, of all the male householders who appeared to be qualified on the basis of a £10 police tax valuation. These lists were then scrutinised by the rival parties, whose agents prepared objections to supporters of the opposing party who seemed to be dubious; four barristers appointed by the government ruled on their validity. On the Liberal notices of objection in 1842 both the name of the agent and his address were incorrectly stated. When Bates challenged them on this ground they were all declared invalid, whereas all the Conservative claimants went on to the roll of qualified voters. The resulting Conservative council appointed Bates (who continued to act as the party's agent) to the posts of Town Clerk and Town Solicitor. As Clerk, he was then responsible for compiling the lists of those who had paid their local taxes and were therefore, barring any other objection, eligible for the burgess roll; anyone who failed to pay any of the five rates could be disqualified. All the collectors appointed were Conservatives who, under Bates's guidance, ensured that as the deadline approached for registration Conservatives paid their rates in time and in full (if necessary they were lent the money to do so, or even issued with receipts without having paid), while Liberals were deliberately neglected. It later emerged that on average every year between 1843 and 1854 nearly half of the people apparently qualified were struck off, most of them Liberals; in 1852 a total of 999 Liberals out of 1,119 were removed, compared with 463 of the 1,322 Conservatives. The Liberals of course complained, but there was nothing much they could do about it. When Bates fell from power in 1855 the collector's office was conveniently burgled and the parish rate books were stolen.[29]

In 1842 the Conservatives were careful to distribute council seats to each of the elements among their supporters. Though Churchmen occupied the leading positions, Presbyterians were nominated for the largest single number of seats. Two supporters of the Donegall interest were also chosen, though not the last Sovereign, who stood as an Independent Conservative and lost. In three of the five wards the Tories were returned unopposed. The Liberals contested only one, St Anne's, where they put up four Protestants and four Catholics. From the start, the Conservative business-men elected were content to ask no questions and to leave all arrangements to Bates, who, it has rightly been pointed out, came to occupy in Belfast a position not unlike that of a city boss in America. One alderman later confessed that he himself did not know the Conservative ward secretary, never campaigned for votes and did not even know of his election until he was told about it.

Local Government

Despite the bigotry and corruption that characterised their complete domination of local government in the 1840s and early 1850s, the Conservatives were both energetic and effective in governing the town. Here one must note that the powers given to Irish town councils by the Municipal Corporations Act of 1840 had in fact been quite narrow. One notable omission, compared with the corresponding legislation in England, was control of the police, but in neither country were the new authorities empowered to carry out large programmes of municipal improvement. In Belfast the Police Commissioners (most of whom in 1842 were Liberals) and Police Committee continued to exist and retained responsibility for policing, lighting, paving and so on. One of the Town Council's first actions, however, was to take over the powers of this rival organisation. The Town Clerk, Bates, secured a legal opinion that the successors to the twelve burgesses of the old corporation, who had been ex officio Commissioners, were all the people on the new, Conservative-sifted burgess roll. In January 1843 the mayor summoned these men to what he claimed to be a meeting of the Police Commissioners but which the existing Commissioners held to be illegal. Packed with Conservatives, this meeting swept aside the objections of the Liberals and voted to transfer to the Town Council the powers of the Commissioners and the Police Committee. A Liberal appeal to Parliament failed when a similar case in the town of Sligo was decided in favour of the council. So in January 1844 the powers of Belfast Town Council were immensely increased when the transfer took effect. So too were the patronage and influence of Bates, who had managed the whole affair.[30]

Thereafter, as in other cities, further powers had to be sought by means of private Acts of Parliament (the expense of which until 1847 fell entirely on the town concerned). In this respect the Conservative council in Belfast demonstrated a zeal for improvement that was matched only by the most progressive Liberal corporations in Britain. Indeed by 1847 only 29 of the 178 municipal corporations in England and Wales had applied for additional powers to carry out improvements, whereas Belfast, established later than any of them, had already obtained three improvement acts – in 1845, 1846 and 1847. (Of the usual public amenities, only water never came under council control. Despite several attempts by the council, the water supply remained the responsibility of a separate elected body, which was established in 1840 to take over the task from the Charitable Society.) The aim of the Conservatives, according to the chairman of their local act committee in 1844, was 'to get the largest amount of good done at the least possible expense'. The three elements of the council's financial strategy were to raise revenue from the rates, to finance improvements by borrowing and to make profits from any improvements undertaken. The level of the rates was kept as low as possible, well below the limit allowed and just enough to pay normal operating charges and the interest on loans. Debts were to be paid instead from the returns on 'productive improvements'. The very concept of productive improvement, by which the council financed street schemes and other amenities by taking more land than was necessary and selling the surplus when improved, was anathema to the Liberals, who saw it as speculation by a public body with private property. In a rapidly expanding town it appeared to work, however. By 1850 the

47

Conservatives could claim that the loan of £150,000 raised under the 1845 Act had been met by the sale of surplus land and the profits from the markets that the council had purchased.[31]

The 1845 Act granted the power to borrow up to £150,000 to widen old streets and make new ones, to pave, clean and light parts of the town, to lay sewers, to buy land for new markets and so on, and it also outlawed thatched roofs in all new buildings and forbade such undesirable practices as the keeping of pigs in dwelling houses and offering rotten meat for sale. The 1846 Act 'for the better lighting and improving the Borough of Belfast' gave power to borrow a further £50,000 to municipalise the gasworks. The 1848 Act and another in 1850 authorised further borrowing, mainly to deal with the 'Blackstaff nuisance' – a euphemism for the notorious health hazard created by the frequent flooding of a tributary of the Lagan which had become an open sewer – and laid down minimum standards for all new housing, including notably that each dwelling should have a small yard and an ash pit. Using the powers gained by this burst of legislation, the Council filled in the old docks along the river and created broad new streets, the most impressive of which were Victoria Street and Corporation Street. Using its powers under the 1845 Act, the Council formed a markets committee and bought up existing markets and market rights, paying over £20,000 to Lord Donegall for the ground of the Smithfield Market and his interest in it.[32] Altogether, markets and manorial rights cost £52,000, and a further £38,000 was invested in the creation of new market facilities which centralised trading in livestock and agricultural produce (one must not forget that in becoming a commercial and industrial centre Belfast never ceased to be an important market town) and put an end to the filth and inconvenience associated with street trading in livestock. The proposed purchase of the gas undertaking had to be abandoned, however, for lack of money. The draining of the Blackstaff was not achieved either, foundering on the reluctance of the Council on the one hand to undertake the scheme unless it was given large powers of compulsory purchase (and hence the prospect of large profits from selling off the land when improved) and on the other hand of the millowners using the stream (most of them Liberals), who obstructed voluntary purchase of their rights. The issue was to run and run, a good deal more vigorously than the polluted stream itself.

The Liberals' revenge, and a long pause in the spate of improvement acts, came in 1854, when a solicitor named John Rea filed a suit in the Court of Chancery in Dublin against the Town Council, naming as special respondents Bates, the Treasurer and sixteen leading councillors. The Council was accused of having exceeded its borrowing powers and of using for unauthorised purposes the money raised to buy the gasworks. Bates himself was charged with fraud and with having exacted exorbitant fees for his professional services as Town Solicitor. The Lord Chancellor's verdict, delivered in June 1855, found all the allegations proved and held the respondents personally responsible for the huge sum of £273,000. Bates resigned at once and died three months later, and the Treasurer also gave up his post (he had run an overdraft with the bank of which he was a director). Moderate Liberals were not unwilling to make an accommodation with the Conservatives, but a more extreme group allied itself with Rea. A private bill to indemnify the respondents foundered on the opposition of the no-compromise faction, but the report of a Royal Commission in 1859 was more favourable to them: apart from censuring the failure to drain the Blackstaff it spoke approvingly of the Council's improvements and referred to arbitration the question of the £273,000.[33]

These exciting events were not without their political effects. In 1855 the disorganised Tory machine managed to remove only 988 names from the list of qualified persons and the local electorate consequently shot up from less than a thousand to over 2,500. In the elections of that year the Liberals got six candidates in, one of whom was Rea himself. As a catalyst he had been superb, as a councillor he was deplorable. In council meetings, his characteristically disruptive and eccentric behaviour (as a solicitor he had a long history of being forcibly ejected from the courts) amused his supporters but alienated moderates, until he was ousted the following year. In an attempt to settle matters the Conservatives, whose electoral machine survived the demise of Bates and soon enabled them to recover their hold on the representation, voluntarily made way for seventeen co-opted Liberals in 1859. Two years later, with half the council seats under their control, the Liberals were able to install their nominee Sir Edward Coey as Belfast's first and only Liberal mayor.[34]

Sectarianism

'Apart from one-party dominance and a penchant for corrupt practices, the Council of the era of John Bates exhibited another unpraiseworthy characteristic, sectarianism. In every election of the period, with increasing emphasis, the close connection between civic prosperity and Protestantism was loudly proclaimed.'[35] This judgement may be illustrated by the story of John Clarke, the second mayor (a supporter of the Donegall interest), who was dropped by the Conservatives because he attended the dedication of the new Catholic church of St Malachy's in 1844 (when he helped to take up the collection and personally subscribed £10) as part of his declared policy of showing no partiality to any party or sect. Such was to be the fate of all moderates in the partisan world of Belfast municipal politics. How did this situation come about? And how did it become a permanent feature of Belfast life?

There was little or no anti-Catholic feeling in eighteenth-century Belfast because there were very few Catholics in the town and because, in a largely Presbyterian community, both denominations shared a common sense of being discriminated against by the Anglican establishment. In the early years of the nineteenth century, however, large numbers of Catholic immigrants came to Belfast to work in the cotton mills, altering the balance between the denominations in a short space of time. Whereas the proportion of Catholics in the population had been only six per cent in 1757 and no more than ten per cent at the end of the century, by the 1830s it was one in three.[36] This Catholic counter-colonisation of an area hitherto perceived as Protestant might not in different circumstances have caused such a hostile reaction. It coincided, however, with political and religious developments which polarised opinion nationally, notably O'Connell's campaigns for Catholic emancipation and for repeal of the union with England, the controversialist evangelical movements in both main Protestant churches and, in the 1850s, the appearance of a much more challenging, ultramontane spirit in the Catholic church associated with the leadership of archbishop Paul Cullen – a spirit which many Protestants, evangelicals in particular, interpreted as 'papal aggression'. These reinforced the division in the community. A property-owning franchise after 1832 gave Catholics little direct voice in Belfast politics, since few had property, but before the introduction of the secret ballot in 1872 they and their equally voteless Protestant counterparts could have what one observer later called 'a warm interchange of opinion on a basis of basalt'[37] at election time. Competition between Catholic and Protestant labourers, if not in the early years of the century then certainly later, added an economic ingredient to this explosive religious and political brew; it is sometimes forgotten that a majority of unskilled labourers were Protestants, though the proportion was smaller than in the case of the skilled. By the 1830s most Belfast Protestants believed that the maintenance of the union with Britain was good for business. At the height of O'Connell's repeal campaign in 1843, a petition that in the event of its coming about the north should either become a separate kingdom or remain within the union was seriously canvassed.[38]

The first reported riot in Belfast was as early as 1813, an Orange and Green affair that was an urban version of the kind of sectarian violence common enough in some rural areas but not typical of the opening decades of the century in Belfast. In fact, apart from a minor scuffle in 1825 between supporters and opponents of Catholic emancipation there were no outbreaks of any significance till the 1830s, the decade when real parliamentary politics arrived in Belfast. In 1832 two mobs stoned each other and four people were killed during the chairing of one of the successful Conservative candidates. The unexpected election of a Liberal three years later caused a clash between rival factions from Sandy Row (Protestants) and Pound Street (Catholics), a sign that the territoriality that was such a striking feature of sectarian strife in Belfast was already becoming established. A similar fracas occurred after the election of 1841. The pitched battle between the Pound Street Boys and the Sandy Row Boys two years later followed the Twelfth of July celebrations rather than an election but happened in the context of O'Connell's campaign for repeal, which reached its climax that year. In 1852 an election held on 12 July, in which the one Liberal member lost his seat, was the occasion of another confrontation in which at least one man was killed, the military had to be called in and (a new feature that was to become a familiar one) numbers of people fled their homes, taking their belongings with them. A much more serious outbreak occurred in 1857, starting with ten days of continuous rioting in which both sides, as well as the armed police who had been drafted in, did a good deal of shooting.[39]

This time the trouble had begun with a fiercely anti-Catholic sermon to a congregation of Orangemen, preached in his own church (which stood on the edge of the frontier or 'shatter zone' between Pound Street and Sandy Row) by the rector of Christ Church, the Rev. Dr Thomas Drew. Drew had been preaching in similar vein at open-air meetings in the town centre since the previous summer, and had been joined in publicising the evils of Romanism by another Church of Ireland clergyman, Thomas McIlwaine, and by a fiery Presbyterian, the Rev. Hugh Hanna. (Indeed the only inhabitants of Belfast entirely safe from sectarian preaching of one sort or another in the mid-nineteenth century were the inmates of the Lunatic Asylum, whose medical superintendent resolutely refused to admit chaplains, on the ground that over-zealous pastors might disseminate

The Custom House (1857), the finest work of the architect Charles Lanyon who left an enduring mark on the appearance of Belfast. The steps were the 'Speakers' Corner' of the town from the time of the building's completion and figured prominently in the riots of 1857; the cobbled street in front provided plenty of ammunition for those unconvinced by argument alone. *Welch Collection, Ulster Museum*

'a wild and dangerous fanaticism amongst the lunatics'.)[40] After the initial outburst had subsided the rioting resumed and continued well into September, despite the fact that the police had been reinforced by the military. When all was over the Liberals demanded an inquiry, which was granted in the form of a Royal Commission. The Commission's report was rather inconclusive but chiefly blamed Drew's inflammatory preaching and the provocation offered to Catholics by the activities of the Orange Order. It also criticised the Town Police as both inadequate and biased.[41]

The 1857 report was to be only the first of many. Though the circumstances and the details of each outbreak were of course different, the basic cause of the continuing conflict – and the essential shape of 'the narrow ground' on which it was fought – was already fixed by 1860. A recent detailed study of the local politics of the period comes to this conclusion:

> Behind the vicious sectarianism there lurked a political question involving a test of strength and a difference of identity: the Roman Catholics, seeing themselves as part of Ireland's overwhelming religious majority, challenged Belfast's identity as a Protestant town where they were regarded as alien intruders; the Protestants, fearful of Ultramontanism and of an Irish identity which Roman Catholics seemed to regard as exclusive to themselves, determined to assert that Belfast remained a Protestant town in a Protestant United Kingdom.[42]

Religion and Education

There were, of course, many quite normal aspects of religious activity in this town where – as Thackeray remarked in 1842 – no stranger could fail to be struck, and perhaps a little frightened, by the number of churches and the esteem accorded to leading clergy.[43] The number of churches had certainly grown since 1800, but not nearly so quickly as the population. A second Church of Ireland congregation was established only in 1816, when St George's was built on the site of the old parish church at the foot of High Street. By the early 1830s, however, when Christ Church (Drew's) was built, the two buildings could accommodate only 2,300 of the nominal 16,000 members of the established church; in fact, since pews were bought and bequeathed as private property, only six seats were left for the poor.[44] By 1850 five more churches had been built, and by 1861 there were ten. Catholics had even greater difficulty in keeping pace with population. A second church, in Donegall Street, was opened in 1815 (like the first, with the help of Protestant subscriptions). By 1861 there were still only three churches, which with the chapels of a religious order and the diocesan seminary served a population of more than 41,000; the observation made (by a Protestant clergyman) in 1863 that only one-third of Belfast Catholics attended Sunday mass was probably true, if for no other reason than lack of a church to go to.[45] There was no Catholic church on the Falls Road until 1866, despite the numbers of Catholics who had settled there by that time. Poverty was a major cause of this time-lag. The much greater number of Presbyterian churches, on the other hand, was a reflection both of numbers and wealth; indeed Belfast was then, as now, the ecclesiastical capital of Irish Presbyterianism. The normal Presbyterian tendency to divide and form separate organisations in fact operated in reverse during this period, apart from the great split over Arianism at the end of the 1820s: in 1840 the two bodies that claimed the allegiance of most of the congregations in the north – the Synod of Ulster and the Secession Synod (the latter itself only united in 1818) – came together to form the General Assembly of the Presbyterian Church in Ireland. By 1861 mainstream Presbyterianism had no fewer than twenty churches in Belfast. A further twenty belonged to other dissenting sects. The Protestant churches at that time were still digesting the effects of an extraordinary outbreak of popular evangelical fervour, which reached a climax in the 'Great Revival' of 1859, an experience which transported many worshippers into hysterics. (The typical Belfast converts were evidently unmarried mill girls. Male shipyard workers, despite all the efforts of evangelists, resisted almost to a man.)[46]

The 1861 census revealed that 30% of Belfast Catholics were illiterate, as compared with 10% of Protestants. Religion and public education were of course closely connected. In the early years of the century two undenominational schools for the education of the poor had been established, the Lancasterian school in Frederick Street (founded by the educational pioneer Joseph Lancaster when he visited Belfast in 1811) and the Sunday School Society school in Brown Street. The priest in charge of the Catholic parish from 1812, Dr Crolly, supported both of these schools for many years and was elected to the committees that ran them. In 1822, however, he was not re-elected to the Brown Street committee, and his offer to supply the Catholic pupils with free copies of the Douay version of the Scriptures was also rejected. As a result, he withdrew the Catholic children from Brown Street and set up a Sunday School in the new church in Donegall Street. Distrust of the Sunday School Society's evangelising policies combined with growing numbers of Catholic children (the new school soon had 1,500 on its rolls) to undermine the co-operation that had existed. Nevertheless, in 1825, when he was made bishop of Down and Connor, Crolly included many Protestants – including the sovereign, who proposed his health, and leading clergy – among his guests at a celebratory dinner, and was entertained in return by 170 of 'the most respectable Protestant inhabitants'. The fact that as bishop he chose to run his diocese from Belfast, rather than Downpatrick, indicates how significant the Catholic population in the town was becoming. As bishop, and later as archbishop of Armagh, Crolly supported the National Schools, introduced throughout Ireland after 1831, which were intended to be undenominational. However, in practice they became denominational because of clerical pressure from all sides. By 1854 there were 28 National Schools in or about Belfast, most of them under the control of the Protestant churches; at this stage, in the absence of sufficient schools of their own, many Catholic children attended what were in effect Protestant schools.[47]

At the secondary level the only establishment in the early years of the century, apart from a few small private schools, was the Belfast Academy, a Presbyterian foundation. A second, the Academical Institution, was founded in 1810 and opened its doors in 1814; one of its subscribers, incidentally, was the Catholic priest, Dr Crolly. The old radical Dr William Drennan (author, in one of his poems, of the epithet 'Emerald Isle' as a description of Ireland) delivered the opening address; and indeed the Academical Institution represented the liberal hopes of enlightened Presbyterians. It had a collegiate department which it was hoped would develop into a university and which in fact soon largely replaced Glasgow University as the seminary for Presbyterian clergy. The presence on the staff of liberal ministers such as the Rev. Dr Henry Montgomery drew down on the Institution the implacable hostility of the reactionary Cooke, who in 1825 accused them of promoting 'Arian' or unitarian doctrines. Cooke's strictures were not upheld by a government investigation in 1829. He did, however, oblige his opponents and their supporters to withdraw from the main Presbyterian body, which thereafter withdrew its students from the polluted teaching at the Institution.[48] (Following the union of the Synod of Ulster and the Secession Synod in 1840 and the opening of the 'godless' Queen's College in 1849, the orthodox Presbyterians built their own seminary, Assembly's College.) St Malachy's College, established in 1833, was the first Catholic secondary school for boys as well as a diocesan seminary. Victoria College, founded in 1859 by a redoubtable widow, Mrs Elizabeth Byers, was the first secondary school of respectable academic standing for Protestant girls. These sectarian divisions in schooling were by no means peculiar to Belfast, however.

The Academical Institution did not develop, as hoped, into a secular college of higher education, but the need and wish for such a college in the north of Ireland became increasingly strong. Trinity College, Dublin, the only university in Ireland, excluded both Catholics and Dissenters from degrees and appointments. In 1845 Peel's government decided to establish and endow colleges in the Irish provinces. The act establishing the Queen's Colleges did not specify where they were to be, and in the north the rival claims of Armagh and Londonderry were canvassed before Belfast was decided upon. The design of the architect Charles Lanyon for a Tudor-style edifice reminiscent of an Oxford college was accepted, work started in 1846 and the opening ceremony was carried out just before Christmas 1849. Though officially non-denominational, the College inevitably reflected the predominance of Presbyterians among its supporters and students: its first two presidents were Presbyterian ministers and it became in effect the college for Presbyterians, just as the Queen's Colleges in Cork and Galway

Queen's College (1849), another of Lanyon's imposing works, as it looked in the 1880s.   *Welch Collection, Ulster Museum*

became colleges for Catholics.[49] At the university level as in primary and secondary education, the ideal of every denomination was to control its own institutions.

The establishment of the Queen's College both confirmed and strengthened the intellectual and cultural interests already evident in the existence of the Academical Institution and other bodies such as the Linen Hall Library, the Literary Society (1801), the Natural History (later Natural History and Philosophical) Society (1821) – which in 1831 established the first museum in Ireland paid for by public subscription – and a Mechanics' Institute (1825). Another self-improvement group, the Historic Society (1810), did not long survive the arrival of real politics in the 1830s. One of its leading lights during its last years was the young Thomas O'Hagan (1812–85), a Catholic educated at the Academical Institution who went on to become Lord Chancellor of Ireland. On the whole, however, Belfast Catholics at this stage lacked both the education and the leisure to take much part in such activities. The town was remarkable in this period for a number of gifted amateur natural scientists, notably the botanist John Templeton, his son Robert, a renowned zoologist, and William Thompson, the leading authority on the invertebrate fauna of Ireland.[50] The visual arts were less well patronised: hopes for an art gallery, first expressed by the promoters of the Academical Institution and later attempted in the Museum, foundered on the philistine indifference of most potential patrons, though there were several local artists of some competence, and the owner of a

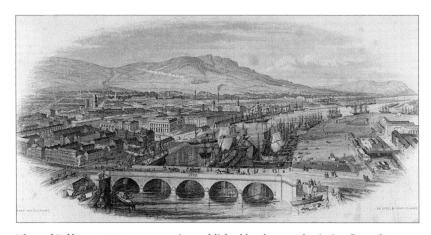

View of Belfast, c.1860, an engraving published by the noted printing firm of Marcus Ward & Co. In the foreground is the Queen's Bridge, which replaced the old Long Bridge in the early 1840s. The new Custom House is just beyond, overlooking Donegall Quay. The schooners on the right brought the coal on which the growing town's industry and domestic comfort depended.   *Ulster Museum*

cotton mill, Francis McCracken, was an early collector of Pre-Raphaelite paintings (unfortunately he had to sell them all when his business collapsed).[51] The linen manufacturers could not even be induced to subscribe half the running costs of a government-sponsored School of Design (1849–55) which aimed to train designers for the textile industry. The theatre in Belfast, formerly well supported, incurred the disapproval of respectable citizens in the 1840s and 1850s (the author of the entry in the *Parliamentary Gazetteer*, for example, remarked that it was much neglected, 'greatly to the credit of the metropolis of the north'). More popular entertainments, however, in the theatre and the Queen's Island pleasure grounds, attracted large crowds in the 1850s and 1860s; so too did the numerous public houses (over 300 by 1861, despite the efforts of the temperance movements that had developed in all the churches during the previous three decades). These diversions, like many other everyday activities, were still common ground in a town which in other respects was steadily growing more divided.[52]

Over the half century or so before 1860, Belfast like other towns in the United Kingdom had been transformed into a major industrial centre. Its urban facilities had similarly expanded as a result of public and private efforts. A social hierarchy of the kind to be found in other industrial areas had also emerged, with a commercial and manufacturing elite replacing aristocratic patronage and pretensions and dominating a growing urban labour force. Untypically, however, in Belfast divisions over nationality and religion were assuming greater importance than those of class and were already stamping their peculiar pattern on the social geography of this 'great and rising town'.

56

References

1. E. Boyle, ' "Linenopolis": the rise of the textile industry', in Beckett *et al.*, *Belfast*, pp. 43–4.
2. F. Geary, 'The rise and fall of the Belfast cotton industry: some problems', *Irish Economic and Social History*, 8 (1981), pp. 30–49; and 'The Belfast cotton industry revisited', *Irish Historical Studies*, 26, no.103 (1989), pp. 250–67.
3. J. L. McCracken, 'Early Victorian Belfast', in Beckett and Glasscock (eds), *Belfast*, pp. 88–9.
4. Boyle, '"Linenopolis"', in Beckett *et al.*, *Belfast*, pp. 46–7.
5. G. N. Wright, *Scenes in Ireland*, London (1834), p. 220.
6. Mr and Mrs S. C. Hall, *Ireland: Its Scenery, Character etc.*, 3 vols, London (1841–3), 3, pp. 53, 56.
7. *Parliamentary Gazetteer of Ireland*, 3 vols, Dublin (1844–6), 1, p. 234.
8. See M. Moss and J. R. Hume, *Shipbuilders to the World: 125 Years of Harland and Wolff, Belfast, 1861–1986*, Blackstaff Press, Belfast (1986), pp. 11–21.
9. See W. E. Coe, *The Engineering Industry of the North of Ireland*, David & Charles, Newton Abbot (1969), pp. 22–32, 46–76.
10. P. Ollerenshaw, *Banking in Nineteenth-Century Ireland: The Belfast Banks, 1825–1914*, Manchester University Press, Manchester (1987), pp. 5–30; N. Simpson, *The Belfast Bank, 1827–1970*, Blackstaff Press, Belfast (1975), chs 1 and 2.
11. Simpson, *Belfast Bank*, p.49.
12. R. E. Glasscock, 'The growth of the port', in Beckett and Glasscock, (eds), *Belfast*, pp. 98–101; Sweetnam, 'Development of the port', in Beckett *et al.*, *Belfast*, pp. 57–8.
13. T. Gaffikin, *Belfast Fifty Years Ago*, Belfast (1875), p. 12.
14. Sweetnam, 'Development of the port', in Beckett *et al.*, *Belfast*, pp. 60–2.
15. Owen, *Port of Belfast*, pp. 38, 48.
16. McCracken, 'Early Victorian Belfast', in Beckett and Glasscock, (eds), *Belfast*, pp. 96–7.
17. Gaffikin, *Belfast Fifty Years Ago*, p. 12.
18. I. Budge and C. O'Leary, *Belfast: Approach to Crisis: A Study of Belfast Politics, 1613–1970*, Macmillan, London (1973), pp. 27–33, appendix to ch.1.
19. The statistics quoted here come from two pamphlets: *Report on the Sanitary State of Belfast*, Belfast (1848); and A. G. Malcolm, *The Sanitary State of Belfast, with Suggestions for its Improvement*, Greer, Belfast (1852).
20. W. M. O'Hanlon, *Walks among the Poor of Belfast, and Suggestions for their Improvement*, Greer *et al.*, *Belfast* (1853), reprinted by S. R. Publishers, Wakefield (1971), pp. 5–6, 13, 16, 44.
21. P. D. Hardy, *The Northern Tourist*, Dublin (1830), p. 137.
22. *Report from the Select Committee on the Municipal Corporations* (1833), pp. v–vi.
23. Budge and O'Leary, *Belfast*, p. 53.
24. W. A. Maguire, *Living like a Lord: The second Marquis of Donegall, 1769–1844*, Appletree Press, Belfast (1983); and 'The 1822 settlement of the Donegall estates', *Irish Economic and Social History*, 3, (1976), pp. 17–32.
25. W. A. Maguire, 'Lord Donegall and the sale of Belfast: a case history from the Encumbered Estates Court', *Economic History Review*, second series, 29, no.4 (1976), pp. 570–84.

26. R. B. McDowell, 'Dublin and Belfast – a comparison', in R. B. McDowell (ed.), *Social Life in Ireland, 1800–45*, Mercier Press, Cork (1957), p. 23.

27. G. J. Slater, 'Belfast politics, 1798–1868', DPhil thesis, New University of Ulster, Coleraine (1982), 2 vols, 2, pp. 333–8. I am greatly indebted to Dr Slater for making his thesis – a major contribution to the understanding of the period – available to me.

28. R. F. Holmes, *Henry Cooke*, Christian Journals Ltd, Belfast, (1981), pp. 113–7.

29. Slater, 'Belfast politics', 2, pp. 248–52.

30. Slater, 'Belfast politics', 2, p. 254.

31. Slater, 'Belfast politics', 2, pp. 264–5.

32. Slater, 'Belfast politics', 2, pp. 264–5.

33. Slater, 'Belfast politics', 2, pp. 255,258; Budge and O'Leary, *Belfast*, pp. 60–2.

34. Slater, 'Belfast politics', 2, pp. 256–7; Budge and O'Leary, *Belfast*, p. 63.

35. Budge and O'Leary, *Belfast*, p. 65.

36. Budge and O'Leary, *Belfast*, p. 32.

37. F. F. Moore, *The Truth about Ulster*, Eveleigh Nash, London (1914), p. 24.

38. McCracken, 'Early Victorian Belfast', in Beckett and Glasscock, (eds), *Belfast*, p. 96.

39. See A. T. Q. Stewart, *The Narrow Ground: Aspects of Ulster, 1609–1969*, Faber & Faber, London (1977), pp. 145–54; and A. Boyd, *Holy War in Belfast*, Anvil Books, Tralee (1969), reprinted by Pretani Press, Belfast (1988).

40. M. Finnane, *Insanity and the Insane in post-Famine Ireland*, Croom Helm, London (1981), p. 200.

41. *Report of the Commissioners of Inquiry into the … Riots in Belfast in … 1857*, HMSO, Dublin (1858). Drew's sermon to the Orangemen, Hanna's public letters to the 'Protestants of Belfast' and McIlwaine's advertisements of his Lent Lectures on Popery – on the theme 'Is Popery Christianity?' – were printed as appendices to the Report.

42. Slater, 'Belfast politics', 2, p. 339.

43. W. M. Thackeray, *The Irish Sketch Book, 1842*, reprinted by Blackstaff Press, Belfast (1985), p. 304.

44. Budge and O'Leary, *Belfast*, p. 97, n. 35.

45. When St Patrick's in Donegall Street opened in 1815, pews were sold to the more affluent parishioners, as in some Protestant churches – incidentally an early indication of social advancement. The practice ceased from the middle of the century.

46. P. Gibbon, *The Origins of Ulster Unionism*, Manchester University Press, Manchester (1975), p. 48.

47. A. Macaulay, 'William Crolly', unpublished paper. I am grateful to Dr Macaulay for kindly providing me with a copy of his useful paper.

48. Holmes, *Cooke*, pp. 34–6, 39–43, 47–76.

49. See T. W. Moody and J. C. Beckett, *Queen's, Belfast, 1845–1949*, 2 vols, Faber & Faber, London (1959), 1, Introduction and pp. 84–115.

50. A. Deane (ed.), *The Belfast Natural History and Philosophical Society: Centenary Volume, 1821–1921*, Belfast (1924).

51. M. Anglesea, 'A Pre-Raphaelite enigma in Belfast', *Irish Arts Review*, 1, no.2 (1984), pp. 40–5.

52. J. Gray, 'Popular entertainment', in Beckett *et al.*, *Belfast*, pp. 106–7; E. Black, *The People's Park: The Queen's Island, 1849–1879*, Linen Hall Library, Belfast (1988).

Chapter 3

Industry, Trade and Society, 1861–1901

Though the basis of Belfast's reputation as a great industrial and commercial centre had already been laid by 1860, it was only during the last forty years of Victoria's reign that this reputation was actually given substance, first as 'Linenopolis' and then as the site of the largest shipyard and the largest ropeworks in the world, a major engineering centre and a great port. This chapter surveys these developments and the society which both produced them and resulted from them.

Linen

The effect of the American Civil War (1861–5) on the Irish linen trade was nothing short of dramatic. With imports of raw cotton from the Confederate states cut off, the demand for linen and also its selling price soared. Both sectors of the manufacturing side of the industry, by then heavily concentrated in the north-east, benefited enormously. In Belfast itself, however, the boom led to the expansion of existing mills and factories rather than the building of new ones: only two mills were built between 1862 and 1871, and by 1866 only twelve of the country's powerloom factories were in Belfast. On the contrary, much of the expansion in production in the 1860s and early 1870s took place in rural areas of Ulster, now well served by railways, where wages were significantly lower than those paid in Belfast. Even so, by 1870 more than 80% of the spindles in use and 70% of the power looms were located in or near Belfast. According to the 1871 census, 8,500 of the town's 'industrial class' workers were employed in the manufacture of flax and linen. The more striking thing in the town, however, was the expansion of the commercial side: by 1870 practically every firm in the country had its warehouse and offices in Belfast and over 99% of Irish linen was being exported through the port; the number of 'linen merchants and manufacturers' listed in the street directory rose from 29 in 1863 to over 150 in 1870. No less than 21,000 workers, out of the 50,000 engaged in industry and commerce, were employed in making or dealing in textiles and dress. At the height of the boom some firms made vast profits, in one case equalling the value of the entire premises and plant two years running. The reappearance of cotton caused some recession in the late 1860s, but in general the good times continued until 1873. By that date Belfast had become the largest linen-producing centre in the world, a position it retained until 1914.

Spinning linen yarn in a Belfast mill in the 1890s. The women and girls who tended the machines (the overseers were men) were probably safer without shoes on the wet and slippery floor, but more liable to contract the foot infection onychia.

Ulster Museum

A number of firms which had extended too far and too fast in the sixties went bankrupt in the later seventies. The next crisis, in the mid-1880s, was precipitated by the collapse of the great spinning firm of John Hind and Co. – a disaster brought on not by commercial failure but by a lawsuit over a will. No further run of bankruptcies occurred till 1898, when the effects of collapse were worse on firms in outlying areas than in Belfast. In fact the outcome of these recurring difficulties was the still greater concentration of the industry in and around Belfast, where the surviving firms struggled with some success to keep up their share of a highly competitive market. This was achieved in part by more efficient production – improved hackling machines were adopted, for example, and spinning machinery was speeded up – but also by a determined search for new markets and new uses for linen, and by more aggressive marketing. Though the number of spindles fell from 925,000 to 828,000 between 1875 and 1900, linen at the end of the century was employing slightly more people than in 1868 because powerloom weaving increased.[1]

This is an appropriate place to add a footnote about cotton, whose displacement by linen was such a striking feature of the decades before 1860. That decline continued so far as manufacturing was concerned: by 1883 only one spinning mill remained and not a single weaving factory. A considerable business developed, however, in bleaching, printing, dyeing

Richardson Sons & Owden's linen warehouse in Donegall Square, early 1880s. Built in the late 1860s at the time of the great linen boom, this palace of commerce later became the head office of the Belfast Water Commissioners; it is now part of Marks & Spencer's store. *Welch Collection, Ulster Museum*

and finishing cotton piece goods from England and Scotland; this led in turn to the local manufacture of cotton goods such as blouses, shirts and pinafores.[2]

The evidence of Linenopolis was to be seen not only in the great mills and factories to which the shawled women and girls hurried early in the morning and from which they poured out in the evening, but also in warerooms and workshops where linen was finished and made up and in the warehouses and offices of dozens of firms. Some of the best buildings that survive from this period were built as linen warehouses. When a foreign visitor admired Richardson Sons & Owden's building in Donegall Square (now owned by Marks & Spencer) and asked which nobleman had built it he was told, 'Duke Linen'. The Robinson & Cleaver building next to it, built in the late 1880s, was also a linen warehouse; so too were the Bank Buildings in Castle Place, while Bedford Street consisted almost entirely of the imposing facades of such premises.[3]

Shipbuilding

If linen was king in the sixties and seventies, shipbuilding rose in the eighties and nineties to share the throne. During the 1860s and 1870s the firm of Harland & Wolff produced a growing number of iron ships, many of them for the Bibby Line. The three launched for Bibby's in 1867 were constructed to a revolutionary new design by Harland which combined great length with narrow width and a flat 'Belfast' bottom. Derided at first by rivals as 'Bibby coffins', they were later admired as the 'ocean grey-hounds' of their day. Harland & Wolff's connection with the Oceanic Steam Navigation Company of Liverpool – the White Star Line – began in 1870 with the *Oceanic*, which made all existing Atlantic liners obsolete, both in performance and in standards of comfort (innovations included cabins amidships, electric bells and lamps instead of candles). By later standards these iron liners were not particularly large (*Britannic* and *Germanic*, launched in 1874, were the first to exceed 5,000 tons), and they carried sail as well as steam, but they were the beginning of real comfort in ocean travel and fast as well. Harland & Wolff were to build increasingly large and more luxurious ships which would make their name and that of the White Star Line famous throughout the world. By 1880 the yard had been extended to forty acres and had ten slips; when it built its own engine works on the Queen's Island in the same year it became practically self-sufficient.[4] Great as these changes were, they were only the beginning. Harland himself, replying in 1879 to the toast of 'The Town and Trade of Belfast', indicated as much when he said: 'It is a new town without a

The partners of Harland & Wolff, c.1880: from left to right, Gustav Wolff, W. H. Wilson (designer), William Pirrie and Edward Harland.   *Ulster Museum*

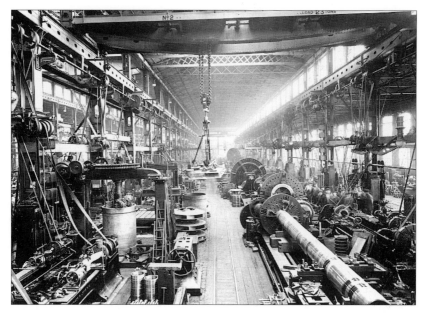

Turning shop in the engine works at Harland & Wolff, c.1890.
Welch Collection, Ulster Museum

history, and in time I have no doubt we will possess a reputation for commerce and industry that will assign us an important place in the history of the United Kingdom'.[5]

By that time Harland & Wolff's was not the only yard in Belfast. Another was founded in the late 1870s by Frank Workman, a local businessman, who was joined in 1880 by George Clark from Glasgow. Workman Clark's 'Wee Yard', as it came to be called, expanded rapidly in the 1880s and 1890s; by the end of the century, having taken over a third, much smaller yard and built up its own engine works, it was operating on a site covering fifty acres and had reached national importance. Its customers included P&O, Royal Mail, Cunard, Orient, Shaw Savill and Ellerman Lines, for whom it built ships of up to 15,000 tons.[6] Although a serious trade depression in the early 1880s had obliged Harland & Wolff to cut its workforce from 5,000 to 3,500 and to reduce the wages of those who remained, a really spectacular growth of shipbuilding in Belfast took place in the late 1880s and 1890s. The halcyon era in passenger liners began with the launching in 1889 of the *Teutonic* and *Majestic* for the White Star Line – steel vessels of nearly 10,000 tons with twin screws, triple-expansion engines and accommodation for more than 1,300 passengers. In the years that followed, Harland & Wolff launches averaged 100,000 tons a year; by 1900 they were employing 9,000 men. Between them the two Belfast yards outstripped those of all other UK regions in their rate of growth right up to the outbreak of the war in 1914, but especially so during the years before

1900.[7] The year 1899, in which Harland & Wolff launched four ships for the White Star Line, including *Oceanic II* – at 17,274 tons the largest ship afloat, and the first to exceed Brunel's *Great Eastern* in length – demonstrated the firm's achievement at the end of the century, when it had become the greatest single shipyard in the world.

Harland himself had begun to withdraw from active management quite early, to enter public life as chairman of the Harbour Commissioners (1875–87), an alderman (1883–7), Mayor of Belfast (1885 and 1886) and finally Conservative MP for North Belfast 1887–95 (when he died). His partner Wolff also withdrew and became an MP, in his case for East Belfast 1892–1910. It was a Belfast man, William Pirrie, who had become a partner in 1874 at the age of twenty-seven, who presided over the firm in its greatest days. The entrepreneurial flair and business acumen of such men were certainly an important factor in the success of Belfast's shipyards. Access to markets, through contacts and connections, was vital in what was almost entirely an export industry. Pirrie had many such contacts, and also arranged for established customers to have the benefit of a secret 'commission club' (members could have their ships built at cost price plus a small percentage fixed commission); the advantage to the yard was that orders could be maintained at a high average level. An abundant supply of cheap labour was also important, for though skilled men in Belfast were paid more than the national average, wages for the workforce as a whole were rather less. A reputation for good workmanship, established under the exacting management of Harland, no doubt helped as well.[8]

Engineering

The success of linen and shipbuilding encouraged the growth of engineering; between 1865 and 1900 the number of engineering workers grew from 900 to 9,000. By 1870 there were twenty foundries in Belfast but, undercut in the making of cast-iron and brass products by English and Scottish firms (both Harland & Wolff and Workman Clark found it cheaper to run foundries on the Clyde), most of them could survive only by making machinery. Steam engines were made by Coates's and Rowan's for use in linen mills (the Ulster Museum has examples of both); Coates's also made water turbines and, at the turn of the century, electricity generation equipment; McAdam Brothers made steam pumps which were used in Nile irrigation schemes; Combe Barbour made engines for cotton mills in India. Even Belfast got its linen looms from Manchester or Leeds, but it became the leading centre in the world for the production of linen machinery for processes which had no equivalent in cotton – hackling, spinning, beetling. The Falls Foundry of James Combe (later Combe Barbour) had been making hackling machines from the 1850s. The Clonard Foundry, established by George Horner from Leeds in 1859, found a world market for its famous 'Duplex' machine, which hackled both ends of the flax. James Scrimgeour, a Scot who came to Belfast to start a textile machinery works, was succeeded when he failed in the Albert Foundry by his manager James Mackie, another Scot, who made a great success of it. Mackie's became a limited company in 1897 and in 1902 took over the Clonard Foundry. By that time Mackie's and Combe Barbour were the largest engineering firms in the city apart from the shipyards, between them manufacturing the entire range of flax-processing machinery. An incidental advantage of having the makers and their chief customers in close proximity was that adjustments and improvements could easily be made.[9]

There were also successful firms in other branches of engineering. Musgrave Bros, for example, became internationally known during this period for its decorative cast-ironwork, patent stable fittings and heating equipment. By the end of the century many of the best stables of Europe were furnished by Musgraves'. The same firm's domestic and institutional heating stoves (the more luxurious in 'ethnic' styles such as the 'Slav', with beautiful coloured tilework) were also to be found all over the British Isles and Europe. By 1900, in which year 'Le Poêle Musgrave' won a gold medal at the Paris Exposition, the firm had a branch in the Rue de Rivoli and was producing a catalogue in French with colour illustrations.[10] One other specialist engineering firm which attained a worldwide reputation deserves mention here. Samuel Davidson spent his early years in the Assam tea plantations, where he devised drying machinery which he patented on his return home. The machines were at first made by a local engineering firm, but when Davidson finally came back to Belfast in 1881 he started his own 'Sirocco' works. By the end of the century Sirocco was producing most of the world's tea-drying machinery and a large proportion of its ventilation equipment; most of the ships of the German Grand Fleet, scuttled at Scapa Flow in 1919, were equipped with Sirocco fans.[11]

Other Industries

Impressive as they were, linen, shipbuilding and engineering were not the whole story. This period also saw the rise of an extensive ropeworks, formed in a small way near the Queen's Island shipyard in 1873 but rapidly expanded after 1876, when it became a limited liability company with Gustav Wolff as chairman and W. H. Smiles (son of the famous Dr Samuel Smiles, author of *Self Help*) as managing director. An early publicity coup was achieved by persuading the French tightrope walker, Blondin, to use its products. By the turn of the century it was the largest ropeworks in the world, covering forty acres and producing not only rope and twine of all kinds but also sash cord, fishing lines and nets, and binder twine for harvesting machines; the number of employees had risen from only one hundred to 3,000.[12]

Ropewalk at the Bloomfield Mill of the Belfast Ropeworks, 1899; fishing lines being made. Overhead is a 'Belfast roof', a distinctive local style of construction using timber trellis. *Welch Collection, Ulster Museum*

Belfast also became a major producer of whiskey, in the days before the Irish variety of the water of life was displaced in world opinion by Scotch. Large-scale production of whiskey began after 1860, when Dunville's gave up their tea business to concentrate on distilling. In 1870 William Dunville, in partnership with James Craig (father of the first prime minister of Northern Ireland), built a huge modern plant on the Grosvenor Road; by 1890 it was producing two and a half million gallons of proof spirit. The Irish Distillery at Connswater in east Belfast was producing two million gallons by 1900, and the Avoniel Distillery about 850,000. In fact Belfast firms were responsible for well over half the total whiskey exports of Ireland.[13]

In a smaller way, soft drinks were also an export success. In the middle of the century there were a dozen small firms producing 'aerated waters' from the exceptionally pure artesian springs on the outskirts of the town at Cromac. The most successful of these were Grattan's, Corry's and Cantrell's (from 1867 Cantrell & Cochrane's), to which was added W. A. Ross and Co. in 1876. Though never so important to the economy of Belfast as extensive advertising and hard selling made them appear, these firms and their products became known throughout the Empire and wherever European settlers found the local water undrinkable. Ross's claimed to have invented the gin and tonic as a way of marketing their tonic water with quinine, Cantrell and Cochrane's to have invented ginger ale (which was also a speciality of Ross's). By the late 1880s, Cantrell & Cochrane's had 500 employees in Belfast and Dublin (the Dublin branch opened in

Bird's-eye view of Thomas Gallaher's new tobacco factory in York Street, c.1900.
Ulster Museum

1869) and was producing over 160,000 bottles of table waters a day; Ross's produced 36,000 a day in Belfast in 1889.[14]

Tobacco, a larger employer of labour, was dominated in particular by the rise of Gallaher's. In 1863 Thomas Gallaher transferred his successful but small-scale operations from Londonderry to Belfast, where his superior pipe tobacco could be produced more cheaply and in greater quantity to meet a growing demand (between 1850 and 1900 per capita consumption of tobacco in Ireland doubled). During the 1870s power-driven machinery began to replace hand-operated methods, and in 1881 Gallaher built a five-storey factory in York Street employing 600 people; a still larger one was added in 1896 on the same site. In terms of customs revenue, tobacco became a major import into Belfast; in 1889 Gallaher's alone paid duty amounting to almost half a million pounds.[15] The other notable firm of manufacturers, Murray Bros, expanded less spectacularly than Gallaher's but it too became a substantial enterprise.

Lastly, three Belfast printing firms achieved national or international reputation during this period. Marcus Ward & Co. had started as paper-makers before developing as chromolithographers and pioneers of the Christmas card. They exhibited at the Great Exhibition of 1851 and thereafter with increasing success at exhibitions all over the world, notably in Paris in 1867 and 1878 (where they gained the highest awards in all the classes in which they exhibited), Philadelphia and Melbourne. At their peak they employed more than fifty artists and designers at their Royal Ulster Works, and also bought in the services of such notable illustrators as

Kate Greenaway. For many years an important bread-and-butter income was derived from a monopoly of printing the Vere Foster writing and drawing copybooks, familiar to generations of schoolchildren. Another firm, McCaw, Stevenson & Orr, which started in the mid-1870s, specialised in commercial and advertising products, such as the 'Glacier' transparent coloured labels which adorned many late-Victorian shop windows. A third firm, David Allen & Sons, became the leading supplier of colour posters for the English-speaking theatrical world. At one point in 1889 it was calculated that they had something like 16,000 theatre posters on London hoardings alone. So good did business become that branches were opened in London and New York, and the firm later transferred its headquarters to the capital.[16]

The Port

The continued expansion of the port and harbour facilities was both a condition of all this industrial and commercial growth and a consequence of it. In 1892 exports from Belfast included 35,000 tons of linen, 24,000 tons of whiskey and nearly 9,000 tons of mineral waters, not to mention almost all the output of the shipyards and engineering works. Agricultural exports included 65,000 head of cattle and 11,000 tons of grass-seed, as well as considerable quantities of cured ham. Imports in the same year included half a million tons of coal, 86,000 tons of iron and castings, more than 160,000 tons of wheat and Indian corn, and most of the flax used in the linen industry. By that time the port was clearing nearly 9,000 vessels a year with a tonnage of just under three million, as compared with 1,372,000 in 1867. The number of ships handled had increased by less than one thousand but they were much bigger vessels and a greater proportion of their space was devoted to cargo. These larger vessels with their deeper draughts made it constantly necessary to improve the port and harbour facilities, a course which the Harbour Commissioners followed with great energy and foresight. On the County Down side of the Lagan, the Abercorn basin and Hamilton graving dock, started in 1863, were opened four years later. In 1872 the Spencer and Dufferin docks opened on the County Antrim side. The Queen's Quay, completely reconstructed, was reopened in 1877 as part of an extensive programme which included the rebuilding of the Donegall Quay, the renewal and extension of the Albert Quay and the widening and deepening of the existing channel. During a visit by the prince and princess of Wales and Prince Albert Victor in 1885 the new Donegall Quay was declared open and the first sod of a new graving dock was cut. Albert Victor returned in 1889 to open the Alexandra dock. The century-old connection of the Chichester family with the Ballast Board and its successor came to an end at this point: when the fourth marquess of Donegall died in 1888 the office of president, which he had held by virtue of being lord of the castle, was abolished.

By the time the duke of York came to Belfast in 1894 to open the dock named after him, all the docks, quays and sheds were lit by electric light, produced by a special generating station erected in 1892 at the Abercorn basin. The rowing-boat ferries across the harbour were replaced by steamboats in 1872. The Harbour Office, built in the 1850s, was greatly extended in the early 1890s, to designs by W. H. Lynn, Lanyon's former partner. As the century neared its end the Commissioners obtained another Act of Parliament to widen and deepen the Victoria channel, to make a new cut with a tidal dock at the end of it, to construct two other docks on the site of older existing ones and to build a graving dock on the County Down side. The first part of this ambitious programme was started in 1899 and the new cut, named the Musgrave channel, was opened in 1903. Compared with other major ports such as Liverpool, Belfast was fortunate in having only a small tidal range. There was no need to enclose the docks by gates; vessels were able to lie alongside the open quays and wharves to discharge their cargoes and could be berthed, docked and undocked at all times without waiting for high water.[17]

Population Change

In the forty years between the census of 1861 and the death of Queen Victoria the population of Belfast almost trebled, from 121,000 to just under 350,000. Part of the increase can be attributed to a boundary extension in 1896 which expanded the physical area of the borough from ten to twenty-three square miles. Officially Belfast's population became larger than that of Dublin, much to the northern city's satisfaction. Most of Belfast's human growth, however, was caused by the immigration of workers attracted by the dynamic industrial and commercial scene described above: the decades of most industrial growth were also those of greatest increase in numbers. The rise in 1861–71, for example, the years of the linen boom, was no less than 43%, the highest in the town's history after the start of censuses in 1821. By contrast the 1870s and 1880s, with decennial increases of 19% and 22%, were periods of lower (if still substantial) growth. The boom years of the 1890s were reflected in a rise of over 36%, only a small fraction of which was due to the boundary extension.[18]

This late-nineteenth century immigration was largely from the eastern, predominantly Protestant counties of Ulster. The proportion of Catholics in Belfast's population consequently declined during this period, from a fraction over one-third in 1861 to just under a quarter in 1901. Their numbers more than doubled, however, from 41,000 to 85,000, and in the circumstances of the time this rise in absolute numbers seemed more significant in sectarian calculations than the proportionate decline. There was comparatively little immigration from farther afield. Though its ship-building and engineering industries attracted skilled workers from Scotland and the north of England (a two-way traffic), Belfast never had any large number of immigrants from outside the British Isles – unlike Liverpool and other places. A few more Italians appeared towards the end of the century. A small Jewish community also developed, starting in the 1860s with a handful of well-to-do families from Hamburg engaged in the linen trade, notably the Jaffés. Gustav Wolff, Harland's partner, was another prominent member of this group. Around the turn of the century a larger influx of poorer refugees from Russia settled in Belfast. Even so, by 1911 the entire Jewish community numbered only 1,140.[19]

At the turn of the century only one-fifth of the city's householders had been born in Belfast. The proportion of native-born was somewhat higher among Catholics than among Protestants, a reflection of the heavier immigration of Protestants (particularly Presbyterians) into the city in the preceding generation or so. Another significant feature revealed by the censuses was the consistently greater number of women. In 1841 there had been 38,000 women and 32,000 men; sixty years later, with 188,000 women and 162,000 men, the ratio was very much the same. Nineteenth-century Belfast in fact provided more employment for females than most other cities in the British Isles, particularly in the textile industry and allied trades; domestic service was less important as a way of escaping from what for some was the unattractively 'restrictive, male-dominated environment of the family farm'.[20] By the turn of the century nearly two-fifths of the city's workforce consisted of women.

Housing and Urban Development

The growth of its industry and population led to a great expansion in the physical size of Belfast in the later nineteenth century. The immigrants of the 1860s and early 1870s mostly settled close to the linen mills and factories where they found employment; the working day started early enough without a long walk to reach the mill gate in time to avoid a fine for lateness. In order to have their workers close at hand, especially where mills were situated beyond the built-up part of the town, millowners them-selves constructed rows of small 'kitchen' houses. Some of these were so badly built that they were slums almost at once: a medical officer in 1873 described mill houses with walls of single brick only four inches thick and flat roofs covered with tarred felt as 'not fit to afford shelter to domesticated animals, much less to our fellow-creatures'. If built recently, however, these deplorable dwellings were probably outside the town boundary, for an Act of 1864 (unique to Belfast, as the Royal Commission on the Housing of the Working Classes noted in 1885) had made landlords responsible for the cost of rates and repairs for all houses with a Poor Law valuation of less than £8 – in effect, all working-class homes. This and stricter building regulations introduced in 1878 made employers uninter-ested in providing houses.[21]

Landowners, even those at a secondary level who held long leaseholds from major proprietors such as Lords Donegall and Templemore, played little or no part in the great building boom of the late-nineteenth century; most of those concerned were professionals. A crucial role was played by developers – individuals or companies with land at their disposal who laid out their property in building plots, which were then sold or (more usually) leased to builders; some developers, such as the Methodist College and Cliftonville Football Club, were in the development business only part-time or incidentally. Building societies, of which there were eight in Belfast by the early 1880s, provided capital by lending to builders rather than occupiers. So too did building-society-type investment companies such as the Royal, the Bloomfield (particularly active in east Belfast), the Ulster and the Belfast Provincial, which themselves built and owned houses. Some estate agents, such as William Hartley in the 1870s and R. J. McConnell & Co. later, were also major developers and building entrepreneurs; McConnell's in particular built all over the city and for every class of inhabitant. Large contractors such as H. & J. Martin (who owned 300 acres of building land and brickfields) and McLaughlin & Harvey did the same, not to mention some of the city's 170-odd smaller builders. In the last thirty years of the century the stock of houses quadrupled; almost 50,000 were built between 1880 and 1900, a figure representing more than half of all the houses built in Belfast between 1861 and 1917. In the latter decade alone the number of inhabited houses rose from 55,000 to 67,000; the total stock included several thousand more lying empty, for a notable feature of all housing development at this period was that dwellings were built speculatively, ahead of actual demand, and could remain unsold for several years. Nearly 2,300 new ones were built in 1895, nearly 3,000 in 1896 and almost 4,500 in 1898. By the turn of the century there was no shortage of houses, only a shortage of decent houses that the poorest could afford.[22]

Building costs in Belfast were low, not so much because wages of labourers were in general low, though that was true (the highest-paid bricklayers could not earn more than 35s. (£1.75) for a 56½ hour week), as because there was plenty of cheap local brick. Indeed ever since Sir Arthur Chichester had fired over a million bricks from the local clay to build his castle, Belfast had been a brick town. By 1900 there were more than thirty brickworks in and around the city producing not only millions of the 'commons' used for general building but also a wide variety of fancy bricks and the terra cotta panels and ornaments so typical of the better houses of this period. H. & J. Martin's brickworks on the Ormeau Road, the largest in Ireland, produced 60,000 bricks a day in 1888; their price of a guinea a thousand in 1885 was half the cost of bricks in Dublin. Furthermore, Belfast was very well placed to import cheaply, and in as much variety as anyone could wish, the timber, slates and other materials not available locally. Most timber for houses came from the Baltic and most slates (even the smallest kitchen house needed at least a ton) from North Wales, apart from a few years in the late 1890s when a labour dispute at Penrhyn led to the importation of large quantities from the United States.[23]

By the standards of the time, Belfast in the late nineteenth century was well-housed, if rather crowded. It had few if any of the dreadful tenement houses to be found in Dublin or Glasgow, for as the well-to-do inhabitants moved out from the centre their homes were made into offices or knocked down for redevelopment as commercial premises (this is why scarcely anything of the Georgian town survived); while its main growth came late enough to ensure that most of its working-class houses were purpose-built to minimum standards, thus avoiding the cellar dwellings and back-to-backs of Manchester and other cities. The great belt of working-class housing that encircled the city centre by the end of the century consisted mainly of 'kitchen' houses, small terrace houses whose front doors (on the street) opened directly into the kitchen/living room that occupied most of the ground floor; the stairs led from the kitchen to the two bedrooms upstairs, the front one of which was usually much bigger than the back one; behind the kitchen on the ground floor were a small third bedroom and a scullery. The rent of a kitchen house was 3s/6d (17½p) to 4s/0d (20p) a week. The up-market alternative to a kitchen house was a 'parlour' house at 4s/6d (22½p) to 5s/0d (25p) a week. Like the kitchen house this had four

Belfast was almost entirely made of locally-produced brick. This view was taken at the Ava brickworks in the Ormeau area in 1910. *Welch Collection, Ulster Museum*

rooms and a small scullery, and was of similar size, but the front door opened into a small hall out of which rose the stairs to the two bedrooms (there were only two) and off which were doors to the parlour at the front and the kitchen at the back. Quite apart from its lower rent, the kitchen house was popular because its three bedrooms better accommodated the large families that were the norm at that time in both Protestant and Catholic households. In the 1890s some larger parlour houses, with a third bedroom in a return over the scullery, were built for renting by the highest-paid artisans at 5s/0d (25p) to 6s/3d (32p) a week; it was the over-production of this type of house that mainly accounted for the 10,258 dwellings listed as empty in the census of 1901.[24]

Transport

The growth of public transport during the later nineteenth century had little effect on the pattern of development of working-class housing in Belfast; most people lived near their work and in any case could not afford to spend money on fares. Cheap and reliable public transport did a great deal, however, to encourage growing numbers of business and professional people to live at a considerable distance from their work. The flight from the town centre had begun earlier with wealthy merchants and manufac-turers who had built country villas on the outskirts, at Malone, Strandtown and the Shore Road. From the 1840s the railways enabled such people to commute easily. It was horse-drawn omnibuses, however, that first conveyed passengers in large numbers across the town and served the nearer suburbs as they grew; by 1870 there were regular services as far as

Artist's impression of the Midland Hotel and railway station, York Street, c.1890.
Welch Collection, Ulster Museum

73

Windsor in the south, Fitzwilliam in the north and Sydenham in the east. From 1872 omnibuses were increasingly challenged by trams, also horse-drawn. The Belfast Street Tramways Company, set up in that year by a group of London businessmen, ran single-decker, one-horse trams to begin with, but introduced double-deckers drawn by two horses from 1878. By that time the lines extended to Dunmore Park on the north side and on the south to Ormeau Bridge and the Botanic Gardens. The omnibuses held their own comfortably enough until the early 1880s. Then a new manager, Andrew Nance, transformed the operation of the tramway company by introducing a twopenny fare for any length of journey and a five-minute service on the main routes. Additional lines soon extended the network in all directions and it was also linked to the Cavehill and Whitewell Tramway (set up in 1882) which served the upper reaches of the Antrim Road. The introduction of a penny stage fare finished off the competition: the last omnibus service ended in 1892. The Corporation, which had an option to purchase the Tramway Company after twenty-one years, postponed the purchase (and the necessary electrification of the system) for another fourteen years, till forced by public pressure for purchase to do so in 1904. By the turn of the century the Tramway Company had almost a hundred tramcars and 800 horses. The number of passengers it carried each year had risen from one million in 1881 to ten times that figure in 1891 and to 28 million by 1904.[25] The vast majority were residents of the new lower-middle-class suburbs of small villas and terraces which had grown up beyond the solid ring of working-class houses that enclosed the city centre.

Sanitation and Health

Though the majority of working-class houses at the end of the century had been built in the previous twenty or thirty years under regulations that should have ensured reasonable standards of construction, some of them had nevertheless been built in ways, and in places, that were anything but salubrious. Giving evidence in 1896 to a public health inquiry, the assistant town surveyor admitted that one site, on the Shore Road, was 'an enormous dunghill' composed of 'horse manure, cow manure, human excrement; everything of the most abominable character … you would have to go on stilts …. No language is too strong to describe it'. One of the chief offenders was Sir Daniel Dixon – seven times lord mayor, knighted in 1892, created a baronet in 1903 and later Unionist MP for North Belfast – whose property company made a fortune by buying large tracts of slobland, filling it with anything that came to hand and creating the maximum number of building plots, which were then leased to small builders for the highest possible rents; 75 acres of mud near the Connswater in east Belfast were thus made to yield ground rents of almost £3,000 a year. A Labour

Derelict court of pre-1878 houses in the Millfield area, photographed for a slum clearance scheme in 1912. The only sanitation for the inhabitants was the communal privy at the far end. *Hogg Collection, Ulster Museum*

councillor rightly lambasted such 'rack-renters, land speculators, jerry-builders, usurers, etc.', who acquired swamps and then used their positions on the corporation 'so that the swamps are filled up at the corporation's expense by ashpit refuse, road scrapings, etc.; after which, street upon street of doggery houses are erected thereon, irrespective of the grave and imminent danger to the public health'.[26]

Apart from such unsatisfactory new houses there were many older ones that caused concern on grounds of health. The 1878 Act ensured that all houses built after that date had back access, but houses without access remained a high proportion. According to the Medical Officer of Health in 1892:

> At present some 40% of houses in the city have the system of privy and ashpit combined in the small back yard, immediately contiguous to the rooms in which the inmates live and sleep. In thousands of cases there is no back passage or means of access to the yard ... save through the house, and hence all the accumulated filth must be removed by carrying it through the kitchen.[27]

In 1896 a special corporation committee, set up to inquire into the city's high death rate, was told by the Sanitary Officer that there were still 20,000 houses (out of a total of about 70,000) without back passages. Until well into the 1890s it was apparently not uncommon for the contents of the cleared privies and ashpits to be left lying in the street to await collection.

Conditions in the old, pre-by-law slum areas off the city centre were worst of all. In the opinion of one witness a piggery in Barrack Street was more fit for human habitation than some of the houses in Millfield Place nearby; and the only sanitation in St James's Square, a foul little court of six houses in the area between York Street and Corporation Street, which had an entrance too narrow to admit a wheelbarrow, was a common pit in front of the dwellings. 'You could not walk through the little narrow passage between the common pit and the houses', reported one who had not forgotten his visit to the place, 'without going over your shoe mouth in human excrement.'[28]

Very few houses in working-class areas had water closets at that date. Belfast's unique addiction to the old dry closet system was to some extent caused by recurring crises in the supply of water, which could not keep pace with the constantly increasing demand, despite the efforts of the Water Commissioners. In dry summers there was never enough: by 1890 the city was using 9½ million gallons a day, twice as much as in 1880. Drinking water was sold round the streets from horse-drawn carts, and in desperation even the filthy River Lagan was used. Not until 1893 was the problem tackled in anything other than a piecemeal way. An Act of that year authorised the Commissioners to commence a long-term scheme to draw water from the Annalong valley in the Mourne Mountains, thirty-five miles away. The first Mourne water, both abundant and pure, arrived in 1901.[29] In anticipation of this happy outcome to an old problem the Corporation in 1899 took powers to compel the owners of houses with cesspits, privies and pail closets to provide them with water closets. All or part of the money could be borrowed from the Corporation, which for its part undertook to provide the necessary sewage works.[30] Under this legislation most of the old privies were replaced by back-yard water closets within the next twenty years.

Victorian cities imported their water but exported their waste as manure or sewage. Belfast was as slow to solve the latter problem as the former, mainly because public health was not taken seriously in official circles until late in the century. It was 1865 before the Corporation appointed a sanitary committee, and the first Medical Superintendent Officer of Health was not appointed until 1880 (following the Public Health (Ireland) Act of 1878). At last in 1887 an Act of Parliament was obtained to sanction the construction of a main drainage system. From the dispersal point at Duncrue Street the untreated sewage was carried, by means of a wooden 'shoot', across the mud flats and out into deep water in the Lough. As early as 1897 the shoot was said to be unsatisfactory because of leaks and bursts, and there were complaints about the smell at low tide. The small tidal range in the Lough, so beneficial to the development of the port, here made matters worse. Nevertheless, and despite continuing problems with flooding in some of the very low-lying areas near the Lagan and along the course of the

Blackstaff (which was culverted in the 1880s), the construction of the sewerage system was a major achievement; though much improved and extended later, it is only now being replaced.[31]

As well as human and industrial waste there was a great deal of animal waste to be disposed of. Inevitably in a world of horse transport, the growth of the city added enormously to the problem, but horses were by no means the only source of it. In 1896 there were more than 800 dairies within the boundary, and many people in the poorer areas kept pigs and fowl. Evidence was given to the 1896 special committee about the danger to health of keeping livestock in densely inhabited streets; one small yard in Percy Street contained 60 pigs and 30 cows, the sewage from which oozed through a wall into the street.[32] Dairies and cowsheds were at least subject to regulation and inspection by the Corporation. The numerous stables were not; the Tramway Company, whose horses were for many years stabled in Wellington Street in the city centre, was merely the largest of many.

The first Medical Superintendent Officer of Health, Dr Samuel Browne, was an elderly former naval surgeon who had been mayor of the town in 1870 and was its Sanitary Officer at the time of his appointment in 1880; he died in office ten years later at the age of eighty-one. His successor, Dr Henry Whitaker, was both elderly and poorly qualified, though an enthusiastic writer of reports. Unfortunately, like most doctors at the time, he believed that miasma (polluted air) was responsible for the transmission of infectious diseases such as typhoid fever, which was not only endemic in Belfast but actually increasing in the 1890s. A seven-year delay in adopting the Infectious Disease (Notification) Act of 1890 masked the true scale of the problem; as soon as the Act was implemented there was an immediate huge rise (or apparent rise) in the number of cases, from 219 in 1896 to 3,269 in 1897. In the following year there were nearly 6,500 cases; 662 people died. The epidemic was largely blamed on the consumption of shellfish, which were gathered from the sewage-polluted shores of Belfast Lough by the poor and sold from barrows in the street, until sale was forbidden by a by-law.[33]

The great killer, however, was tuberculosis, which caused as many deaths as all the other communicable diseases put together, over a thousand a year in most years between 1889 and 1906. The death rate from tuberculosis ('phthisis' to doctors, 'consumption' to most laymen) for Ireland as a whole at this period was higher than for the rest of the British Isles. Arguably Belfast was no worse than other parts of Ireland, except in one respect: the very high death rate among women in the age-range 25–44. This was one of the occupational hazards of working, as so many Belfast women did, in the linen mills and factories. The risk of industrial accidents was much the same in Belfast as in any other manufacturing city of the period. Like factory owners elsewhere, Belfast employers opposed the introduction and enforcement of legislation requiring them to fence off dangerous machinery;

in 1855 the linen manufacturers had affiliated to the Manchester-led National Association of Factory Occupiers, the body Dickens styled the 'Association for Mangling Operatives'.[34] Shipyard accidents were also common; working with red-hot rivets on high scaffolding was particularly dangerous. The leading opthalmic surgeon in Belfast during this period made his professional name with an operation to remove metal fragments from the inner eye of a Harland & Wolff apprentice by means of a magnet.

Working Conditions

Conditions of labour in the Belfast linen industry may not have been exceptional in United Kingdom terms – in the Lancashire cotton industry the hours of work were just as long, the workers contracted similar occupational diseases and the risk of accidents with machinery was just as great – but they were altogether exceptional in Ireland, and there can be no doubt that their effect on the health of women and children in particular set Belfast apart. About 70% of all linen workers were female, about a quarter juveniles under the age of eighteen. The proportion of children under thirteen increased during this period from 2% in 1868 to 9% in 1890, then began to fall. Hours of work in linen spinning mills and weaving factories were restricted by the same factory acts as in the cotton and woollen mills of England, and reductions were greeted with similar cries of woe by the employers ('It will ruin our trade, and perhaps leave Belfast a forest of smokeless chimneys', said the president of the Belfast Chamber of Commerce of the 1874 Factory Act, which limited the working week to 56 hours).[35] Workshops, as distinct from factories, were not covered by this legislation until 1878. Till then, certain linen operations continued to demand very long hours; the linen lappers in 1861 complained of being made to work sixteen or seventeen hours a day.

But it was the risks and dangers to health specific to the various processes of spinning and weaving linen that drew the attention of factory inspectors and medical officers. The effect of fine dust on the lungs of workers was worst in the processes by which flax was prepared for spinning. Hackling (which involved roughing, machine combing and sorting) was carried out by men and boys; the certifying medical officer for the Belfast factory district remarked in 1877 that roughers and sorters were so well known to have bad lungs that the Army was forbidden to recruit them. Preparing (which involved spreading, drawing and roving) released even finer, and therefore more dangerous, dust. To make matters worse, the temperature in the preparing rooms was kept high. The women in these departments were subject to dreadful attacks of coughing and diseases of the lung; one manager described spreading in particular as 'sure death'. The carding of tow (a by-product of hackling), which was done by young women, was described in 1867 as the 'dirtiest, most disagreeable as well as the most unwholesome and most dangerous of all the departments connected with the spinning of flax'; the average working life of a carder was reckoned to be only seventeen years or so. Many workers, male and female, could get through the day only by drinking large quantities of alcohol, which added to the already considerable risk of accidents with the machinery.

The hot and moist conditions needed for the wet-spinning process produced anaemia and 'mill fever' among the women and girls who formed the vast majority of the workforce in the mills. The spinners were also liable to get a very particular occupational condition known as onychia, a painful inflammation of the big toe nail which was caused by working barefoot on floors covered with hot contaminated water. Onychia became less common with better drainage and the more frequent wearing of shoes (though bare feet were often safer than shod ones in the wet conditions). The process called dressing – treating the yarn with a mixture of carrageen moss, flour and tallow prior to weaving it – was a very unhealthy one because of the high temperatures used (90–125 degrees Fahrenheit); only fit adults were employed, and they were paid much higher wages than the rest. Even weaving, regarded as more desirable work, was pretty unhealthy. Workers frequently suffered from chest trouble caused by the hot and damp atmosphere in the weaving sheds and the stooping posture they had to adopt. The death rate in weaving was high partly because women whose health had already been ruined in the preparing processes were recruited to it. Not all employers were indifferent or hostile to attempts to make working conditions less unhealthy. In the 1870s one large firm pioneered the use of steam to purify the atmosphere in its hackling, preparing and carding departments (many workers in these dangerous areas resisted well-meaning attempts to make them wear respirators), and it was the largest, the York Street Flax Spinning Co., that introduced localised exhaust fans over the hackling benches, long before such measures were made compulsory in 1906. Nevertheless, at the turn of the century the certifying officer of health for the Belfast factory district (Dr H. S. Purdon, who succeeded his father in the post) found still rife all the diseases and ailments reported a generation earlier by his predecessor, with the sole exception of onychia.

Whatever the effect on their health, and despite the low wages they earned (linen was a low-wage industry, even compared with jute), women were glad to be employed in flaxspinning and weaving and anxious not to lose their jobs. In many poorer households, where the husband had an unskilled labouring job or none, the wife's wages from the mill were essential to keep the family out of the workhouse. As little time as possible was taken off to have children. The children themselves, often raised by 'baby farmers' on a diet of tea, whiskey and laudanum, were taken to work at the mill as soon as they reached (or would pass for) the minimum age (before 1874 eight, thereafter ten).[36]

Education

Being employed at the mill did at least ensure that children received some schooling, as 'half-timers'. One Belfast millowner, giving evidence to the Powis Committee in 1870, thought half-timers would be better employed and educated on alternate days rather than half-days, being 'not in a proper state of dress when leaving work to go into school, and vice versa'. And indeed the Committee's report found that the mill children were separated from other pupils not only by educational backwardness but also by the disagreeable evidence of their employment:

> … the afternoon set come to school in a state of personal dirt and squalor, which makes association with them disagreeable and offensive in the extreme. The room is pervaded with the nauseous odour of the oil with which flax is impregnated; the children's faces are smeared with the oil and dust which adheres to their fingers after their work; their scanty ragged clothing, with an old shawl thrown over their shoulders to protect them from the rain, distinguishes them painfully from their companions, who are apt to shun them as an inferior class….[37]

After 1874 alternate days became the rule. The system began to decline when the Education Act of 1892, which made full-time attendance compulsory to the age of eleven, took effect, but it was not officially abolished until 1920.

Attendance might be compulsory, but the National Schools in Belfast at the end of the century were in general so badly financed, staffed and equipped and so lacking in adequate accommodation that they could scarcely cope with the numbers on their rolls. Some millowners provided schools for their half-timers, and a few were owned by trusts or individuals, but the great majority belonged to and were run by churches. In Belfast in the 1860s the Presbyterian church owned and ran most of the National Schools – 70 out of the 80, according to the new Catholic bishop, Patrick Dorrian, who was greatly concerned at the number of Catholic pupils attending them, for want of schools of their own. Dorrian's resolve to change this state of affairs was strengthened by Pope Pius IX's official condemnation of the 'mixed' principle in December 1864. His success during the next twenty years in establishing schools under church control, though naturally a source of great satisfaction to the Catholics of Belfast, inevitably also brought about what lack of resources and the caution of his predecessor Bishop Denvir had hitherto prevented – namely the more or less complete separation of Catholic and Protestant schoolchildren. On a practical level, some schools in poor areas faced severe problems. An extreme example, perhaps, was one described by an unsympathetic critic in 1868 as having 64 Presbyterian and 18 Catholic pupils, more than half of whom were illegitimate and 'hard to manage', and an assistant teacher who was reputedly a prostitute.[38] In the absence of school boards, such as existed in Great Britain after 1870, no local body – least of all the Town Council with its concern for the rates – was prepared to take responsibility for schooling. It is only fair to note that, despite all the difficulties, real progress was made. In 1861, according to the census, 30% of Catholic children were illiterate, compared with 8% of Presbyterians; the figures in 1891 were 14% and 5%.

Secondary education expanded to meet the needs of a growing professional and commercial middle class, also along sectarian lines (the tutorial colleges which crammed candidates for entry to the armed forces or the civil service were perhaps an exception). The Methodist College, opened in 1868, was in its early years both a seminary for theological students and a secondary school for boys and girls. Campbell College, a Presbyterian foundation for boys on the lines of an English boarding school, was established in 1890. On the Catholic side, St Malachy's College was enlarged and rebuilt in 1867 and St Dominic's High School for girls was opened on the Falls Road in 1870. The Christian Brothers, invited to Belfast by Bishop Dorrian in the 1860s to provide primary teaching for poor boys, later offered secondary-level instruction as well.[39]

Churches and Charities

As the city grew, all the main denominations built new churches (often with schools attached) and scores of gospel halls and mission huts sprang up as well. The late-nineteenth century, in fact, was the greatest church-building period in Belfast's history, as Christians of all kinds strove to catch up with the needs of an ever-increasing number of adherents – not to mention the many lost souls who had no connection with any organised religion. The Church of Ireland, which had eight or nine churches serving a nominal membership of 30,000 in 1861, built another sixteen during the next four decades and laid the foundation of a new cathedral (which replaced the eighteenth-century parish church). Mainstream Presbyterianism started the period with twenty churches for 42,500 people and finished it with 47 congregations for a membership of 120,000. The Roman Catholic community, with five churches and 41,500 members in 1861, built another six, including the pro-cathedral of St Peter's in Derby Street; in 1901 there were just under 85,000 Catholics in the city. All denominations sought to organise into regular membership the irregular or unattached. Churchgoing may have become almost universal among the middle classes and the respectable working class which adopted middle-class morals and ethics, but it was far less common among the working class in general. In 1888, when Methodist lay missioners surveyed the situation in the Shankill area, the very heartland of militant Protestantism, they found scores of homes with no church connection and where no clergyman had ever called; in one street alone, 55 of the 110 homes were

81

'unchurched'. All the denominational missionaries, in their quest to reach these lost souls, had to face the realities of life at the lowest level of urban society. The annual report of the Belfast Central Mission for 1893 refers to 'work in slumdom' among people who were 'debased and debauched to the last degree'; volunteer workers were said to 'descend into hell every Saturday afternoon'. As well as the moral squalor in which the inhabitants of the poorer quarters lived, their physical condition became a matter of immediate concern to mission workers.[40]

The poor, the sick and disabled, and those who had fallen on hard times were the objects of charity for the many voluntary societies that operated to alleviate the lot of the deserving poor. The most successful in attracting general public support were those which dealt with the victims of natural handicap, such as the Society for Promoting the Education of the Deaf and Dumb and the Blind, the Association for the Employment of the Industrious Blind and the Cripples' Institute; the fact that all three still exist testifies to an enduring appeal. The Coal Relief Fund, set up to meet severe distress during the winter of 1878–9, also became a permanent – if seasonal – feature. Even the most successful societies brought relief only to small numbers, however; Prison Gate missions for released prisoners, the Home for Friendless Females, Lady Johnston's Bounty and other such, however well-intended, made little impression on the problems they attempted to address.

As in the provision of schools, the main impulse of those concerned in charitable work was religious; and because this was the case, charity, like education, became largely a denominational matter. In a city where most of the population belonged to one or other of the Protestant churches, and where most of the wealth was in Protestant hands, the main voluntary societies were inevitably controlled by Protestants. Few, apart from avowedly denominational organisations such as the orphan societies, excluded Catholics from benefit, with the exception of the Cripples' Institute, but the Deaf, Dumb and Blind School in practice required all its boarders to attend Sunday worship at either St George's Church of Ireland or Fisherwick Presbyterian church. A recent study has concluded that by the end of the nineteenth century in Belfast 'the division between catholic and protestant benevolence was almost complete'.[41] Apart from occasional co-operation, as when Bishop Dorrian sat on the committee of the Coal Relief Fund in 1879, the Catholic church set up its own structures. Catholic charity was organised through the religious orders and the lay workers of the Society of St Vincent de Paul. The first St Vincent 'conference' was established in 1850; many more appeared after 1860. Their work covered a wide range of the activities undertaken by a number of separate Protestant-controlled societies; women volunteers assisted the efforts of the Sisters of Charity and the Sisters of Mercy. In 1867 Bishop Dorrian invited the Good Shepherd Sisters to come to Belfast to work among fallen women. Their convent on the Ormeau Road, built in 1867,

The Theatre Royal, Arthur Street, after its destruction by fire in 1881 (it was replaced by an equally grand building). Respectable Belfast citizens, much influenced by evangelical clergy, were for a long time hostile to the theatre – the Royal was the only one until the Grand Opera House opened in 1895 – but music hall and popular plays were rowdily supported by large numbers of less puritanical people.

Hogg Collection, Ulster Museum

Laundry at the Edgar Home, Sunnyside Street, c.1901. The Home, established by a Presybterian clergyman for 'penitent victims of seduction', had recently moved to the Ormeau Road area from a much grimmer building in the city centre.

Hogg Collection, Ulster Museum

was enlarged and rebuilt in 1893 and again in 1906. Like the Presbyterian-controlled Ulster Female Penitentiary and the Anglican-controlled Ulster Magdalene Asylum, the Convent of the Good Shepherd ran a profitable laundry. Whatever their religious denomination, fallen women did a lot of washing.[42]

The late nineteenth century brought a great expansion in hospital services. Apart from the workhouse infirmary, the refuge of the desperate or the fever-stricken, most of the public hospitals were charitable institutions dependent on subscriptions and donations; patients who could afford to pay were treated in private clinics or nursed at home. The main hospital was the Belfast Royal Hospital in Frederick Street, an institution which had started as a fever hospital in 1817 and had later become a general hospital (it got its royal charter in 1875). The growth of the city made its facilities increasingly inadequate, until at last plans to replace it got under way in the late 1890s. The new Royal Victoria Hospital was named in 1899 and opened four years later on the site of the old County Antrim lunatic asylum on the Falls Road (the 'insane poor' were removed to Purdysburn, a 300-acre estate purchased by the Corporation from the Batt family in 1895). Even medicine could not entirely escape the tendency towards sectarian organisation: a second general hospital, the Mater Infirmorum on the Crumlin Road, originating in the work of the Sisters of Mercy, was established in 1883 under Catholic control. Apartheid did not extend to admissions, however.

A number of specialised hospitals also appeared. The Hospital for Sick Children, originally established in King Street in 1873, acquired new premises in Queen Street in 1885. The Hospital for Skin Diseases (1865) was given a fine new building in Glenravel Street in 1875 by a notable benefactor, Edward Benn. The Ulster Eye, Ear and Throat Hospital (1871) was nearby in Clifton Street. The Ophthalmic Hospital in Great Victoria Street (1867) replaced an earlier Ophthalmic Institution. The Samaritan Hospital for Women, on the Lisburn Road, another of Edward Benn's gifts, was founded in 1872. The Samaritan charged 9s. or 10s. (45–50p) a week for each of its intern patients. The Throne group at Whitehouse comprised a children's hospital, a convalescent home and a small hospital for consumptives endowed by Forster Green, another notable benefactor. Lastly, the Ulster Hospital for Children and Women, in Fisherwick Place, provided twenty beds for children and ten for women.[43]

A particular medical problem arose from the scale of prostitution in the poorer quarters of the town. Poor Law records suggest that there were 500 or so full-time prostitutes in Belfast in the latter part of the century; in Ireland only Dublin had more. The Guardians were so concerned about the spread of syphilis in the Union Infirmary that they twice tried to have the Contagious Diseases Act (under which, until 1886, prostitutes in garrison towns could be compulsorily examined by doctors) extended to Ireland. Objections from local clergy and others, however, overrode even arguments based on the likely saving to ratepayers. In the 1880s the Infirmary alone was treating about thirty patients a week, and the General Hospital, which had closed its doors to such cases 'on moral grounds', had to admit them again. One indication of the scale of the problem is the fact that in 1880 the Belfast garrison had the highest VD rate of any of the main Army establishments in the British Isles – no less than 428 per thousand – and was always among the first six. So far as possible, official Belfast preferred not to face such unpleasant realities.[44]

By the end of Victoria's reign in 1901 Belfast had become a city of 350,000 people, the major port in Ireland and one of the leading industrial and commercial cities of the United Kingdom. Its linen, ships, ropes, tobacco and mineral waters were known throughout the British Empire and the trading world. Though not equally notable for cultural interests and achievements, except in natural and applied science, it had a high opinion of the value of education (and self-education). A lively press reflected these achievements, but also reflected (and at times exacerbated) ever-sharpening political and sectarian divisions within local society.

References

1. E. Boyle, '"Linenopolis": the rise of the textile industry', in Beckett *et al.*, *Belfast*, pp. 47–50; and 'The economic development of the Irish linen industry, 1825–1913', unpublished PhD thesis, Queen's University, Belfast (1979), pp. 96, 100–101. See also P. Ollerenshaw, 'Industry, 1820–1914', in

L. Kennedy and P. Ollerenshaw (eds), *An Economic History of Ulster, 1820–1940*, Manchester University Press, Manchester (1985), pp. 74–84.

2.   Owen, *Belfast*, p. 301.
3.   Brett, *Buildings of Belfast*, pp. 53–4.
4.   Moss and Hume, *Shipbuilders*, pp. 21–44.
5.   Quoted in Chambers, *Faces of Change*, p. 189.
6.   D. J. Jeremy (ed.), *Dictionary of Business Biography*, 5 vols, Butterworths, London (1984–6), 5, pp. 891–3 (Workman) and 1, pp. 683–5 (Clark); also Ollerenshaw, 'Industry', in Kennedy and Ollerenshaw (eds), *Economic History of Ulster*, pp. 94–5.
7.   F. Geary and W. Johnson, 'Shipbuilding in Belfast, 1861–1986', *Irish Economic and Social History*, 16 (1989), pp. 43, 45–52. See also Moss and Hume, *Shipbuilders*, pp. 46–92.
8.   *Dictionary of Business Biography*, 4, pp. 702–8 (Pirrie); Ollerenshaw, 'Industry', in Kennedy and Ollerenshaw (eds), *Economic History of Ulster*, pp. 89–94.
9.   Coe, *Engineering*, pp. 64–7; *Dictionary of Business Biography*, 4, pp. 38–40 (Mackie).
10.   Coe, *Engineering*, pp. 114,120.
11.   *Dictionary of Business Biography*, 2, pp. 18–20 (Davidson).
12.   *Dictionary of Business Biography*, 5, pp. 194–7 (Smiles).
13.   Owen, *Belfast*, p. 311; A. Bernard, *The Whisky Distilleries of the United Kingdom*, Harper's Weekly Gazette, London (1887), reprinted by David & Charles, Newton Abbot (1969), pp. 426–7, 428–9; also J. Vinycomb, *Historical and Descriptive Guide to the City of Belfast*, Marcus Ward & Co., Belfast [1895], p. 38.
14.   *Dictionary of Business Biography*, 1, pp. 720–1 (Cochrane).
15.   *Dictionary of Business Biography*, 2, pp. 461–3 (Gallaher); *The Industries of Ireland: Part 1, Belfast and the Towns of the North*, Historical Publishing Co., London (1891), p. 96.
16.   Extracts from *The Pictorial World*, 1889–90, in *Industries of the North*, Friar's Bush Press, Belfast (1986), pp. 10–14; *Industries of Ireland*, pp. 98–9.
17.   Owen, *Port of Belfast*, pp. 41–6.
18.   Census reports; Budge and O'Leary, *Belfast*, ch.1, appendix.
19.   L. Hyman, *The Jews of Ireland, from Earliest Times to the Year 1910*, Irish Universities Press, Shannon (1972), pp. 203–9.
20.   L. Clarkson, 'The city and the country', in Beckett *et al.*, *Belfast*, p. 156.
21.   Housebuilding in Belfast between 1861 and 1900 is analysed in detail in P. G. Clery, 'Spatial expansion and urban ecological change in Belfast, with special reference to the role of local transportation, 1861–1917', unpublished PhD thesis, Queen's University, Belfast (1979), ch.6, pp. 285–339; for a useful summary of this material see J. Bardon, *Belfast: An Illustrated History*, Blackstaff Press, Belfast (1982), pp. 137–41.
22.   Cleary, 'Spatial expansion', pp. 308–28.
23.   Cleary, 'Spatial expansion', pp. 333–4; A. C. Davies, 'Roofing Belfast and Dublin, 1896–98', *Irish Economic and Social History*, 6 (1977), pp. 26–35.
24.   B. Collins, 'The Edwardian city', in Beckett *et al.*, *Belfast*, pp. 172–3.
25.   Cleary, 'Spatial expansion', ch.5, pp. 180–207.
26.   C. E. B. Brett, *Housing a Divided Community*, Institute of Public Administration, Dublin (1986), pp. 19–20 and caption to pl. 10.

27. Quoted in R. Blaney, *Belfast: 100 Years of Public Health*, Belfast City Council and Eastern Health and Social Services Board, Belfast (1988), p. 21.
28. Quoted in Blaney, *Belfast: 100 Years*, p. 11.
29. J. Loudan, *In Search of Water, being a History of the Belfast Water Supply*, Wm Mullan, Belfast (1940), pp. 52–95.
30. *Belfast Corporation Act, 1899* (62 & 63 Vict., Ch. ccxlvi), para. 43.
31. Blaney, *Belfast: 100 Years*, pp. 21–4.
32. Blaney, *Belfast: 100 Years*, p. 12.
33. Blaney, *Belfast: 100 Years*, pp. 25–9; Budge and O'Leary, *Belfast*, pp. 109–11.
34. D. L. Armstrong, 'Social and economic conditions in the Belfast linen industry, 1850–1900', *Irish Historical Studies*, 7 (1951), pp. 235–8.
35. *Belfast News Letter*, 1 July 1874, quoted in Armstrong, 'Social and economic conditions', p. 243.
36. Armstrong, 'Social and economic conditions', pp. 245–53, 258–60.
37. Quoted in A. McEwen, 'Half-timing in Belfast', *The Northern Teacher*, 14, no.1 (1983), pp. 1–5; see also Armstrong, 'Social and economic conditions', pp. 260–2.
38. Macaulay, *Dorrian*, pp. 271–4, 270.
39. R. Marshall, *Methodist College Belfast: The First Hundred Years*, Belfast [1968], pp. 1–11, 44; Macaulay, *Dorrian*, p. 280.
40. Census reports and Belfast street directories; Eric Gallagher, *At Points of Need: The Story of the Belfast Central Mission, Grosvenor Hall, 1889–1989*, Blackstaff Press, Belfast (1989), pp. 10, 33.
41. A. Jordan, 'Voluntary societies in Victorian and Edwardian Belfast', PhD thesis, 2 vols, Queen's University, Belfast (1989), 2, p. 582; and *Who Cared?: Charity in Victorian and Edwardian Belfast*, Institute of Irish Studies, Queen's University, Belfast (1992), pp. 191–8, 222–8.
42. R. S. Casement, 'History of the Mater Infirmorum Hospital', *Ulster Medical Journal*, 38 and 39 (1970).
43. R. S. Allison, *The Seeds of Time, being a Short History of the Belfast General and Royal Hospital, 1850–1903*, Brough, Cox & Dunn, Belfast (1972); H. G. Calwell, *The Life and Times of a Voluntary Hospital: The Royal Belfast Hospital for Sick Children, 1873–1948*, Brough, Cox & Dunn, Belfast (1973); R. S. Allison, *The Very Faculties: A Short History of the Development of Ophthalmological and Otorhinolaryngological Services in Belfast (1801–1964)*, W. & G. Baird, Belfast (1969); R. Marshall and K. N. M. Kelly, *The Story of the Ulster Hospital*, Brough, Cox & Dunn, Belfast (1973).
44. D. S. Johnson, 'Prostitution and venereal disease in Ireland during the second half of the nineteenth century', unpublished paper. I am indebted to the author for allowing me to make use of this material.

Chapter 4

Party Politics and Local Government, 1861–1901

Economically and physically, and in the matter of municipal enterprise, Belfast during the latter part of the nineteenth century developed in very much the same ways as other British industrial cities. Politics was another story altogether. Here sectarian and ethnic considerations increasingly distorted the picture in a way that made Belfast different to the point of being unique.

Sectarian Violence and Party Politics, 1861–1886

The rituals of sectarian conflict which had become established during the decades before 1860 continued after that date, with some significant variations which reflected the development of the town itself and of the national political scene. The next major outbreak after 1857 occurred in 1864, when at least a dozen people were killed and hundreds injured in rioting which went on for ten days in August. The trouble began on 8 August with the return from Dublin, by train, of a large party of Catholics who had attended a great nationalist demonstration to mark the laying of the foundation stone of a monument to Daniel O'Connell. The Sandy Row Protestants particularly resented such a display at a time when Orange parades in the north were illegal under the Party Processions Act of 1850, and showed their displeasure by burning a huge effigy of the Catholic hero at the boundary between Sandy Row and the Pound. Though the occasion of the clash was novel, in that it arose out of a national political event rather than a local one, the conflict that ensued between the two sets of partisans at first followed the by now traditional pattern, escalating from mutual provocation, through increasingly serious confrontations between rival mobs, to armed skirmishes with the police and military who tried to restore order.[1] What was different, however, was the more widespread nature of the disorder and the significant part played in it by Catholic navvies and Protestant shipyard workers.

The navvies had come to Belfast to work on the construction of new docks. On 15 August, a Catholic holy day, they ransacked the town centre, seizing guns and looting shops before marching to the Shankill Road and attacking Brown's Square National School. This foray led to a Protestant attack on St Malachy's Church and a convent nearby. An attack on Bishop Dorrian's house was answered by one on the home of Dr Cooke, the Presbyterian divine. Next day the Protestant shipwrights marched into the town centre and plundered gun shops and hardware stores before attempting to attack the Catholic pro-cathedral in the Falls, where a Methodist church had been the target of a Catholic mob. When thwarted by the military they demolished Malvern Street National School, working (as the principal said later) 'calmly and deliberately … like furniture removers'. The day after, the navvies were caught at work by the shipyard workers and, their retreat cut off, had to flee across the mud flats or swim the harbour; one man was killed by a blow from an adze, many were wounded.[2] There was little sympathy for the navvies from any shade of Protestant opinion. The Liberal newspaper, the *Northern Whig*, had observed the previous day:

> The prosperity of our town, which is the envy of the rest of Ireland, brought to it for the formation of our new docks this horde of assassins; and the greatest punishment that could be inflicted upon them would be, not to send them to jail, but to dismiss them, and send them starving from our town, as starving they came to it.[3]

The 1864 riots, like those of 1857, were the subject of an official inquiry, this time conducted by Serjeant Barry, QC. The Conservative magistrates came in for much criticism for failing to take prompter action against Protestant mobs. The Town Police were particularly censured for their highly sectarian composition (all but half a dozen of the 160 were Protestants, some of them Orangemen) and their partiality. Recent research, however, suggests that their failure to do better was due less to partiality (for which there is little evidence) than to the inadequacy of any untrained local force to deal with prolonged conflict between two determined sets of urban rioters. Nevertheless, the main recommendation of the inquiry's report was that the Town Police should be disbanded and replaced by a much larger number of men from the national police force, the Irish Constabulary (or Royal Irish Constabulary, as it soon came to be called).[4] The recommendation was promptly carried out. The 480 constables subsequently stationed in Belfast, the majority of whom were Catholics from the south of Ireland, were resented by the Town Council and most of the Protestant population and were to be no less a target in future confrontations than their predecessors had been.

In local politics, the Conservative stranglehold on the Corporation, which had been interrupted briefly by the co-option of a large number of Liberals in 1857, soon resumed as strongly as ever. Co-opting Liberals had not proved to be an effective strategy. Early in 1861 five of them refused to act (although the Liberal mayor, Coey, managed to persuade four to change their minds) and another two had to be replaced later in the same year. One even went so far as to get himself struck off the burgess roll so that his resignation would have to be accepted. The return of Rea to the Council further discouraged moderate Liberals from attending. From twenty in 1860 their numbers fell to twelve in 1863 and eight in 1868.[5] The report of the inquiry into the 1864 riots remarked that the Town Council

Sir Edward Coey (right), ex-mayor, with the current mayor, John Lytle (wearing his chain of office) and a future mayor, William Ewart; the Town Clerk, James Guthrie, is on the left. The photograph was taken in London c.1864, at the time of the proceedings which settled the chancery case begun ten years earlier.

Coey Album, Ulster Museum

was then, and appeared likely to remain, anti-Liberal; the chairman of its Police Committee, Samuel Black (who was later for many years Town Clerk), startled the inquiry by stating that he could usually tell a man's religion by the look of him. In the general election of 1865, even with a single candidate untainted by local associations (Lord John Hay), the Liberals failed to get sufficient support among Presbyterian and Catholic voters. On polling day, thoughtfully fixed by the Conservative mayor and returning officer, John Lytle, for the Twelfth of July, there were rowdy scenes inside the Court House, which Lytle allowed to be taken over by a crowd of Conservative supporters, described by the Liberal press as 'a gang of ferocious Orange ruffians armed with bludgeons of a most formidable character'; outside, a Catholic mob wrecked Protestant houses and stoned the constabulary.[6]

After 1865, however, there was a brief Liberal revival. An Ulster Liberal Society was formed to look after the registration of voters and to bring together Liberal Protestants and Catholics. A young solicitor named Charles Brett took responsibility for registration in Belfast and managed it with uncustomary efficiency. When the 1868 election came the Liberals had a single, local candidate, Thomas McClure, while their opponents were for once seriously divided. The Belfast Conservative Association had nominated the architect and former mayor Sir Charles Lanyon and the millowner John Mulholland for the two seats, despite the presence in the field of an existing Protestant candidate – a leading Orangeman named William Johnston, who was proclaimed at a mass meeting of Protestant working men at which the dictation of the Conservative clique in the Town Hall was denounced. The Conservative vote was inevitably split and McClure and Johnston (who had made contact with the Liberals and received a contribution from them towards his expenses) were elected.

The election of McClure was to be the last Liberal success in Belfast, and did not last long (he lost the seat at the next general election in 1874). The election of Johnston, on the other hand, signalled the emergence of a new force in local Conservatism. The Irish Reform Act of 1868, by reducing the borough franchise from £8 to 'over £4' and extending the boundaries of the Belfast parliamentary constituency to the municipal boundaries of 1853, increased the number of voters by about 7,000 to just over 12,000 (there were 3,243 municipal electors).[7] The bulk of the new-comers were skilled working men, the kind of unionised craftsmen who in England would probably have voted Liberal but who in Belfast espoused Toryism or a populist Orangeism – working class, democratic and sectarian – which opposed a Liberalism that embraced Catholic voters. Thus the arrival of democracy increased rather than diminished the sectarian nature of Conservative rule in Belfast.

The membership and influence of the Orange Order had grown considerably since the middle of the century, when it had 35 lodges and some 1,300 members in the town. In 1864 a separate Belfast Grand Lodge was formed, and by 1870 there were more than a hundred lodges and over 4,000 members. During the later 1860s the national leaders of the Order, predominantly episcopalian clergy and gentry, accepted the Party Proces-sions Act and were more concerned about the threat to disestablish the

Church of Ireland than about the right to march. Many Belfast members, on the contrary, deeply resented the Act and welcomed the defiance of it (and their own leadership) organised by William Johnston in 1866 and 1867. Hence the establishment of the Ulster Protestant Working Men's Association (UPWA) in 1868, when Johnston was arrested and jailed, and its support for his candidature. Johnston of Ballykilbeg, as he was usually called, was a somewhat impoverished small landowner from County Down, a law graduate of Trinity College, Dublin and author in his early days of several anti-Catholic novels; in 1852 he joined the Orange Order and by the mid-sixties was a district master in Belfast and prominent in both the County Down Grand Lodge and the Grand Lodge of Ireland. As MP for Belfast he introduced the private member's bill that led to the repeal of the Party Processions Act in 1870, supported the secret ballot the following year (even resigning from the Orange Order for a time because it opposed the reform), spoke in favour of the extension of the 1874 Factories Act to Ireland, to the delight of Belfast linen workers and the chagrin of the millowners and the Chamber of Commerce, and voted for the Merchant Shipping Bill (which established the famous Plimsoll Line).[8]

The Conservative leadership in Belfast was obliged to come to terms with the forces that had ensured Johnston's election. In 1872 it was agreed that in future the UPWA would be consulted about the selection of candidates. This arrangement worked well in the general election two years later, when Johnston and a leading shipowner, J. P. Corry, were chosen and easily elected. Four years later, however, when Johnston created a by-election by resigning to take up a post as inspector of fisheries (which he had accepted because of financial embarrassment), the Conservative leadership in Belfast engineered the nomination of William Ewart, owner of a large spinning mill, by calling a meeting at short notice and at a time inconvenient to working men. The UPWA retaliated by putting up a candidate of its own, a barrister named Seeds. Seeds was no Johnston, however, and Ewart beat him by more than 3,000 votes. Seeds was nominated again at the general election in 1880. This time it took all the efforts of the Conservative bigwigs to get their two candidates, Corry and Ewart, safely in; Ewart topped the poll with 8,132 votes, Corry got 7,638, Seeds 6,119.[9]

By that time, however, the political battleground was changing. In 1880 the Irish Home Rule party won more than half of the Irish seats and chose Parnell as its leader. Thereafter the politics and parties of Belfast were increasingly dominated by national politics and parties, to the virtual exclusion of local issues. This development was not the cause of the elimination of the Liberals in Belfast, however; that had already happened by 1874, as their inability to take advantage of the division in Conservative ranks after 1868 demonstrates. They not only failed to attract a sufficient number of the new working-class Protestant voters, they failed to keep the support they had had among Catholics and even among the Presbyterian middle class. After McClure's defeat in 1874 the *Northern Whig* wrote despairingly: 'Five years ago the Liberal party was thoroughly organised. Yesterday there seemed no organisation at all. Nobody seemed to know what to do. It was painfully evident there was no directing mind.'[10] But it was more than a matter of organisation. The Tories received increasing support from influential groups such as shipowners (alienated after 1852 by the stance of the Liberals on free trade and further alienated later by Liberal backing for Plimsoll's legislation) and new entrepreneurs in shipbuilding and engineering. More and more professional men, dependent for business on goodwill, followed this lead; it is a striking fact that by 1874 the Conservatives could call on the free services of fourteen Belfast solicitors, whereas the Liberals had two. Even the linen barons who had been the backbone of the party became less and less willing to finance it; McClure spent nearly £5,000 in 1868 but less than half that much in subsequent contests.[11]

The ruin of the Liberals was completed in 1885–6. In the early 1880s they had made belated, and half-hearted, attempts to secure the support of the more liberally-minded working-class voters. The first Liberal Working Men's Association did not appear till October 1885, however, and its inaugural meeting, addressed by speakers who were all employers, made no reference at all to working-class grievances. Following the reforms of 1884 and 1885, which quadrupled the number of Irish voters and redistributed the seats, in the general election of 1885 Parnell and his party won every seat in Munster, Leinster and Connaught and 17 of the 33 in Ulster. In Belfast the redistribution created four seats in place of the previous two – the constituencies of North, South, East and West Belfast. West Belfast, which contained Sandy Row, Shankill and Falls Road, emerged as a marginal seat, a prominent Orange merchant, J. H. Haslett, just defeating the Home Rule candidate, Thomas Sexton. The other three seats were won easily by Conservative or Independent Conservative (i.e. Orange) candidates: Ewart in North Belfast, where his opponent, Alexander Bowman, secretary of the Belfast Trades Council and a former employee in Ewart's mill, was the first working-class candidate in Irish history; the revenant William Johnston without a contest in South Belfast, which he was to hold unopposed until his death in 1902; and E. S. de Cobain in East Belfast, where he defeated the official Conservative, Corry, in a close contest. Since the Home Rule party held the balance of power in the new House of Commons, home rule at once became the leading issue in British politics. In 1886 the Liberal leader, Gladstone, announced his conversion to the policy of granting home rule, came to power with the support of Parnell and introduced a bill to bring it about. This virtually destroyed the Liberal party in Belfast. Faced with the prospect of a Dublin parliament dominated by Catholic nationalists with little appreciation of the vital interests of northern industry and commerce, most Liberals became Liberal Unionists almost overnight and made common cause with the Conservatives against home rule. In May 1886 a large majority at a meeting of Liberals in the Ulster Hall condemned Gladstone's new policy as one 'fraught with danger to the industrial, social and moral welfare of the country'. The Town Council and other bodies such as the Chamber of Commerce and even the General Assembly of the Presbyterian Church – to say nothing of dozens of Orange and loyalist meetings, including a monster demonstration in the Ulster Hall at the end of February addressed by Lord Randolph Churchill – had already expressed their opposition. From 1886 onward Belfast elections were fought by parties organised on national lines and campaigning on national issues.

The first Home Rule Bill was defeated in the House of Commons on 8 June when 93 Liberal MPs joined the Conservatives in voting against it. The tension its proposal had created in Belfast had already started what were to be the most serious riots of the century. After the outbreak of 1864 things had been comparatively quiet until 1872, when thousands of Belfast Catholics took part in a great Nationalist parade and demonstration. This event marked the first public appearance of the hitherto shadowy Ancient Order of Hibernians, a secret, oath-bound society as exclusively Catholic and nationalist as the Orange Order was Protestant and unionist; 'Lady Day' (15 August) was to become the AOH equivalent of the Orange Twelfth of July.[13] Attacks on the 1872 parade by Protestants were followed by a week of rioting in which five people were killed, more than 200 injured and hundreds driven from their homes. On the occasion of a similar 'Lady Day' (15 August) procession in 1880 two were killed and ten injured in four days of rioting. Now, on 4 June 1886, shipyard workers attacked Catholic navvies working on the Alexandra dock who had expelled a Protestant navvy with the message that, once home rule was achieved, 'none of the Orange sort would get leave to work or earn a loaf of bread in Belfast'. One young Catholic drowned trying to escape and ten others had to be taken to hospital. The mayor, Sir Edward Harland, sent to Dublin for more police and soldiers. The constabulary had no sooner arrived than they were sent into action against Protestant looters. Battles between police and Protestants, rather than those between Catholic and Protestant mobs, became the predominant pattern of these riots. The worst of the early fighting took place on 9 June when police, besieged in their barracks by a mob of 2,000, fired indiscriminately and killed seven people, five of them perfectly innocent. The Presbyterian minister of St Enoch's, Dr Hugh Hanna, denounced from his pulpit this massacre of 'seven martyrs ... sacrificed to avenge the resistance of a loyal people to a perfidious and traitorous policy'.

There was a lull until July, when another general election was held in which Ewart, Johnston and de Cobain were returned without a contest, as was the Nationalist, Sexton, in West Belfast (his election gave Parnell's party 86 of the Irish seats – the '86 of '86'). Thereafter rioting was sporadic until mid-September, when prolonged heavy rain dampened the ardour of the mobs; the riots petered out altogether the following month. The worst

Bower's Hill RIC barracks on the Shankill Road in June 1886, the day after the rejection of the Home Rule Bill. Besieged by a Protestant mob of more than 2,000, the police had opened fire and killed at least seven people, only two of whom proved to be rioters. **Welch Collection, Ulster Museum**

of the bloodshed occurred in this later period, which featured a Catholic attack on a Sunday School outing (St Enoch's) accompanied by Orange bands and a Protestant attack on a Catholic outing the following day, as well as the sacking of York Street, the expulsion of Catholics from the shipyards and determined assaults on the police. When all was over, about 50 people had been killed (including a soldier and a policeman) and 371 policemen had been injured; 31 public houses had been looted and property worth £90,000 destroyed. The report of the inquiry into the riots, which with the minutes of evidence ran to over 600 pages, put much of the blame on the politicians and other public leaders who had earlier talked of resorting to force to oppose home rule. As a Liberal Unionist witness remarked, it was 'exceedingly unwise on the part of respectable people' to use such words, 'as they were likely to cause the poorer classes to carry out what they had only talked about and threatened ...'.[14] Quite apart from the widespread fear that Home Rule would mean Rome Rule, Protestant workers feared that it would destroy the manufacturing industry which made Belfast prosperous and gave them their livelihoods: in the mid-1880s, a period of recession in shipbuilding and engineering during which Harland & Wolff laid off hundreds of men, locked out the riveters for a month and reduced everyone's wages, it must have seemed a serious threat when William Pirrie, the chairman of the firm, let it be known that he would transfer the shipyard to the Clyde if home rule became a reality.[15]

Town Government

While all this was going on, municipal affairs on a practical level were developing in ways similar to those in other great urban centres of the period. The chancery case was at last laid to rest in 1864 by the Belfast Award Act, which implemented the recommendation of arbitrators that the Corporation should be responsible for debts of £120,000, while the respondents should pay their own costs and those of Rea (about £50,000 in all). Resisting compromise to the last, Rea had to be forcibly removed by police from a House of Lords committee hearing.[16] Almost everyone, including most Liberals, greeted the settlement with relief. The way was thus clear for further improvement acts. In 1866 powers were taken to establish the first municipal cemetery, outside the town boundary on the Falls Road. More important than this act of colonisation by the dead, local Acts in 1865 and 1868 extended the responsibilities of the Corporation over parts of the borough which lay in the counties of Antrim and Down and had therefore been subject in some respects to the county grand juries and liable to pay county taxes.[17] From 1866 the town had a separate Quarter Sessions court, presided over by a Recorder. In 1869 a new public abattoir was opened, after a deputation of councillors had visited Paris and other continental cities to view the facilities there. Expanding functions and civic pride justified not only jaunts to Paris but also the building of a new Town Hall, which was opened in 1871 in Townhall Street. Three years later powers were taken to purchase the gas undertaking, for £386,550 (the final cost, with interest, was £430,000). This was a lot more than the £50,000 secured for the purchase in 1846, the diversion of which had been one of the charges in the chancery suit. It was to prove an excellent investment nevertheless: the profits from the Gas Works later paid for the City Hall and other things. The corporation had a Sanitary Committee from 1865, but it was not until 1877 that some limited improvement on sanitary grounds was undertaken in the Smithfield area, and then under Local Government Board legislation dealing with artisans' and labourers' dwellings, rather than the usual private act. Such general acts were to be increasingly important as a spur to social improvement; left to themselves the town fathers were slow to do anything that would add to the burden of the rates.

The enormous and rapid growth of the town, and the desire to emulate more enterprising places such as Birmingham, nevertheless made activity unavoidable. A major improvement Act in 1878 shaped the future street geography of a large part of the centre by taking powers to lay out a grand new thoroughfare between Donegall Place and York Street, sweeping away in the process the old butchers' quarter in Hercules Street and a warren of alleys and entries. Royal Avenue, as it was named, took shape during the 1880s, and very impressive it proved to be with its tall uniform frontages, even if the central railway station that was planned by developers did not

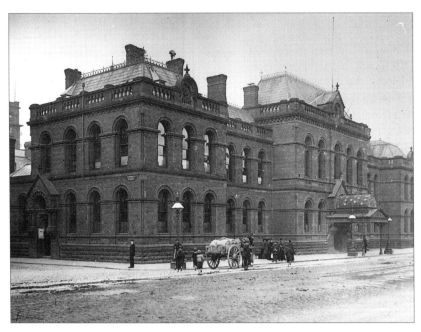

The Town Hall, Victoria Street, c.1900. Opened in 1871, the building was too small – and too modest in style – for the activities of the City Council (1888), which immediately set about acquiring a site for a City Hall. At the height of the Home Rule crisis in 1913–14 these premises were the headquarters of the Ulster Volunteer Force.

The old Town Hall is still there, having survived a number of explosions aimed at the magistrates' court which occupied the back of the building. The fire brigade also had its headquarters there until recently; the station tower can be seen on the left of the picture. *Hogg Collection, Ulster Museum*

materialise (beyond a Grand Central Hotel which was a notable feature of the street until recent times). Under the same Act the long-standing nuisance of the Blackstaff river was at last tackled, the old mill dam near its mouth drained and Ormeau Avenue and the streets between that thoroughfare and Donegall Square completed. Ann Street, Cornmarket, Millfield and the street along Donegall Quay were also widened and improved. Another Act in 1884 led to the widening of the Queen's Bridge, the enlargement and improvement of St George's Market and the improvement of Arthur Square, Rosemary Street, North Street, University Road and Stranmillis Road. This fury of paving and sewering continued into the 1890s as more and more houses were built and as action on the grounds of public health became ever more necessary and unavoidable. In this respect the Main Drainage Act of 1887 was a major (and long overdue) achievement. Apart from the powers it gave to construct a proper system of sewers, it also contained public health provisions such as a prohibition against carrying the corpses of victims of infectious diseases in public conveyances.[18]

View of Royal Avenue in the 1890s. This imposing thoroughfare, built in the 1880s to replace Hercules Street and a warren of alleys off it, became an important extension of the central business district.　　　　*Welch Collection, Ulster Museum*

The Main Drainage Act is of interest in another, rather curious way: it led to the introduction of household suffrage in local elections more than ten years sooner in Belfast than anywhere else in Ireland. Though Catholics had no direct representation or influence on the Town Council after 1878, when the last remaining Catholic member died, the power of the Nationalist party at Westminster could be exerted on their behalf whenever the Corporation sought an improvement act. The price for allowing the Main Drainage Bill to pass into law was an amendment to the Municipal Corporations (Ireland) Act of 1840, so far as it related to Belfast, enabling any householder (including women) to be a burgess without the £10 property qualification.[19] A new Council was to be elected, one-third of its members retiring in rotation. It was not until the boundaries were extended and the wards changed, however, that the next Catholic councillors were elected.

Improvement during these years was not entirely a matter of drains and paving stones, though no fewer than 857 previously private streets were handed over to be 'sewered and paved' between 1878 and 1896. In 1869 the Corporation acquired the abandoned demesne of the Donegalls at Ormeau and made part of it into the first public park, thus doing what Professor James Thomson (father of the future Lord Kelvin) had advocated nearly twenty years before. Others followed – Alexandra Park in

1885, Woodvale three years later, Dunville and Victoria in 1891, the Botanic Gardens (in existence since the late 1820s but not in public hands) in 1894. A new cemetery for the eastern part of the city was opened at Dundonald in 1899.[20]

Up to the 1890s Belfast had no separate provision for the insane poor, as lunatics in public care were called; these unfortunates went either to the County Antrim Asylum on the Falls Road or to the County Down institution in Downpatrick. In 1892, however, the city became a separate district for such purposes. Three years later the Purdysburn estate was acquired. (What happened to well-to-do lunatics is something of a mystery. In the late nineteenth century there was only one private licensed asylum in the Belfast area, a small establishment for up to five men run by a Ligoniel doctor; when inspected by the commissioners of lunatics in 1895 it had only two patients, and by the turn of the century it had closed altogether. Presumably there were discreet, unlicensed places as well; if so, they are undetectable in the directories).

Another municipal service which was overhauled and expanded at this time was the fire brigade. In 1891 it consisted of 40 men, only ten of whom were full-time. Following reorganisation in 1892 it was staffed by 40 full-time officers and was housed in a new headquarters in Chichester Street.

Pepper Hill steps, which led to Pepper Hill Court, one of the worst old slums in Belfast. The photograph was taken in 1894, when the property was being demolished.
Ulster Museum

The brigade was responsible for a public ambulance service (horse-drawn waggons to begin with), an arrangement which was copied by cities throughout the kingdom and remained standard until the coming of the welfare state (it is still the case in Dublin). The Fire Brigade is a good example of the expansion of municipal employment as the Corporation took on new functions or developed existing ones. The wages paid were actually higher than in Great Britain; by 1912 a first-class fireman had a basic 30–34 shillings (£1.50–£1.70) a week plus allowances and a possible bonus for good conduct, at a time when the average unskilled wage was 15–18 shillings (75–90p).[22]

Extension of the boundary had been advocated on a number of occasions before 1879, when the lord lieutenant agreed to a public inquiry into the subject. The Council argued for the inclusion of new suburbs at Strandtown, Ballyhackamore, Knock, Malone and Ballymurphy on the usual grounds, namely that they were a danger to public health because they had no sewerage and that they ought to share the burden of the rates because they shared many of the town's amenities. The commissioners

Members of the Northern Cycling Club in Ormeau Park, c.1880. At club meets these middle-class fitness fanatics were marshalled by calls on a hunting horn, here carried by the man third from right. The invention of the modern-style safety bicycle with pneumatic tyres (developed first by J. B. Dunlop, a Belfast veterinary surgeon) was soon to revolutionise cycling and bring it within reach of many more people than could afford – or manage to ride – these machines. *Ulster Museum*

agreed, and also proposed increasing the number of wards from five to eight. Nothing was done, however. In 1885 the area of the parliamentary borough was extended by 15,000 acres. Three years later Belfast was granted the dignity of a city, after the Council had assured itself that this could be done without incurring much expense, and in response to pressure from the Chamber of Commerce; the Mayor became a Lord Mayor in 1892. These developments increased the demand for an extension of the boundary. Eventually in 1895 a bill was prepared to extend the municipal boundary to correspond, more or less, with the parliamentary one, a move which would increase the area of the city from ten square miles to twenty-three and its electorate from 39,603 to 47,294.

In political terms the 1895 bill proposed the creation of fifteen wards, based on population and valuation, radiating from the centre. This was immediately seen by Catholics as a threat to their interests. A Catholic Representation Association, presided over by Bishop Henry (who played a dominant role in Catholic politics in the city), drew attention to the fact that they had had only three councillors elected in fifty years despite being a quarter of the population, that the proposed new wards would all have a Protestant majority, that Protestants would not vote for Catholics, and that Catholics were virtually excluded from Council employment. When questioned by a Select Committee, the Liberal Unionist lord mayor, William Pirrie, had to admit that under the new scheme the Catholics could not be sure of a single seat, and that so far as he knew not a single Catholic contractor was employed by the Council. The solicitors largely responsible for drawing up the Catholic case claimed that they ought to have control of at least two wards. Following a meeting with a deputation from the Catholic Association the Council capitulated: two wards, Falls and Smithfield, were to be so drawn as to ensure a permanent Catholic majority. Joseph Devlin, active earlier in the protest but excluded from the deputation, who was later to become the Nationalist boss of Belfast, thought this arrangement was the worst possible outcome, one that was sure to perpetuate sectarian politics in the city – and so it proved. It is hard to see what else was practicable in the circumstances, however.[23]

The first general municipal election under the new arrangements was held in November 1897. Only Catholic candidates came forward in Falls and Smithfield, only Protestants elsewhere. Nearly one-third of the sixty seats (three entire wards) were uncontested; henceforth, indeed, local elections were to be of interest only for the internal squabbles of the two main blocks or the efforts of a third force such as Labour to break the sectarian stranglehold. Catholics, for example, were for some time sharply divided between Bishop Henry's Catholic Association and the Irish National Federation (the central Nationalist organisation). The Nationalists put up candidates in Falls and Smithfield but all eight seats went to the Association. Among Protestants the Liberal Unionists remained nominally separate from the Conservatives. All five of their candidates were elected, including the lord mayor, Pirrie, and a future lord mayor, Otto Jaffé, the only Jewish holder of the post. The Conservatives got 33 seats, Independents (basically Conservatives) eight. The six 'Labour' candidates nominated by the Belfast Trades Council to promote action on social issues were also successful; Alexander Bowman was one of them. Neither they nor the Catholic group, even acting together as they often did, could make any impression on the entrenched Conservative majority which, whatever may be said about it, undoubtedly represented the will of a large majority of the citizens.[24]

Sectarian Politics and the Labour Movement, 1886–1901

National politics, and therefore inevitably local politics, were dominated in the early 1890s by the renewed hope or threat of home rule. In 1892, when the Conservative government resigned and Gladstone again sought office, promising to introduce home rule if elected, local Conservatives and other supporters of the Union again organised themselves to oppose it. Well aware that their cause had been damaged in Britain by the disgraceful scenes in 1886, they arranged a great demonstration in Belfast in June 1892 which was impressively orderly and well-behaved. The rowdy scenes that usually accompanied gatherings such as the Twelfth of July celebrations were entirely absent, along with bands and party songs. Instead, 12,000 delegates from all over the province met in a huge, specially-constructed hall (said to be the biggest temporary structure in existence). Before the political speeches started the assembly listened to prayer and bible reading by the Church of Ireland primate and the ex-Moderator of the Presbyterian Church and sang the hymn 'God is our refuge and strength'. Afterwards, crowds estimated at anything up to 300,000 thronged the Botanic Gardens. In the general election that followed, Wolff, Johnston and Harland were returned unopposed and the Nationalist, Sexton (an anti-Parnellite in the recently-divided Irish party), was beaten in West Belfast by a Liberal Unionist, H. O. Arnold-Foster.[25]

Gladstone came to office nevertheless, and the second Home Rule Bill passed the Commons in April 1893, only to be thrown out by the Lords. This time there were no riots in Belfast. All four Belfast members were returned without a contest in 1895, when the Conservatives began another spell in office which was to rule out any likelihood of home rule for the next ten years. In the general election of 1900 there was again no contest in three constituencies; in the fourth, North Belfast, Sir J. H. Haslett (who had succeeded to the seat on the death of Harland in 1896) easily defeated an independent Liberal Unionist.

The sectarian basis of politics and the intensity of feeling on the national question effectively prevented the development of a strong class-based Labour movement in Belfast. The year 1893 did indeed see the formation

Nationalist procession along the Falls Road in 1898, to celebrate the centenary of the rebellion of the United Irishmen. *Ulster Museum*

in the city of a small Independent Labour Party, whose meetings – regularly the target for anti-socialist objectors – were addressed by Tom Mann and other notable cross-channel socialists. The leading activists were William Walker, a member of the Carpenters' Union, and John Murphy of the Typographical Association. Even the normal development of trade union organisation was affected by sectarian politics. As a great industrial centre with an unusually high proportion of skilled craftsmen, Belfast was a natural stronghold of the craft unions that dominated the labour movement in the later nineteenth century. In addition to many small local bodies, the 'New Model' British unions organised in Belfast from the 1850s. The Amalgamated Society of Engineers was followed by lithographic printers, boilermakers, carpenters and joiners, cabinetmakers and bricklayers, and a Belfast United Trades Council was formed in 1881. There was a rapid growth of unions in the 1890s, among the increasing number of municipal employees for example; by the end of the century there were 57, with a membership of 19,000, affiliated to the Trades Council. The importance of Belfast in the movement was recognised when the Trades Union Congress met there in 1893. However, dissatisfaction among Irish delegates with the scant consideration given to the concerns of their members led to the formation in the following year of an Irish Congress of Trade Unions. At the time this was not at all a nationalist organisation, and was not intended to supersede the TUC itself, but inevitably it soon began to reflect the diverse opinions of its membership on the national question.

The extent to which Belfast craftsmen were part of the British labour scene as well as players in the drama of Irish politics is well illustrated in the 1890s. In 1892–3 the shipyard engineers were an essential element in the background of Unionist opposition to the threat of home rule. In 1893, in a period of recession, they were obliged to accept reduced wages. Subsequently the shipbuilding section of the Belfast engineering employers' federation entered into an agreement with the shipbuilders on the Clyde jointly to resist wage demands. Thus when engineering workers on Belfast in 1895 demanded an increase of two shillings (10p) a week in order to recover what they had earlier lost, the employers refused to negotiate except through joint machinery which included the Clyde employers. And when the union called an official strike in November 1895 (which went on into the new year and put out of work large numbers of unskilled men as well), Clydeside employees were dismissed in order to put pressure on the union. Following a joint intervention by the lord mayor of Belfast and the provost of Glasgow, the union accepted a slightly better offer from the employers and cut off strike pay from its members to force them back to work. Belfast prided itself on its good industrial relations, however, and the action of the employers – and of the local MPs, two of whom were Harland and Wolff – did not escape criticism in the press. In any case, trade union activity in the 1890s did little to advance the cause of socialism.[26]

The cause of labour in general at the turn of the century was affected by renewed stirrings of sectarian feeling, which had on the whole been notably absent during the previous decade. Catholic celebrations of the centenary of the 1798 rising had provoked controversy but confrontation had been prevented. In 1900, however, the Boer War provided a focus for conflict. The news of the defeat of British armies was greeted with bonfires on the Falls Road. In reply, when Pretoria fell to the British, Protestant workers left work to parade the streets and sing patriotic songs, bonfires were lit in Sandy Row and the Shankill, and some minor rioting took place. The dominant role of the Catholic Church in local nationalist politics provoked increased support for the extremist Belfast Protestant Association, which preached anti-popery and organised an attack on a Corpus Christi procession in 1901. When the Association's leader was arrested and imprisoned there were attacks on Catholic navvies and shipyard workers. Against such a background, the sole working men's candidate in the general election of 1900 was easily defeated in North Belfast, despite massive support from his fellow trade unionists for a prolonged strike of carpenters and joiners which was going on at the time.[27]

In 1899 the *Belfast News Letter*, the organ of the Conservatives who controlled the city, could write with some justification: 'We Belfast people are proud of our city and its many activities. We are in the very front of the race of civic development … and we have a laudable ambition to keep there …'.[28] That pride in economic and social advancement would have been shared by many Catholics, who despite great disadvantages had also come a long way. But whereas in other British cities politics and cultural pressures had operated to assist the assimilation of Catholic Irish minorities, in Belfast the opposite had happened.[29] By the end of Victoria's reign the Catholics as a community had become both more deeply rooted in Belfast and also more separate and distinct from the majority of its inhabitants.

References

1. See Stewart, *Narrow Ground*, p. 148.
2. See Boyd, *Holy War*, pp. 44–89, for a detailed and racy account of the 1864 riots; for a sociological analysis of Belfast rioting in the nineteenth century see Gibbon, *Origins of Ulster Unionism*, pp. 67–86.
3. *Northern Whig*, 16 August 1864.
4. *Report of the Commissioners of Inquiry into the Riots in Belfast in 1864*, Parliamentary Papers, 1865, xxviii, HMSO, Dublin (1865), p. 22. The report in fact acknowledges that the local constables were too few in number to do much.
5. Slater, 'Belfast politics', 2, p. 259.
6. D. Dunlop, *Brief Historical Sketch of Parliamentary Elections in Belfast*, Belfast (1865), p. 11, quoted in Budge and O'Leary, *Belfast*, p. 98, n. 55; *Belfast News Letter*, 15 July, 1865.
7. The property qualification for the parliamentary franchise had been reduced in 1850 from £10 to £8. The Irish Act of 1868 was less democratic than the English Act of 1867, which established household suffrage in boroughs. The property qualification for the municipal vote in Belfast remained £10.
8. For an account of Johnston's chequered career, see A. McClelland, *William Johnston of Ballykilbeg*, Ulster Society Publications, Lurgan (1990). His first attempt to repeal the Party Processions Act, in 1869, was seconded by The O'Donoghue of the Glens, a great-nephew of Daniel O'Connell and Liberal MP for Tralee. Johnston, incidentally, was a son-in-law of the Rev. Dr Thomas Drew, the Orange cleric, who after leaving Christ Church became rector of Loughinisland, a rural parish in County Down whose Catholic priest was Patrick Dorrian, the fervently nationalist bishop of Down and Connor.
9. Budge and O'Leary, *Belfast*, pp. 102–3.
10. *Northern Whig*, 6 Feb. 1874; Gibbon, *Origins of Ulster Unionism*, p. 102.
11. Gibbon, *Origins of Ulster Unionism*, pp. 104–7.
12. Budge and O'Leary, *Belfast*, p. 103.
13. There is no reliable published history of the Irish AOH (the movement was organised separately in the USA); its early records, in any case scanty, perished in 1922. The best source for most purposes is M. T. Foy, 'The Ancient Order of Hibernians: an Irish political-religious pressure group, 1884–1975', unpublished MA thesis, Queen's University, Belfast (1976).
14. Quoted in Boyd, *Holy War*, pp. 172–3.
15. Moss and Hume, *Shipbuilders*, pp. 52,55.
16. Slater, 'Belfast politics', 2, p. 284.

17. Slater, 'Belfast politics', 2, pp. 291–3.
18. *Belfast Corporation Gas Act, 1874* (37 & 38 Vict., Ch.cxxv); *Local Government Board (Ireland) Provisional Orders (Artizans and Labourers Dwellings) Confirmation Act, 1877* (40 & 41 Vict., Ch.cxxii); *Belfast Improvement Act, 1878* (41 & 42 Vict., Ch.clxxx); *Belfast Improvement Act, 1884* (47 & 48 Vict., Ch.xciii); *Belfast Main Drainage Act, 1887* (50 & 51 Vict., Ch.cxxvii).
19. *Municipal Corporation of Belfast Act, 1887* (50 & 51 Vict., Ch.cxviii); see Budge and O'Leary, *Belfast*, p. 117.
20. Sir R. Meyer, *City of Belfast Public Parks*, Belfast Corporation, Belfast (1922), pp. 21–63, 98.
21. *Report of the Inspectors of Lunatics … in Ireland, 8 July 1895* (1895 [C 7804], liv, 435), p. 174.
22. K. D. Brown, 'The Belfast Fire Brigade, 1880–1914', *Irish Economic and Social History*, 16 (1989), pp. 65–72.
23. Budge and O'Leary, *Belfast*, pp. 116–9.
24. Budge and O'Leary, *Belfast*, pp. 119–21.
25. Gibbon, *Origins of Ulster Unionism*, pp. 131–6; H. Patterson, *Class Conflict and Sectarianism: The Protestant Working Class and the Belfast Labour Movement, 1868–1920*, Blackstaff Press, Belfast (1980), pp. 19–23.
26. A. Boyd, *The Rise of the Irish Trade Unions, 1729–1970*, Anvil Books, Tralee (1972), pp. 65–7; Patterson, *Class Conflict and Sectarianism*, pp. 32–5.
27. Patterson, *Class Conflict and Sectarianism*, p. 42.
28. *Belfast News Letter*, 12 Sept. 1899.
29. See G. Davis, *The Irish in Britain, 1815–1914*, Gill & Macmillan, Dublin (1991), pp. 51–82 and 148. It should be noted, however, that the Irish minorities in Britain, even in Glasgow and Liverpool, were comparatively small.

Chapter 5

Heyday and Crisis, 1901–14

In retrospect, the period in the history of Belfast between the death of Queen Victoria and the outbreak of the First World War reveals more clearly than any other the contrast between social, economic and municipal advance – the 'British' aspects of the city – and the effects of sectarian and ethnic division – its Irish or at any rate Ulster character.[1]

The Social Pyramid

The population of Belfast continued to rise in the early years of the twentieth century, though at a much less spectacular rate than in previous decades. Reaching 349,000 in 1901, it was 386,000 in 1911 and by the outbreak of war three years later must have been about 400,000. The rate of increase between the censuses of 1901 and 1911 was 10.8%, compared with 36.4% in the 1890s; this reflected slower economic growth after 1900 in the linen industry and the less skilled sectors of other employment, such as building, which had attracted so many immigrants in the late nineteenth century. The continued importance of linen, however, was still reflected in the preponderance of women in the population – 188,000 women as compared with 162,000 men in 1901 – and in the large proportion of households (a quarter of Protestant, a third of Catholic ones) headed by women. Among all immigrants in the age-range 15–24 the ratio of women to men was 100 : 71, among those of them who were Catholics as high as 100 : 58. The population as a whole was youthful – 77% were under the age of 40 – the marriage rate high at 8.2 per thousand (the figure for the whole of Ireland in the 1890s was 4.8) and the birth rate correspondingly high at 30.4 (23.1 for Ireland in the decade 1901–11); the first evidence of birth control, by middle-class Protestants, can be found in the low figure of 20.1 in the College district in 1914.[2]

Many such details about Edwardian Belfast can be gleaned from the records of the censuses of 1901 and 1911, which are available to historians in full manuscript form as those for other British cities are not (the nineteenth-century detailed records for Belfast, on the other hand, were all destroyed). At the apex of Belfast society was a solitary aristocrat, the ninth earl of Shaftesbury (his mother, the only surviving child of the third marquess of Donegall, had inherited the Donegall estates in 1883), who kept up a residence in Belfast Castle with a staff of nineteen indoor servants and played an active part in public affairs; he was lord mayor in 1907 and

The ninth earl of Shaftesbury (ninth also from right in the front row) with a party of his tenants at Belfast Castle, c.1905. He lived in Belfast for part of every year and took an active interest in the city, despite the fact that his family no longer owned most of it: these tenants would have been from country areas of south Antrim.

Ulster Museum

first chancellor of the Queen's University from its creation, out of Queen's College, in 1908. It is worth noting here that few of the men who made fortunes in Belfast felt the need to gentrify themselves to the extent of withdrawing from business. For instance Andrew Mulholland, proprietor of the York Street Flax Spinning Company, who became a major landowner in County Down in the 1840s, remained in control of the firm; more remarkably, so too did his son John, who was raised to the peerage as Baron Dunleath in 1892. Dunleath died in 1895 worth nearly £600,000.[3] His nearest, but even wealthier, equivalent in the late nineteenth and early twentieth century was William Pirrie, chairman of Harland & Wolff, who achieved a peerage in 1905. The Pirries could, and quite often did, sit 160 guests down to dine at Ormiston; and for a banquet in 1896 Pirrie chartered an entire ship to sail from London to Belfast, complete with all the staff, cutlery and linen needed for the feast. When the Pirries set out to dazzle London society in 1898 they rented Downshire House in Belgrave Square, and the head office of the firm was removed to London in the same year. Pirrie subsequently purchased an estate in Surrey, where in later years he entertained most of his guests, including employees of the shipyard, so he and his wife were seen less often in Belfast.[4] At least two other Belfast businessmen of the period, both of them distillers, left over a million each; neither made any attempt to match the conspicuous consumption practised by Pirrie, however.

Below this thinly-inhabited stratosphere of the seriously wealthy the 'social profile' of the city was dominated by a group of three hundred or so families. They formed a tight-knit community of family and business interests, were much intermarried, controlled interlocking companies, were members of the same golf and sailing clubs, and sent their children to the same boarding schools in England or Scotland. Many belonged to the same church congregations, usually Presbyterian, the wives and daughters

110

meeting constantly in church activities and charitable work as the husbands and sons did in the Ulster Club or the Reform Club. Most of the men personally managed their own businesses. These families lived in substantial villas in the spacious suburbs to the east, north and south of the industrial and commercial centre and employed gardeners and coachmen as well as indoor servants (mostly female, though there were 283 butlers, valets and footmen in Belfast in 1911).[5]

Next in the scale were five or six thousand families of the middle classes – an elastic term which included everything from 'aspiring barristers to gasworks' clerks'. They were distinguished from those below them not only by their white-collar occupations but also by the incomes (anything from £200 to £500 a year) that enabled them to buy or rent suburban houses, to send their children to fee-paying schools, to employ at least one maid (there were 6,360 female domestic servants in 1911) and to save something for seaside holidays, sickness and retirement.

The working classes which formed the large majority of the city's population were sharply divided between the skilled on the one hand and the semi-skilled or unskilled on the other. Skilled artisans – the labouring elite of apprentice-trained shipbuilding, engineering and building craftsmen who made up 26% of the male and 16% of the entire manual workforce – earned wages of 35 to 45 shillings (£1.75 to £2.25) a week, enough to enable their wives to stay at home instead of going out to work. Typically such families lived in a terrace house of five or six rooms, costing five to six shillings (25–30p) a week in rent, and the children attended the local National School and perhaps went on to study at the Technical College; holidays were an occasional day trip to the seaside at Bangor. The father belonged to a trade union which protected his rights both against the employer above and the encroachment of the unskilled (and generally unorganised) workers below. His spare time might be spent on union or church business, attending meetings of his Orange lodge or cultivating an allotment. Except for the manual nature of their work and their membership of a trade union such men conformed more to the beliefs and outlook of the lower ranks of the white-collar middle class than to those of the working class as a whole.

The remaining 40% of the population – those who, as one historian has pointed out, could not afford to buy a £3 plot in the city cemetery but had to rest content with a public grave – were much less well-off. Whereas the wages of the skilled in Belfast were at least as high as those of similar workers elsewhere in the United Kingdom, the unskilled were often paid less, no more than half the earnings of the craftsmen they worked with. Since their numbers were constantly being added to by new arrivals, and since they were scarcely unionised at all till after 1907, they could put little pressure on employers. Even at the best of times, unemployment and casual employment were more likely for labourers than for craftsmen. Housebuilding, which traditionally provided for many, was at a low ebb during this period. Even when in work, only those who worked with craftsmen (who had a 54-hour week) could be sure of reasonable hours; tram conductors worked 60 in all weathers, carters 68. Such families could not avoid destitution without the earnings of wives and children; in bad times they could afford only a share of a kitchen house.[6]

In recent years the census figures of 1901 and 1911 have been analysed in particular for evidence as to the social and economic position of the city's Catholic minority. So far as social class is concerned, one study concludes:

> The figures demonstrate … that the Catholic population of Belfast did not occupy an inferior class position in relation to Britain as a whole, but rather that the Protestant population had obtained for itself a relatively advantaged position.

Protestant workers as such did not constitute an aristocracy of labour. Within the working class the majority of both Catholics and Protestants were semi-skilled or unskilled in 1901. But whereas few Catholics belonged to the elite of skilled craftsmen, substantial numbers of Protestants did – and were much better placed, through the way the apprenticeship system operated in most firms, to transmit these skills to the younger generation. There is no doubt that the high-wage industries were predominantly Protestant and that Catholics were under-represented in them in proportion to their numbers, as they were also in the better-paid linen jobs; they were correspondingly over-represented in the unskilled, less secure and less well-paid occupations such as carters, dockers, tailors, shoemakers and hairdressers. It is worth noting that Presbyterians were significantly better placed than other Protestants, to the extent that 'Episcopalians as a group could have found a basis for feeling under-privileged had they had any ideological stimulus to seek one'.[8]

Standards of Living

While many of the working classes, when in work, could afford to shop at the new chain stores such as Lipton's and the Home & Colonial for groceries, or the Co-ops with their better bread ('the same quality all year round') and more hygienic milk, and even to sample the novel delights of the new Italian ice-cream and fish and chip shops (there were nearly fifty of these by 1914), many others were restricted to the staple labouring-class diet of tea, white bread, sugar and condensed milk, occasionally supplemented by margarine and American bacon and cheap foreign meat bought from barrows in the street. Women who worked in the mills had neither the time nor the facilities to do much in the way of cooking. In 1901 only a quarter of the kitchen houses had a gas supply. The free installation of coin meters by the Gas Department two years later encouraged the use of gas lighting and, more slowly, gas cooking. Another measure of domestic comfort was the number of fixed baths, far more common (one in six) in

Protestant than in Catholic homes (one in sixteen) – another illustration of relative economic and social status and of the high concentration of Catholics in the old slum areas of the city. Many kitchen houses, especially in these areas, remained without water closets, despite earlier by-laws; nearly one-third still had ashpits in 1914.[9]

Prices rose faster than wages in the years after 1900. The decline in real wages made life even harder for the families of poorly-paid labourers. When the pawnbrokers (whose numbers rose from a hundred in 1900 to 117 in 1914) and all other sources of temporary help had failed, the Poor Law Guardians might have to be resorted to. The Guardians were permitted to give outdoor relief but, under Local Government Board regulations, as little as possible and to as few as possible. They excelled themselves in this task, publicly displaying in each district the names of recipients. By such means Belfast maintained the lowest pauper rate in the United Kingdom. The numbers did in fact rise, from 238 in 1901 to 888 in 1914, but the figure for Glasgow was in the region of 18,000.[10] One category of pauper was largely removed, in Belfast as elsewhere, by the granting of old age pensions in 1908, for which some 7,000 people qualified, but that was no thanks to local charity.

Children who came under the care of the workhouse were treated better after 1900, most of them being transferred to foster homes, some apprenticed, others helped to emigrate. But the workhouse was a last resort for any family, and many children ended up on the streets instead, practically encouraged to beg by being licensed, under a by-law of 1903, as street traders, or working as errand boys or flower sellers. Many came before the

Paupers outside the Belfast Workhouse. The women, in their bonnets, can be seen in the background. The occasion was probably the visit to the city of King Edward and Queen Alexandra in 1903. *Hogg Collection, Ulster Museum*

courts if they evaded the sheltering care of the missions and sought a precarious independence in the numerous filthy lodging houses. Even these were beyond the resources of those who slept rough. The Central Mission dealt with scores of them every night, such as a group of sixty-five, average age twenty, in the Springfield brickworks. The Mission's 'waifs' excursion' to the seaside in 1914 catered for 2,600 children, and in the same year it dispensed 50,000 free meals. One nameless infant rescued from a lodging house by a Mission Sister, and passed on to Barnardo's, was baptised Grosvenor Hall.[11] Newsboys acted as runners for illegal street betting; betting shops were also illegal, and the public libraries even blacked out the racing news in the newspapers. There are no reliable statistics of the extent of prostitution during these years, but it remained considerable. A vigilance committee forced the police to close brothels in the city centre, but this only moved the problem to streets farther out. The Irish Council for Public Morals blamed the situation on the extreme condemnation to which unmarried mothers were subjected and on low female wages, especially when the linen mills worked short time.[12]

Drink was the refuge for many. There was one public house or off-license (the latter used mostly by women) for every 328 inhabitants, and whiskey cost only a penny a tot. The prevalence of drunkenness and its deplorable effects on the morals and living conditions of the poor stimulated the efforts of the temperance reformers. The Pioneer movement, established in 1901 by a Jesuit priest, had considerable success among the devout Catholics at whom it was exclusively aimed (Catholic piety, total abstinence and nationalist fervour were a potent combination). Protestant churches had their own, such as the Catch-My-Pal movement, launched by an Armagh Presbyterian minister in 1910, which was so successful that the Orange parades that year were remarkable for their sobriety. Missioners working among the poor, such as the Rev. William Maguire of the North Belfast Mission, were fervently opposed to liquor and campaigned hard for its restriction. The Corporation was even persuaded in 1906 to issue municipal temperance posters. In fact the licensed vintners in that year complained that Belfast had 'the most aggressive so-called temperance party to be found anywhere'. Nevertheless, those who stood as temperance candidates in the municipal elections in 1902 and 1904 were notably unsuccessful, despite strong support from Presbyterian clergy. It is true, however, that when William Walker was trying to become MP for North Belfast in 1905–7 he sought support from the temperance bodies in the constituency by stressing his own teetotalism.[13]

Religion and Education

The influence of the churches, based upon strong, even fervid, religious faith in a host of individuals, pervaded public life. Almost everyone claimed to belong to a church of some sort; in the 1911 census only 620 people

114

refused to answer the question about religious affiliation and scarcely any claimed to be atheists or free-thinkers. Church attendance was almost universal in middle-class and Catholic areas and high among the respectable working class in general, but it held little appeal for many sinners; it was estimated in 1908 that only one in fifteen of the population of the parish of Ballymacarrett attended church. The building of churches continued, though at a much slower rate than before. The first part of the Church of Ireland cathedral was consecrated in 1910, and a new headquarters for the Presbyterian Church – built in Fisherwick Place in the city centre, on the site of a church which had migrated, like its congregation, to the suburbs – was completed in 1904.[14]

Sectarianism in education, long almost universal in primary schools, extended to technical education in the early 1900s. From 1901 the Corporation was responsible for technical schools, and proceeded to build a splendid new College of Technology to house classes hitherto held in scattered unsatisfactory premises. Staffed by Protestants (almost inevitably, since most industrial skills were at that stage in Protestant hands), the new college was not welcomed by the Catholic authorities, who set up a trades school in Hardinge Street, run by the Christian Brothers. The Brothers' constant emphasis on the importance for Catholic boys of becoming skilled workers was to bear fruit in a growing number of apprentices. The extent to which the Municipal Institute, supported by the rates of the population at large, was regarded as Protestant territory was strikingly demonstrated during the Home Rule crisis of 1912–14 when – in common with the City Hall and other Corporation property – its resources were put at the service of the Unionist cause; there exists a photograph of Sir Edward and Lady Carson inspecting an Ulster Volunteer Force bakery on the premises.[15]

A happy exception to the sectarian trend was the Queen's University, as Queen's College became under the Irish Universities Act of 1908. Independent status and an accompanying gesture of goodwill by which a department of scholastic philosophy was established with a Catholic priest in charge brought to an end the ban on Queen's hitherto proclaimed by the Catholic bishops. The proportion of Catholic students soon rose rapidly, from 5% in 1909 to 25% in 1915. In the education of women too Queen's was comparatively enlightened, taking its first female undergraduates in 1881 and admitting women ten years later to the medical course (its dissecting rooms were the first in Europe to be shared by students of both sexes). By 1911 just over a quarter of the 585 students were women.[16]

Industry and Trade

The industry and trade of Belfast continued to expand between 1901 and 1914, but expansion was uneven. Apart from the contraction in house-building already mentioned, shipbuilding experienced difficult times after the end of the Boer War, which had caused a boom in demand for merchant ships. Concerned about the future, and determined to preserve his own freedom of action in a period of intense competition and threatened mergers, Pirrie diverged from the policy adopted by the owners of other British yards and in what was seen by some as an unpatriotic move negotiated with the American tycoon J. Pierpoint Morgan to form a syndicate called International Mercantile Marine. Pirrie operated brilliantly in these shark-infested waters, though international dealings and his own social ambitions meant that he spent more and more of his time in London rather than Belfast. His style of management became increasingly autocratic, no-one but himself and one trusted subordinate having access to the financial records of Harland & Wolff.

During 1904 and 1905 Pirrie saved the business by accepting orders at or below cost and by building ships for which Harland & Wolff would not normally have tendered. Of the twenty vessels delivered during those years nine made a loss. Output slumped from 73,264 tons in 1903 to 48,404 the following year and workers had to be laid off. Refit work and Admiralty orders helped to keep the yard going, though the collapse of part of the Alexandra graving dock meant that some work had to be sent elsewhere. Despite this, Pirrie invested heavily in modernisation – a new generating station in 1904, which enabled all the tools to be electrified the following year; new engine shops; higher gantries to accommodate even larger vessels the year after that. At the end of 1907 Harland & Wolff was employing nearly 9,500 men (2,429 in the engine works). The fluctuation of the labour force even in busy times is shown in the fall in numbers to 5,785 in 1909–10 as finishing work ran out; by the end of 1910, however, the figure was up to 11,389, and it reached 14,000 by 1914. Repair yards had earlier been acquired at Liverpool and Southampton. Now in 1911, at the height of the boom, another shipbuilding yard was bought in Govan on the Clyde (Pirrie had already sold a majority shareholding in his firm to John Brown). In 1912–13 he planned the expansion of work there, lest civil war should break out in Ulster and he might have to close the Queen's Island. The climax of this era of shipbuilding was the launch of the 45,000-ton *Olympic* in 1910 and her even larger sister-ship *Titanic* the following year. The other yard, Workman Clark & Co., did not approach this tonnage in individual ships – its largest before 1914 were the 14,500-ton *Ulysses* and *Nestor*, built for the Holt 'Blue Funnel' Line – but its total yearly output was the sixth largest in the United Kingdom and it achieved an enviable reputation for excellent design and workmanship, especially in the construction of the specialist ships used to carry frozen meat from America and Australasia and fruit from the West Indies. By 1914 the combined output of the two Belfast yards was nearly one-eighth of the world's production. Between them they were then employing some 20,000; their weekly wages bill, £15,000 – £18,000 at the turn of the century, rose to £35,000 in 1915.[17] Splendid as all this achievement was, and much as the work and wages of the shipyards contributed to the prosperity of

Olympic (right) and her sister ship *Titanic* in the slips at the Queen's Island. The largest ships afloat when they entered service, these huge liners were built by Harland & Wolff for the White Star Line. *Olympic* was launched in October 1910, shortly after this photograph was taken.   *Welch Collection, Ulster Museum*

Belfast, it is well to remember that it was not only hard and dirty but also frequently dangerous work: nearly half of the fatal accidents in Ulster in an average year happened in the Queen's Island.[18]

The continued growth of the shipyard was matched by the continued expansion and improvement of port and harbour facilities. The annual tonnage of shipping cleared, nearly 2.5 million in 1900, rose to 3.2 million by 1913. Over 200 ships, totalling more than 300,000 tons, belonged to Belfast owners, which created a lot of business for local repairers, chandlers and agents. Though not always willing to respond to the pressure for additional space for shipbuilding (Pirrie even tried to bully them by making well-publicised approaches to the Dublin port authorities), the Harbour Commissioners made further major improvements. The Musgrave Channel, begun in 1898, was opened in 1903. The Thompson graving dock, the largest in the world at the time and costing over £300,000, was opened in 1911; its first occupant was the liner *Olympic*. A giant electric floating crane was acquired. As well as being what a French visitor, L. Paul-Dubois, described in 1908 as 'amongst the most thrilling industrial centres of Britain', Belfast in its heyday was above all a great port.

Industrial Relations

Relations between employers and skilled workers such as shipwrights and engineers were good for most of the Edwardian period. After the bitter strike of 1895–6 Pirrie was careful to ensure that the unions were consulted about important matters affecting their members' interests. Harland & Wolff refused to take part in the national lockout of engineers in 1897; instead, Pirrie stole a march on his competitors by conceding a shorter week of 47 hours in return for three-shift working. Two years later, when the Shipbuilders' Employers' Federation was formed, both Belfast yards refused to join. Demarcation disputes between the many shipyard unions were a likelier source of industrial strife during these years than confrontations with the management. The numerous craft unions not only secured good wages for their members when in work but also provided them with benefits when laid off. However, the attempts of labourers to secure higher wages and better conditions through unionisation were seen by the craft unions as a threat to their privileged position. From the early 1890s the National Amalgamation Union of Labour had some success in organising shipyard labourers, but there was no great improvement in the relative position of the unskilled working for the skilled before the First World War. In 1907, when engineering labourers at the Sirocco works went on strike and set up a branch of the union, they were locked out and only allowed back if they signed a document repudiating the union.

Linen workers, who could easily be replaced, were in an even weaker position. Despite attempts to organise them, by 1914 only about one-tenth belonged to any union. Apart from the hostility of employers, occupational jealousies made organisation difficult. The women who worked in the spinning mills, weaving factories and warerooms were intensely conscious of differences in status between those three workplaces and between the various occupations within each. In the mills, for example, reelers (who wore coats to work as a mark of their superiority) looked down upon the shawled spinners. An economic upturn from 1906 nevertheless encouraged an outbreak of militancy amongst unskilled workers. In May 1906 a strike in the linen mills, the first in ten years, secured a wage increase, and in the spring and early autumn of 1907 there were strikes by engineering labourers and coal heavers (as well as by bakers, printers and machine makers). These conflicts reached a climax in the dockers' and carters' strike of 1907, which was led by the charismatic labour organiser James Larkin, who came to Belfast in January of that year as an official of the British-based Transport and General Workers Union.[20]

In 1907 there were 3,100 labourers employed (or sometimes employed) at the Belfast docks. Just over a thousand of them were permanent, the rest casual, none a member of any union. There were also 1,500 carters, a few of whom belonged to an ineffective union. The dockers were to a considerable degree divided along religious lines: most of those employed in the cross-channel docks, where work was constant and regular, were Protestants, while the deep-sea docks, where work was more occasional, were manned mainly by Catholics. It was among the cross-channel dockers that the dockers' part of the great strike was concentrated, hence Larkin's boast that he, a Catholic and a nationalist, led a band of Orangemen in the cause of labour. Within a short time of his arrival he had persuaded all the carters and all but a couple of hundred of the dockers to join the union. Larkin's chief opponent among the employers was Thomas Gallaher, the tobacco magnate, who was also chairman of the Belfast Steamship Company. As a large employer of women and casual labourers, Gallaher saw 'Larkinism' as a threat to all his interests. A number of dock employers were willing to recognise the union, but Gallaher refused to have any dealings with it. When some of the dockers employed by the Belfast Steamship Company struck at the end of May in favour of a closed shop he brought in labour from Liverpool and refused to take the men on again when they tried to return to work.

Larkin's answer to this early setback was to rouse all unorganised workers to give their support. Thousands attended the strike meetings at which he thundered against the employers, Gallaher in particular, and encouraged militant action. The employers in their turn formed an Employers' Protection Society and imported more blackleg labour. Sympathetic strikes by the carters and coal heavers, with active picketing to prevent the movement of goods about the city, stretched the resources of the police and soon threatened Belfast's trade and industry. Cavalry were drafted into the city in July to protect vans from interference by pickets, and there were some minor outbreaks of violence. At the end of that month half of the constabulary in Belfast attended a meeting to protest against the long hours of unpaid extra duty they were obliged to work because of the strike, whereupon three hundred of them (mostly from the Falls area) were transferred to other parts of the country and replaced by 1,200 troops. The first serious rioting began on 11 August in the lower Falls, where vans were overturned and police and soldiers stoned. Next day two people were killed and many injured when the army fired into a crowd.

When the master carriers conceded both union recognition and a wage demand (though their right to employ non-union labour was accepted by the men), the strike was quickly settled by union officials from England who excluded Larkin from their negotiations. The dockers were then obliged to accept an unconditional return to work. Larkin's expressed belief that the co-operation of Catholic and Protestant workers during the strike meant that 'the old sectarian curse had been banished for ever from Ulster'

**Soldiers of the Essex Regiment, camped in Ormeau Park in 1907 during the dockers'
and carters' strike.** *Welch Collection, Ulster Museum*

was soon proved to be a delusion. When he went on in 1908 to establish
the Irish Transport and General Workers Union the Belfast dockers
divided, Catholics joining the new, nationalist-led body, Protestants not;
the Belfast Trades Council also split on the national question.[21]

Any hope of replacing sectarianism by working-class unity was finally
demolished when the home rule question approached its dramatic climax.
After a lull of several years, broken only by a two-day riot in 1909 caused
by an attack on an Orange procession along the Grosvenor Road, in 1912
Catholic workers (and Protestant socialists as well) were expelled from the
shipyards, despite the disapproval of Pirrie and other employers. There
was little they could do. Even in normal times the police hardly dared enter
the yards. As the Belfast commissioner of police testified at the time:

> In ordinary times they did not do duty in the shipyards and their
> presence there was regarded as an intrusion and an insult. Even in
> ordinary times, a policeman in uniform has missiles frequently thrown
> at him if he has to go down about the Queen's Road. Missiles were
> thrown at the police marching to and from duty by men working on the
> ships.[22]

The belief, expressed by most nationalist and labour commentators, that
recurring riots were the result of clever manipulation by bourgeois politicians who wanted to thwart home rule and socialism by keeping workers
at each others' throats, greatly underestimated the genuine strength of
sectarian feeling among the Protestant working class – an attitude of mind
matched, in truth, by that of their opponents. The proclamation in 1908 of
the papal decree *Ne Temere*, which applied new strict, and exclusive, canons
to the validity of marriages between Catholics and Protestants, roused
great resentment in Protestant circles, especially when the new regulations were held to have been responsible for a Belfast Catholic named

McCann deserting his Presbyterian wife in 1910. The McCann case was widely reported and was debated at some length by the Presbyterian General Assembly. Not surprisingly in the circumstances of the time, the issue strengthened Protestant fears that Home Rule would indeed mean Rome Rule.[23]

Municipal Enterprise

The Edwardian period was, as it turned out, the heyday of Belfast. In municipal affairs nothing symbolised better its prosperity and civic pride than the splendid new City Hall, opened in 1906. Designed by a young London architect, Arthur Brumwell Thomas (who was knighted on its completion), and built by the Belfast firm of McLaughlin & Harvey, it cost the enormous sum of £360,000, twice the original estimate. The increase was due partly to the fact that only the finest and most expensive materials were used – the marble work alone cost over £21,000 – and partly to the insistence (by Labour and Nationalist councillors in particular) that Corporation labourers and local contractors should be employed on the work, despite the fact that Corporation wages for labourers were on average three shillings (15p) a week more than usual and that English firms sent in lower tenders for furnishings. 'A precious stone, I suppose?', said the Local Government Board inspector when told that the foundation stone cost £500. The architect subsequently had to sue the Corporation for the balance of his fee.[24] Another major building achievement, completed in 1907, was the College of Technology, built on a city centre site unwisely

The new City Hall in course of erection, 1903.   *Hogg Collection, Ulster Museum*

The new City Hall in 1904, when the exterior was almost finished. The building was opened two years later. *Hogg Collection, Ulster Museum*

sold by the governors of the Academical Institution, the view of which has been spoiled ever since. The College, which also housed the former Government School of Art, was equipped with the latest facilities for teaching engineering and science (it was the Tech that provided practical courses for the university). A third building was the Fever Hospital at Purdysburn, opened in 1906. The Ulster Hall in Bedford Street, the usual venue for large public meetings as well as for concerts and exhibitions, was purchased by the Corporation in 1902 for £13,500. In the same year the Corporation opened its model lodging house for working men, Carrick House, which was twice extended within a few years because of the demand for its 6d. (2½p) a night accommodation. Additional branch libraries were also provided and, not before time in 1913, a new abattoir. From 1910 the horse-drawn engines and ambulances of the Fire Brigade were gradually replaced by motorised ones. Money had to be spent also on improving the new drainage system, after a combination of heavy rain and high tides flooded the whole city centre with a mixture of sewage and sea water in 1902.

The greatest extension of the Corporation's responsibilities, however, was its acquisition of the tramways. The main part of the system, belonging to the Belfast Tramways Company, was purchased in 1904. A separate

Floods in the city centre, September 1902, when the new sewers proved unable to cope with a combination of high tides and heavy rain. The partly-built City Hall is in the background.   *Hogg Collection, Ulster Museum*

system, operated by the Cavehill and Whitewell Tramway Company along the upper part of the Antrim Road, was bought six years later. The bill to authorise the purchase was held up by the Nationalist party at Westminster until the Corporation agreed to include forty acres of recreational land at Bellevue – an example of the minority group's power in anything requiring legislation. The electrification and extension of the tramways cost well over a million pounds but greatly increased the service and the number of passengers.[25] The employment of Corporation labourers on the electrification of the trams was a convenient response to public pressure during a slump but, as in the case of the City Hall, it made the work more expensive. The lavish scale of municipal entertainment during these years was less justifiable.

Critics accused the Council not only of extravagance but also of incompetence. The Citizens' Association, a pressure group of businessmen and professional people formed in 1905, was particularly concerned about public health and was partly responsible for persuading the authorities in Dublin to set up the Vice-Regal Inquiry of 1906. Its report, published two years later, was pretty damning, though it must be said that by comparison with ten other major cities Belfast was found to have a lower overall death rate than Dublin and about the same as Manchester and Liverpool. The death rate from typhoid, however, was very much higher than anywhere else and the tuberculosis rate was higher even than that for Dublin. 'Inefficient sanitary administration extending over many years' was found

123

to be the main cause. The appointment in 1906 of a new Medical Officer of Health did not at the time appear to promise much improvement, for Dr H. W. Baillie was not only less well qualified than other applicants but had been a Conservative alderman on the Council until he resigned in order to apply for the post. His appointment was derided in the medical press as well as elsewhere, but he proved to be an able administrator and, together with an active chairman of the Health Committee, tackled the typhoid problem so vigorously that by 1911 the Fever Hospital rarely saw a case.[26]

Apart from public health, with which it was not unconnected, one of the chief ways in which Belfast Corporation lagged behind other municipalities was in its reluctance to build houses for the poor. Not until 1910, by which date Liverpool, Glasgow and even Dublin had already carried out several schemes, was an Improvement Order adopted and a plan to replace 700 of the worst slums in the Millfield area drawn up. Even then little was done for many years; the first house was not completed till 1917. The delay was largely caused by objections from Nationalist councillors, who did not want those of their voters who were unfortunate enough to live in the area to be re-housed elsewhere. The Unionist majority on the Council, anxious as ever to keep down the rates, did not press the issue.[27]

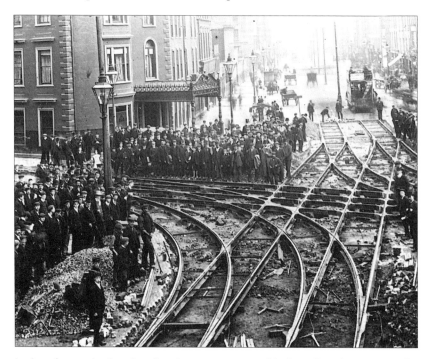

Laying the tracks for the electric trams, 1905. This busy junction was at the intersection of York Street, Donegall Street and Royal Avenue.

Hogg Collection, Ulster Museum

Houses in Abbey Street, off Peter's Hill, photographed in 1912 for a slum clearance scheme.   *Hogg Collection, Ulster Museum*

Party Politics

The political balance in the Council did not change significantly during these years, despite the advance of labour and, to a lesser extent, socialist activity. Labour could never get more than the six seats they gained in 1897. The labour movement was divided both by socialism and by nationalism. The two 'Labour Socialist' councillors elected in 1904, William Walker and John Murphy, both lost their seats in 1907. After 1911 Belfast Labour candidates stood only in Catholic wards, apart from an unsuccessful attempt in Dock Ward in 1913 by James Connolly (the future nationalist martyr), who was the local organiser of the Irish Transport and General Workers Union from 1909 to 1914; the mixture of socialism and nationalism he advocated was a double vote-loser in Belfast. In the Catholic wards until 1905, when it was disbanded, Bishop Henry's Catholic Association secured all the seats, despite the opposition of official Nationalist candidates and the refusal of their leader at Westminster, John Redmond, to recognise the Association on the grounds that it was sectarian. In the Smithfield Ward in 1904, however, the defeat of the Nationalist nominee was a very narrow one and the contest aroused strong feeling against clerical interference. After 1905 the Nationalist leader in Belfast, Joseph Devlin, gained control of the two wards, winning all the seats up for election in 1907 and completing the business in 1909. As we have seen, although they formed a permanent minority on the Council, the Nationalists exercised considerable influence of a mainly negative sort through their allies at Westminster. The only serious challenge to the Conservatives, however, came from the Citizens' Association, which won five seats in 1907 and seven the following year. In 1910 one of its councillors, R. J. McMordie, was elected both lord mayor (a post he was to hold until 1914) and MP for East Belfast in succession to G. W. Wolff. Backed by the Unionist *Belfast News Letter*, the Association did not really differ much from the Conservatives; in the 1908 elections, indeed, all but one of its candidates was a joint choice. From 1911 the Association was practically absorbed by the Conservatives into a new Belfast Unionist Municipal Association, formed to make a united front against the threat of home rule, though it remained nominally independent until 1922.[28]

For much of the period it was national rather than local issues that determined the course of politics. In the early 1900s the Conservative cause in the city was weakened by the rise of an independent Protestant movement deeply dissatisfied with what its adherents regarded as complacency in the face of the Conservative government's 'Romanising' policies. In the by-election in South Belfast that followed the death of William Johnston in 1902, Thomas Sloan defeated the official Conservative, Dunbar-Buller, by 800 votes. Four years later, in the general election, he beat Lord Arthur Hill by a similar margin. Sloan's success in 1902 was achieved with the support of three Orange lodges, which were expelled from the Order. They formed an Independent Orange Order in 1903, which within a year had twenty lodges in Belfast. This weakening of Orange unity created an opening for Labour, which in 1903 formed a Labour Representation Committee and chose William Walker to contest the North Belfast seat at the next election. In a by-election in the seat in 1905 Walker was narrowly defeated by the property speculator (and former lord mayor, hence his baronetcy) Sir Daniel Dixon. Walker might well have won if – hoping to gain Protestant support – he had not lost Catholic votes by revealing his prejudices in replying to a public questionnaire, devised by the extremist Belfast Protestant Association to test his soundness on the only issue that mattered to them. In the general election of 1906, in a larger poll, Walker increased his share of the vote but failed by fewer than 300. When he contested the seat a third time in 1907, in a by-election caused by Dixon's death, the Conservatives had recovered their strength and he lost by more than 1,800. His election agent in 1905, incidentally, was the future Labour prime minister Ramsay MacDonald. Walker was undoubtedly hampered by the fact that the British labour movement with which he strongly identified was in fact, if not officially, sympathetic to home rule, though Walker himself was not.

Catholics in West Belfast were also divided in the early 1900s, between supporters of the Catholic Association and those who favoured the wider

Platform party at the anti-Home Rule rally in the Ulster Hall on the evening of 27 September 1912, the day before the signing of the Solemn League and Covenant. The Unionist leader, Sir Edward Carson, stands at the table in the front row.

Hogg Collection, Ulster Museum

Sir Edward and Lady Carson visiting the UVF bakery in the Municipal College of Technology in February 1913. Behind Carson is James Craig, the future prime minister of Northern Ireland. *Hogg Collection, Ulster Museum*

aims of Redmond's reunited Home Rule party. The sitting Liberal Unionist member, Arnold-Foster, returned unopposed in 1900, was faced three years later (in a by-election caused by his appointment as Secretary for War) by a Nationalist, Patrick Dempsey, who came within 240 votes of him. By 1906, with the Catholic Association disbanded, the Catholic voters were united behind Joseph Devlin, who defeated a Unionist candidate, Capt. J. R. Smiley, by the narrowest of margins (16 votes). Thereafter Devlin held the seat more easily.[29]

By 1907, then, the Unionists had seen off the challenge from both Labour and their own dissidents, and the Nationalists were united behind Devlin, who could call on the powerful Home Rule party in parliament. The landslide victory of the Liberals in 1906 brought to an end a long period of Conservative power during which home rule had ceased to be an active issue. For a time the Liberals, though committed in theory to another Home Rule Bill for Ireland, had such a large overall majority in the Commons and so many other urgent priorities that the threat to the Union remained more potential than actual. The elections of 1910 transformed this situation by reducing the Liberals' majority and making them dependent on the votes of the Irish party. This immediately brought home rule to the top of the agenda and, with the passing in 1911 of the Parliament Act, which removed the veto hitherto exercised in favour of the Unionists by the House of Lords, the way was opened for Redmond at last. In 1910 the Unionists chose Sir Edward Carson as their leader and began to prepare to resist home rule. Increasingly from 1905, when the Ulster Unionist Council had been formed to bring together Unionist associations, Orange lodges, MPs and other defenders of the Union, Belfast had been at the centre of anti-home rule activity. Now it became the headquarters of the Unionist conspiracy to defy the will of parliament. The great demonstrations of September 1911 and Easter 1912, designed to show the government that home rule if it came would be resisted, were both staged in Belfast; and the Solemn League and Covenant campaign reached its dramatic climax in the Ulster Hall and the City Hall in September 1912. The organisation of the Ulster Volunteer Force in 1913, its arming with rifles smuggled from Germany in 1914 (which replaced the wooden ones bought from an enterprising local firm) and the arrangements made to establish a provisional government in the event of home rule all centred on Belfast; the old Town Hall in fact became the headquarters of the UVF. Only the outbreak of hostilities in Europe, seemingly, postponed a showdown in which the city would have become a war zone.[30]

It may indeed be true, as one historian has argued, that the very determination of Belfast Protestants to fight to keep the city British may, paradoxically, have made it 'no longer a British, but an Irish city'.[31] Certainly in Britain itself such recourse to extremes in the cause of religious conviction or prejudice was no longer fashionable.

References

1. For a perceptive discussion of the dual identity of Edwardian Belfast, see S. Gribbon, 'An Irish city: Belfast 1911', in D. Harkness and M. O'Dowd (eds), *The Town in Ireland*, Historical Studies XIII, Appletree Press, Belfast (1981), pp. 203–20.

2. Census reports, 1901 and 1911; S. Gribbon, *Edwardian Belfast: A Social Profile*, Appletree Press, Belfast (1982), pp. 47 and 56 (n. 90).

3. When making the family firm a limited liability company in 1865, John Mulholland took the opportunity to sell off part of his holding in order to buy more land, and he subsequently went into politics (*Dictionary of Business Biography*, 4, pp. 374–7).

4. Moss and Hume, *Shipbuilders*, p. 92; *Dictionary of Business Biography*, 4, pp. 702–8 (Pirrie); Collins, 'The Edwardian city', in Beckett *et al.*, *Belfast*, pp. 179–80.

5. Gribbon, *Edwardian Belfast*, pp. 13–14.

6. Gribbon, *Edwardian Belfast*, pp. 16–20; A. C. Hepburn, 'Work, class and religion in Belfast, 1901', *Irish Economic and Social History*, 10 (1983), p. 34.

7. A. C. Hepburn and B. Collins, 'Industrial society: the structure of Belfast, 1901', in P. Roebuck (ed.), *Plantation to Partition*, Blackstaff Press, Belfast (1981), p. 226.

8. Hepburn, 'Work, class and religion', *Irish Economic and Social History*, 10, pp. 49–50.

9. Gribbon, *Edwardian Belfast*, p. 34, and 'An Irish city', in Harkness and O'Dowd (eds), *Town in Ireland*, p. 207.

10. Gribbon, *Edwardian Belfast*, pp. 30–1, 35–6.

11. Gribbon, *Edwardian Belfast*, p. 39; Gallagher, *At Points of Need*, pp. 52, 44.

12. Gribbon, *Edwardian Belfast*, p. 27.

13. Gribbon, *Edwardian Belfast*, p. 26; E. Malcolm, *'Ireland Sober, Ireland Free': Drink and Temperance in Nineteenth-Century Ireland*, Gill & Macmillan, Dublin (1986), pp. 316–21; R. J. Patterson, *Catch-My-Pal: A Story of Good Samaritanship*, Hodder & Stoughton, London (1910); Budge and O'Leary, *Belfast*, pp. 123 and 134 (n. 87).

14. Gribbon, *Edwardian City*, p. 23; Brett, *Buildings of Belfast*, pp. 67–8.

15. Budge and O'Leary, *Belfast*, p. 126; J. Gray, *City in Revolt: James Larkin and the Belfast Dock Strike of 1907*, Blackstaff Press, Belfast (1985), p. 19; Hogg Collection, Ulster Museum, Belfast, H62/02/10.

16. T. W. Moody, 'Higher education', in T. W. Moody and J. C. Beckett (eds), *Ulster since 1800*, second series, BBC, London (1957), p. 202; Moody and Beckett, *Queen's*, 1, pp. 317–8, 342–4, 407–12.

17. Moss and Hume, *Shipbuilders*, pp. 118, 122–74.

18. Moss and Hume, *Shipbuilders*, pp. 89–90; Patterson, 'Industrial labour', in Kennedy and Ollerenshaw (eds), *Economic History of Ulster*, p. 177; Gray, *City in Revolt*, pp. 9–10.

19. Sweetnam, 'Development of the port', in Beckett *et al.*, *Belfast*, pp. 68–70; Gribbon, *Edwardian Belfast*, p. 13.

20. Patterson, 'Industrial labour', in Kennedy and Ollerenshaw (eds), *Economic History of Ulster*, pp. 167–8, 178; and *Class Conflict and Sectarianism*, pp. 66–7.

21. Gray, *City in Revolt*; Patterson, *Class Conflict and Sectarianism*, pp. 66–7.

22. Quoted in Patterson, *Class Conflict and Sectarianism*, p. 90.

23. Patterson, *Class Conflict and Sectarianism*, pp. 66–7; R. F. G. Holmes, *Our Presbyterian Heritage*, Presbyterian Church in Ireland, Belfast (1985), p. 136.

24. Budge and O'Leary, *Belfast*, pp. 121–2; Brett, *Buildings of Belfast*, pp. 65–7.

25. *The Belfast Book: Local Government in the City and County Borough of Belfast*, Belfast Corporation, Belfast (1929), relevant chapters; Budge and O'Leary, *Belfast*, p. 135 (n.99).

26. Budge and O'Leary, *Belfast*, pp. 111–2, 131 (n. 37–8), 133 (n. 82).

27. Budge and O'Leary, *Belfast*, p. 127; Brett, *Housing a Divided Community*, pp. 20–1.

28. Budge and O'Leary, *Belfast*, pp. 119–21, 122–5, 125–6.

29. J. W. Boyle, 'Belfast and the origins of Northern Ireland', in Beckett and Glasscock (eds), *Belfast*, pp. 133–7; Patterson, *Class Conflict and Sectarianism*, pp. 44–6, 58–61.

30. Boyle, 'Belfast and the origins of Northern Ireland', in Beckett and Glasscock (eds), *Belfast*, pp. 137–41.

31. Gribbon, 'An Irish city', in Harkness and O'Dowd (eds), *Town in Ireland*, p. 219.

Chapter 6

The First World War and After, 1914–39

The First World War and the two decades that followed brought great economic and social changes to Belfast, changes which closely resembled those in other British cities despite some particular local problems. Still greater were the political changes that gave Belfast a new role as the capital of a new, semi-autonomous state, Northern Ireland, in which Protestants were a distinct – if rather insecure – majority. In these circumstances the traditional sectarian divisions in the city assumed still greater prominence and ferocity.

War and Peace

The First World War affected Belfast, as it affected the rest of Ulster and indeed Ireland, in two main ways. One was the high number of casualties suffered by those (all volunteers, for there was no conscription in Ireland) who joined the forces and ended up largely on the Western Front. In 1914, when war broke out, Carson and Craig offered Kitchener 35,000 UVF volunteers. In return, their request for a distinctive organisation for these men was granted and the 36th (Ulster) Division thus came into existence. The division fought heroically and suffered appalling losses in the battle of the Somme in 1916, no fewer than 5,500 being killed or wounded on the first day alone. The Twelfth of July celebrations were abandoned that year; instead, in an act of remembrance anticipating Armistice Day, everything stopped in Belfast at the stroke of noon. As in other cities and towns where local lads joined local regiments, the effect of the casualties in Flanders was devastating. As one historian has put it: 'In house after house blinds were drawn down, until it seemed that every family in the city had been bereaved'.[1] The sacrifice was shared, for many National Volunteers, encouraged by Redmond as Carson encouraged the UVF, also joined up. By contrast, more extreme nationalists saw the war as an opportunity to overthrow British rule; the Easter Rising in Dublin in 1916 and its aftermath served to polarise opinion in the country still further. About half of the 49,000 Irishmen killed in the war came from the six counties that later became Northern Ireland, and a high proportion of them came from Belfast.[2]

The other main effect of the war was a prolonged economic boom that brought increased employment and prosperity to the city. The war itself created a great demand for linen for military purposes – tents, haversacks, hospital equipment, aeroplane fabric (some 90 million yards of it) – which more than made up for the loss of overseas markets. Half of all the cordage needed by the Royal Navy was produced by the Belfast Ropeworks. Munitions were produced on a comparatively small scale, though Davidson's Sirocco works made submarine parts as well as fans and heaters for war purposes, and other engineering firms were organised to produce shells, hand grenades and aeroplane parts.[3] But it was in the building of ships that Belfast made its outstanding contribution to the war effort. By 1916 German U-boats were sinking each month three times the tonnage that was being built. Shipbuilding became a high priority for the government, which brought all the shipyards in the country under its own control and embarked on a crash programme of building standard ships, the first of which was launched in Belfast. When the yards failed to meet their targets, Lord Pirrie was appointed to the new post of Controller General of Merchant Shipbuilding. Under his ruthless leadership the two Belfast yards broke all records. Altogether Harland & Wolff launched 400,000 tons of merchant and naval shipping, Workman Clark 260,000 tons.

The shipyards worked day and night, and by the end of the war were employing nearly 30,000 people. Because some skilled men had joined up, the labour force had to be diluted to a certain extent by less skilled replacements, and flat wage increases narrowed the differential between craftsmen and labourers. The craft unions did not like it but accepted the situation. There was no serious trouble of the kind that occurred on the Clyde, apart from a short strike by shipyard engineers in 1917. Enormous amounts of overtime had to be worked in order to reach production targets; in 1917 the Time Office at Harland & Wolff joked that H & W stood for Harrassed & Worried. In the early years of the war, overtime was needed to maintain living standards, as wages lagged behind rising prices, but from 1917 wages rose faster than prices and with overtime working shipyard hands were financially well-off. In addition to ships Harland & Wolff produced aeroplanes during the latter part of the war, after Pirrie offered to open an aeroplane works. Starting with De Havilland 6 machines, of which a hundred were made, the firm went on to build 300 Avros and twenty of the giant Handley Page V-1500 bombers, which were intended to reach Berlin but were finished too late in the war to be needed. It was Pirrie who acquired the land at Aldergrove, now the site of Belfast Airport, for use with these planes.

The war boom was followed by a postwar boom which lasted till the latter part of 1920 as the losses of war were made good and a public starved of consumer goods such as linen was at last able to spend its accumulated wealth. The number of spindles and looms at work in the province reached its highest between 1918 and 1920, and the shipyards were never again to employ as many as they did in 1919, when Harland & Wolff and Workman Clark were respectively first and second among United Kingdom yards in terms of tonnage launched.[4]

The ending of the war, however, did bring to an end an era of harmonious labour relations, despite the attempts of Unionist leaders, faced with an immediate election on a wider franchise after the 1918 Representation of the People Act, to maintain a united front on the constitutional question by establishing a Unionist Labour Association, three of whose nominees were accepted as official candidates and duly elected. Long hours and the suspension of normal trade union rights were tolerated while the war lasted, but with the coming of peace the shipyard workers at once demanded a significant reduction in the working week, from 54 hours to 44, three hours fewer than the unions' national leadership was prepared to accept in a negotiated settlement. The Belfast branches rejected the result of the national ballot and went on strike in January 1919, calling out not only their members in the shipyards and engineering works but also those in the city's gas and electricity stations. By the end of the first week 60,000 workers in over forty firms were affected, directly or indirectly, there were no trams or street lights and most homes were without normal lighting and cooking facilities, newspapers were reduced in size or (in the case of the *Irish News*) closed down completely, and there was a serious threat to supplies of bread and coal. Strikers smashed the windows of shops which remained open by using whatever power the authorities managed to produce with volunteer labour. At a time when the Bolsheviks had seized power in Russia, when revolutionary socialists were trying to seize power in Germany and Italy and when a general strike was paralysing Glasgow, local extremists hoped and local moderates feared that the strike represented the rising of the workers against the capitalist system – or even a sign of disillusionment with Unionism (the *Belfast News Letter* emphasised the encouragement that was being given to Sinn Fein). In fact the strikers were mostly Protestant workers who had no interest in socialism and no intention of overthrowing the Union; they simply wanted better conditions. Unionist leaders hesitated to act against them but called in the troops after pressure from the authorities in Dublin. On 14 February soldiers occupied the gasworks and the electricity station and the strike quickly collapsed.[5]

The Representation of the People Act of 1918 had replaced the four Belfast constituencies by nine, eight of which were won in the elections of the same year by Unionist candidates. The remaining one was taken by Joseph Devlin, who found himself leading a rump of only six Nationalists at Westminster when Sinn Fein, the heirs of 1916, swamped the Nationalist party at the polls yet refused to take their seats. Devlin himself easily defeated the Sinn Feiner de Valera. Lloyd George's government attempted to settle the Irish question by the Government of Ireland Act of 1920, which allowed for separate home rule regimes in Dublin and Belfast. The north reluctantly accepted this arrangement, and thus Belfast became in name what it had long been in fact, the capital of Ulster. The first Parliament of a six-county Northern Ireland was opened in Belfast City

Sinn Fein poster for a lecture in St Mary's Hall, Belfast, at the end of 1917.
Hogg Collection, Ulster Museum

Hall by George V on 22 June 1922 (it later met for some years in the Presbyterian college, before moving to Stormont in 1932). The 73 Sinn Fein MPs, however, rejected the 1920 Act, having already set up their own assembly in Dublin, Dáil Eireann, which proclaimed an Irish Republic in January 1919. Their military wing, the Irish Republican Army, intensified the guerilla war against the British begun in 1919, and in 1920 extended it to the north in order to prevent the establishment (or survival) of the Unionist regime there.[6]

The reaction of Protestant workers in Belfast was to expel all 'disloyal' elements – Catholics and socialists – from the shipyards and engineering works. This in turn led to a period of serious rioting in east Belfast, in which seven Catholics and six Protestants were killed. As well as reflecting the extremely tense political situation, the expulsions also reflected the fact that a significant number of Catholics had been recruited into skilled trades during the war and were now seen as non-combatants occupying the jobs of ex-servicemen who could not get work. The beginning of what was to be an increasingly serious slump thus added economic rivalry to political and religious division, to bring about communal strife far more serious and prolonged than any in the nineteenth century, a local civil war in everything except name. From 1920 to the end of 1924 Belfast lived under military curfew. Despite this and severe action by the new government's police force, the Royal Ulster Constabulary, and its special constables, the troubles became steadily worse, reaching a climax in 1922. By that time the death toll in Belfast had reached 453, of whom 257 were Catholics and

Falls Road public library, fortified as a base for the Special Constabulary, in August 1923. The poster on the right advertises an Ancient Order of Hibernians excursion to Dublin. *Welch Collection, Ulster Museum*

37 members of the security forces – not to mention those injured and terri-
fied in communal warfare of extreme viciousness on both sides. Up to
10,000 Catholics lost their jobs, and more than twice that number were
forced to flee from their homes. Protestants suffered death and displacement to a lesser extent, while many businesses on both sides were destroyed.
The outbreak of the civil war in southern Ireland, which diverted the
attention of the IRA, and the arrest of some of the worst Protestant thugs
brought peace at last.[7]

Municipal affairs in this postwar period were also not without excite-
ment. At the end of the war, as at the beginning, the City Council was
completely dominated by Unionists (who included the first women councillors, co-opted because there were no elections after 1916). In 1919,
however, Lloyd George's government put through the Local Government
(Ireland) Act, which altered the voting system in Irish boroughs to
one of proportional representation. Much against its inclination, Belfast
Corporation was obliged to draw up a suitable scheme for nine wards,
corresponding to the new parliamentary constituencies in the city. The
first election took place in January 1920. The result, if not quite the 'death-
blow to the Unionist clique' that the *Irish News* thought, reduced their
numbers from 52 to 29. The Nationalists and Sinn Fein each won five.
Belfast Labour Party, the official labour group, won no fewer than ten,
independent Labour candidates another three, while the Labour Unionists
won six. This outcome significantly altered the social composition of the
Council as well as its political balance. At the start of the century all but
five of its sixty members had belonged to the upper-middle or middle class,
in 1914 all but ten; now no fewer than nineteen were working-class. This
situation did not last long. Determined to maximise their power in local as
in provincial and national politics, the Unionists got an abolition bill
through Westminster in 1922. The old ward boundaries were thereupon
restored, and with them the old absolute majority. Without PR Labour
could not capitalise on its support, which was thinly spread throughout
a number of wards. In the local elections of 1923 its representation was
cut to two. The Nationalists, on the other hand, recovered their former
control of Falls and Smithfield and were thus the other group besides the
Unionists to benefit. Sectarian politics were thus firmly reinstated.[8]

The Economy: Trouble and Change

The population of Belfast continued to rise after 1911. At the next census,
in 1926, it was 415,151, an increase of 7.3% in the fifteen years. By 1937
it had reached 438,000 – getting on for one-third of the total for the
province. At about 5% in each decade this rate of growth was very much
less than it had been in the nineteenth century, and not much more than
half of what it had been in the years before the war. The figures reflected
the difficulties experienced by Belfast's staple industries, which depended

almost entirely on export markets. In retrospect we can see that these were not merely temporary setbacks; in reality they marked the end of the long and virtually uninterrupted period of expansion that began in the mid-nineteenth century and the beginning of a long decline. So, just when Belfast became a capital city of a sort, changes in international trade began to undermine the industries that had made it great. If it had not been for the growth of jobs in the service sector, some of them created by the establishment of the new provincial government, things would have been even worse than they were between the wars; the number employed in such jobs in Northern Ireland rose from about 80,000 in 1926 to 100,000 in 1937, and most of them were in Belfast.[9]

Production of linen in Ulster, which had amounted to well over 200,000 million square yards in the years before the war, fell by 1924 to 161 million and by 1930 to 116. In 1935 it was up to 146 million, but the general trend was downward. The numbers employed in the industry inevitably fell sharply, from a postwar peak of 90,000 to 75,000 in 1924 and to 57,000 in 1935. In the later 1920s the United Kingdom's return to the gold standard and high tariffs on linen imports in the United States – the main export market – made things difficult for employers, but they fought back in the 1930s and in fact held their own with foreign competitors most of the time in the American market. It was not that Belfast firms failed to maintain their share of the market, but rather that the market itself shrank, worldwide and for good. Cloth as expensive and durable as linen was no longer in such demand for female fashion, skirts were shorter and required less underwear, the modern fashion for polished wood tables and an increase in eating out lessened the demand for fine linen tableware, fewer domestic servants were employed to give it the care it needed. In these changed circumstances, cotton was a cheaper and more attractive alternative for the mass market that came into existence.[10]

In shipbuilding too it was the state of the world market rather than a failure of enterprise that accounted for the decline that took place. In general between the wars there were too many ships for the level of trade, and too many of them recently constructed during the postwar boom to need replacing; in 1921 the world's shipping was much newer than before the war. During the war, too, the United States and other countries had developed their own shipbuilding industries, which made the market still more competitive. In fact Belfast during the 1920s suffered less than some other areas of the United Kingdom, because there was still some demand for the passenger liners and large merchant vessels in which Harland & Wolff specialised. Between 1922 and 1930 the firm launched 9.7% of the merchant shipping tonnage produced by UK yards, the same proportion as before the war, and in 1929, as so often before, it launched both the largest tonnage in the world and also the biggest ship, the third *Britannic*. Pirrie's foresight (he died in 1924, appropriately at sea) in becoming involved with the firm of Burmeister & Wain in the development of the diesel engine was

Damask linen looms in Belfast, 1920s. Though the linen industry in the 1920s and 1930s was never quite so successful as it had earlier been, it remained an important, if uncertain, employer of labour, especially women.

Hogg Collection, Ulster Museum

one advantage, cheap imported steel (not available to other British yards because of a voluntary embargo) another. Even so, Pirrie had lost most of his fortune in keeping the firm afloat. After 1930, as the slump in world trade took effect, orders ceased and more and more men had to be laid off. By the winter of 1932–33 employment was only a tenth of the 1929–30 level. After the launch of the *Georgic* in 1931 grass began to grow on the slipways at Harland & Wolff, and for two years running the firm did not launch a single ship. It survived, however, partly by building things other than ships – the first diesel electric train in the British Isles (made for the Belfast & County Down Railway), locomotives for companies in America and Australia, engines for an oil pipeline in the Middle East, grain silos, steelwork for shops and cinemas. There was a strong suspicion, possibly justified, that it got less than a fair share of Admiralty contracts – one cruiser out of fifteen and one aircraft carrier out of five, but no battleships or destroyers.

The other yard, Workman Clark, did not survive the slump and went out of business early in 1935, when its south yard and engineering works were taken over by Harland & Wolff, the rest sold. Its failure was in large part due not to the slump but to difficulties caused by financial sharp practice back in 1920 which left Workman and Clark themselves very rich (one left £800,000, the other £1,500,000) but saddled the firm with a huge burden of debt. After a court case for fraud in 1927 the business was financially reorganised as Workman Clark (1928) Ltd, but orders began to dry up. Its last ship, a tanker launched in January 1935, was the 536th completed since the firm began in 1879.[11]

Where the two great staple industries struggled to survive, other smaller concerns fared better. Gallaher's – whose Irish sales were hard hit in the 1920s, first by a boycott of Belfast goods in the Irish Free State and then by prohibitive duties there – recovered well after becoming a public company in 1928, increasing its export of tobacco and cigarettes from 4,000 tons in 1930 to 10,000 in 1936. Employing over 3,000 people, mainly women, it was still the largest independent tobacco factory in the world. Davidson's Sirocco works continued to produce nearly three-quarters of the world's tea-drying machinery, as well as heating and ventilating equipment (also produced by Musgrave's, as the market for expensive stable fittings and solid-fuel stoves contracted). The Ropeworks continued to employ more than 2,000 people. The decline of shipbuilding was partly compensated for by the employment of some of its skilled workers in the only important new industry to be attracted to Belfast between the wars. Short Brothers of Rochester, makers of flying boats, received a large order for Sunderlands from the RAF and needed to expand. Facilities at Belfast were ideal: skilled labour, a deepwater dock, sheltered water suitable for flying boats and an adjacent airport (on 400 acres of slobland recently reclaimed by the Harbour Commissioners). By 1939 the firm was employing 6,000, and was soon to employ many more.[12]

Living Standards and Unemployment

It is well to remember that, despite the misfortunes of some, the majority of insured workers between the wars remained in employment throughout the period and indeed improved their position in terms of real income. The improvement was a modest one, only 10–15% in Northern Ireland compared with about 25% in the rest of the United Kingdom. Incomes per head in the province, though, already in 1924 only 61% of those in the rest of the UK, fell to 57% in 1937. In other words, the base line for Belfast workers, already low compared with that in similar British cities, fell lower still. In the worst years of the slump, 1931 and 1932, more than a quarter of the city's working population – over 50,000 people – were out of work. In these circumstances the nature and extent of public relief were a matter of vital concern.[13] Workers who were covered by national insurance were eligible for the dole, but only until their entitlement, based on the stamps gained while in work, ran out. Economy measures introduced by the British government in 1931 also applied to Northern Ireland, which since the late 1920s had the same level of insurance as the rest of the UK. Benefit was limited to a maximum of 26 weeks a year. After that, claimants had to seek 'transitional benefit', but many of the unemployed did not qualify for such help and had to fall back on outdoor relief from the Guardians (made possible by an Act of 1928). In September 1932 there were 48,000 registered unemployed in Belfast, almost half of whom were not receiving benefit. Of that number, 14,500 were not receiving transitional benefit and therefore had to seek outdoor relief.

Unemployed men queueing in High Street for assistance with the cost of dog licences, March 1933. The size of the crowd illustrates both the number of unemployed and also their anxiety to remain respectable by obeying regulations.
Hogg Collection, Ulster Museum

Successful applicants had to pass a stringent means test – some relieving officers obliged people to sell furniture and even the linoleum on the floor – and were subjected to insulting inquisitions; the chairman of the Guardians, a Mrs Coleman, gave great offence by remarking that if the poor worked as hard at finding a job as they did under the blankets there would be less of a problem. Even when successful, applicants were put to outdoor tasks, such as breaking stones, for which many of them were unfit. If unable to get a place on one of these schemes (of which there were never enough) they got no cash, only payment in kind. Single men who failed to get places were entitled to nothing, and single women got no assistance. To make matters worse, the relief rates in Belfast were exceptionally low, ranging from only 8s. (40p) a week for a married man with no children to a maximum of 24s. (£1.20) for a family with four or more; single men got only 3s.6d. (17½p) if they were lucky enough to get a place on a scheme. These rates, as local clergy pointed out, compared very unfavourably with those in other cities. In Manchester a family with one child got 21s. (£1.05), in Liverpool 23s. (£1.15), in Glasgow 25s.3d. (£1.26), in Bradford 26s. (£1.30), and some got a rent allowance in addition. In one of those rare outbreaks of working-class solidarity that occasionally raised false hopes among socialists, an Outdoor Relief Workers' Committee in October 1932 organised a strike of workers engaged on task schemes. A protest demonstration, led by a band playing 'Yes, we have no bananas', the only non-sectarian tune in its repertoire, headed a crowd of 60,000 from the Labour Exchange in Frederick Street to a torch-lit rally at the Custom House. Next day 7,000 accompanied a delegation to the Workhouse. When pleas of starvation failed to move the Guardians, rioting broke out, and when the government banned all marches there was a violent confrontation between the unemployed and the police. A curfew had little effect, and when police opened fire on looters in the York Street area one man was killed and over thirty wounded. Summoned before an alarmed cabinet at Stormont, the Guardians gave way and announced substantial increases in benefit – to 20s. (£1.00) for a man and wife and up to 32s. (£1.60) for a family with four children, all to be paid in cash; single men and women living on their own were also to receive assistance. It was a notable victory.[14]

Sectarian Violence and Municipal Government

This brief period of co-operation between Catholic and Protestant workers did not put even a temporary end to outbreaks of sectarian feeling, which had a life of its own. Its climax in the 1930s was the York Street riots of 1935, which began with an attack on or by (it proved difficult afterwards to establish which) a parade of Orangemen and their supporters returning from the Twelfth of July celebrations. For more than a month mobs on both sides vented their fury on each other and on the armed police who tried to keep them apart. Troops and a curfew had little better success in the maze of narrow streets, in which a mixed population lived cheek by jowl. By the time it was all over eight Protestants and five Catholics were dead. Most of the wounded were Catholics, however, and over five hundred Catholic families (2,240 people) were driven out of the area to take refuge in the Ardoyne district of north Belfast, where they took over a partially-completed housing estate. The fact that 95% of the £21,699 later paid out in compensation was paid to Catholics illustrates the balance of damage inflicted.[15]

Belfast Corporation played little or no part in these events. In some respects the establishment of a provincial government with a permanent Unionist majority simply reinforced the undesirable attitudes of the permanent majority in the City Hall, for the prime minister, Craig, was anxious not to stir up trouble with local authorities. In 1924, in the course of a dispute with the Corporation about public housing, he told a junior minister: 'We always have to bear in mind that the city represents in many respects one-half of Northern Ireland and therefore requires careful handling'.[16] At the same time, anxious to achieve parity in social services with the rest of the UK, the government felt obliged to put pressure on the City Council. In housing this precipitated a clash and exposed the most serious municipal scandal since 1855. Under the Irish Local Government Act of 1919 the Corporation had prepared a housing scheme and had established a Housing Committee (chairman Sir Crawford McCullagh, vice-chairman T. E. McConnell, an estate agent) and a Housing Department. Valuers and agents were appointed. Most of the proposed houses were to be built by direct labour under the supervision of the city surveyor, the rest by outside contractors. In 1925 the auditor of the new Ministry of Local Government wrote to complain of irregularities in the accounts and extravagance in the purchase of materials. The Housing Committee was obliged to set up an inquiry, which was led by a KC appointed by the Minister of Home Affairs. The Megaw Report, published in October 1926, disclosed scandalous negligence, the purchase of inferior materials, contracts awarded without tenders, members and officials of the Committee (and even the Town Solicitor) with a financial interest in sites chosen for development – sites chosen 'for profit to the vendor and not suitability for working-class housing'. In one case thousands of missing bricks were said to have been used to build a cinema owned by a Committee member. Many similar things may not have come to light, for Megaw complained that officials were unco-operative and failed to produce all the documents he asked for and that members of the Committee were unwilling to give evidence. The outcome was that both the Town Solicitor and the Surveyor resigned, and several contractors were prosecuted.[17]

These revelations led to a demand for reform and a general investigation of the city's administration, which was carried out by a London accountant named Collins. In his report in 1928 Collins said that Belfast was being run on lines more suitable for a village; that there were far too many committees, whose members encroached on work that ought to be left to officials and interfered too much in the hiring and firing of staff (five whole meetings of the Education Committee or its sub-committee were taken up with sifting through 1,460 applications for a porter's post); and that the reviewing of all decisions by the full Council, instead of delegating powers to committees, was long out of date (it had been in operation since 1842). Collins made more than thirty recommendations, all of which were accepted. Apart from those concerned with better financial control and the replacement of patronage by competition in the making of staff appointments, the greatest change was the reorganisation of the committees and their reduction from twenty-one to fourteen (Housing was among those abolished). Sir Crawford McCullagh, whose chairmanship had been criticised by Megaw, was opposed in the 1929 municipal elections by an Independent Unionist, a member of a reform group based on the Chamber of Commerce. McCullagh was defeated (and thus deprived of the lord mayorship for 1929, for which he had already been chosen), but he got back for a different ward two years later and thereafter was lord mayor for no less than sixteen years. This was testimony not only to his lavish style of hospitality but also to the tight discipline of the City Hall Unionist Party that developed under his leadership. One-party rule in the 1930s resulted in apathy rather than scandal. In the 1932 elections only three of a possible twenty-two seats were contested, in 1931 and 1934 only two out of fifteen, though the 45% turnout of electors in the contested wards was much the same as that in other British cities.[18]

One by-product of the housing scandal was that the Corporation decided not to proceed with the building of 870 houses already approved. None at all were built after 1930, by which date only 2,562 had been completed (and 375 of those were for sale, with low-interest loans to approved buyers, rather than for rent). Instead, estate agents and developers built cheap houses for sale, with the help of housing subsidies, such as the 2,500 planned for the Glenard estate in north Belfast which cost £200 each. It was these, still uncompleted, that the refugees from York Street took over. Having got there and arranged to pay rent, they conducted a successful rent strike, which made the place so notorious that in 1937 all the street names were changed in an attempt to attract buyers. In all, 28,450 houses were built in the county borough between the wars. Excuses can be found for the Corporation's dismal record. The financial position in Northern Ireland was different from that elsewhere – per capita income was not much more than half the average for the UK as a whole, and there was no equivalent of the Wheatley Act (which had stimulated subsidised council house building in Britain) – and the city's housing stock was still better than most. Nevertheless, at the bottom end, conditions were far from satisfactory and the failure to do anything effective about them was to create even greater problems later.[19]

Education

In primary education, on the other hand, the Corporation's record was a creditable one. The Lynn committee, which reported in 1923, estimated that at least 12,000 children of school age could not be accommodated in the city's national schools and that many of the places available were in dirty and insanitary buildings. The 1923 Education Act which resulted from the committee's recommendations proposed to increase grants and to make local authorities responsible for primary schools. There was to be no denominational religious instruction within school hours in state-funded schools. The Belfast Education Committee was set up in October 1923 under the chairmanship of Alderman James Duff. The Committee found that only six of the city's elementary schools could be classed as satisfactory. Another twelve could be made satisfactory. Most of the rest 'would not be tolerated in any other part of the United Kingdom'; about forty of them were 'a direct menace to the health and physical development of the children', who might have been better off on the street. Within five years fifty schools had been closed down, many improved and sixteen large new ones either built or started.

The new schools, built entirely out of public funds and entirely under the control of the Education Committee, were described as 'provided' schools. In addition to these the 1923 Act allowed for the transfer of existing schools from the managers or trustees (in most cases churches) to the Committee; thereafter the schools would be run by management committees on which the 'transferors' would be represented. A third category consisted of voluntary schools which did not want to transfer completely but did wish to qualify for a substantial degree of financial help by agreeing to have management committees composed of four representatives of the managers and two of the Education Committee, hence the name 'Four and Two' schools. Lastly, voluntary schools which preferred to remain outside the system would get no help from public funds except the salaries of teachers and half the cost of lighting, heating and cleaning. It was hoped that a large number of Catholic schools would come in as 'Four and Twos', but the Church authorities wanted to retain complete control. In any case, strongly opposed to Partition, they did not wish to recognise the new government, and thus missed an opportunity to negotiate changes to the system.[20]

As in the nineteenth century, the attempt to avoid sectarianism in the state schools by excluding denominational teaching was defeated by the churches. The Protestant churches were very unhappy with the parts of the Act that permitted the Education authority to 'afford opportunities' for religious instruction but did not permit them to provide it. Under great pressure from a joint action committee and in the absence of his Minister of Education (Lord Londonderry), who subsequently resigned, Craig agreed to make important concessions. The amending Act of 1925 enabled

144

(but did not compel) education authorities to make provision for religious teaching and to allow management committees to appoint teachers. In practice the Belfast authority agreed that Bible instruction would be given daily by teaching staff. This persuaded many Protestant church schools to transfer. The early trickle – only five in 1924–5 and six in 1925–6 – became a flood in 1926–7, when 34 transferred. By 1929 the number had reached 73. Some Protestant clergy remained unsatisfied with anything less than 'simple Bible instruction' in all religious education lessons and places for clergy by right on the management committees of transferred schools. The Belfast Education Committee, which had an acrimonious meeting with a deputation of these clamorous divines, led by the Presbyterian Dr Corkey (manager of nine schools in the Shankill area), urged the Minister of Education not to increase clerical representation, but its stand was not supported by the City Council. The 1930 Act gave the Protestant churches all they wanted, in effect ensuring that only Protestant teachers were appointed to state schools attended by Protestant children. Bible teaching accompanied by church teaching, which was essential so far as Catholics were concerned, was forbidden in state schools by the 1930 Act. In these circumstances the transfer of Catholic schools was out of the question (it probably was in any case), but Bishop Mageean was successful in his campaign for better financial treatment. The church schools henceforth received half the cost of building and repairs, which in fact was more than similar schools got in Great Britain.[21]

Separation in education extended to the training of teachers. In 1922 a state training college for primary teachers of both sexes (later to be known as Stranmillis College) was established in Belfast. The following year it was agreed that St Mary's, the Catholic training college for women, would receive government support, while remaining entirely under church control. The small number of Catholic male students at first enrolled in the state college. Since canon law prohibited mixed education, however, the Catholic authorities refused to let this arrangement continue – despite an offer from the government to build a separate, clerically supervised hostel for the students – and argued instead for a Catholic men's training college as well as a hostel. This was refused, but the government did agree to fund male students at the Catholic college at Strawberry Hill, Middlesex. Thus from 1925 Stranmillis College inevitably became a Protestant institution. Not only that, but the joint committee of the three main Protestant churches, which had triumphed in 1925 and again in 1930, was thus enabled to put such pressure on the government that in 1932 the prime minister, Lord Craigavon, once again ditched his Minister of Education and agreed to appoint three clergy to the college's management committee of nine.[22]

Expenditure on new and improved primary schools in Belfast continued even during the depressed 1930s. One of the ancillary services provided was a schools' medical service which by 1929 was carrying out more than a quarter of a million inspections a year; the Medical Officer reported in 1933 that many of the children he saw were suffering from malnutrition and anaemia. The school attendance service, taken over from the national school system, was improved and made more efficient. 'Necessitous children' were provided with free books and free meals, the latter with considerable help from Toc H, St Vincent de Paul and other volunteers. No more was done for secondary education, however, than to provide fifty scholarships (30 boys, 20 girls) each year to the city's grammar schools, a wholly inadequate response by comparison with other UK cities. At university level there was no advance on the five scholarships, each for £160, awarded since 1913.[23]

Health

To turn to public health, the voluntary hospitals were expanded or rebuilt to meet a growing need. The Royal Victoria Hospital was considerably enlarged between the wars. A new Royal Maternity Hospital, with a hundred beds, was opened on the same site in 1933. A new Royal Belfast Hospital for Sick Children had been opened the year before. At the Union Infirmary the Jubilee Maternity Hospital was completed in 1935, but despite this and an extension to the children's wards and the appointment of more specialised staff, the Infirmary was overcrowded with patients and constantly short of nurses, and the food was abominable. Another, macabre shortcoming was that visiting clergy had to conduct funeral services in the mortuary, where mourners were surrounded by corpses. In 1939 the Board was dissolved and replaced by two commissioners appointed by the government. Like other places, Belfast suffered from the great postwar epidemic of influenza, which reached the city in 1920. So many staff died in the Union Infirmary that the Guardians were moved to order that nurses should be issued with an extra ounce of butter and a half-ounce of Bovril every day. The Infirmary, dealing with the poorest, also experienced epidemics of measles and scarlet fever in the early 1920s which carried off many children. A more unusual occurrence, which reached the proportions of a minor epidemic, was an outbreak of encephalitis lethargica or sleepy sickness in the years after 1922. Many who did not die of the disease were permanently afflicted. The historian of the Infirmary recalls 'a bizarre band of zombies shambling along in their workhouse clothes'. More and more, as medical costs rose, the voluntary hospitals were obliged to consider charging in-patients. In the postwar period it was notable that 'a great change had taken place in the class of patients who now attended hospitals'; they were no longer used only by charity cases. At the Infirmary, according to one recollection, any patient staying overnight had to do a day's work the next day before being discharged.

Public health improved in Belfast between the wars. The general death rate declined and life expectancy at birth increased. The improvement

146

during the same period in other large cities of the United Kingdom was much greater, however, so the relatively poor standing of Belfast was maintained and in some respects became worse. A comparison of average death rates for various diseases, per thousand of the population, between Belfast in the late 1930s and English county boroughs in 1938 shows similar figures for scarlet fever, syphilis and diphtheria but far greater mortality in Belfast from whooping cough (11 compared with 4), measles (19 to 5), influenza (24 to 11), epidemic influenza (46 to 13), pulmonary tuberculosis (88 to 66) and other tuberculosis (21 to 12). The greatest killer everywhere was pneumonia (97 to 75), which often developed as a complication of some other condition, especially in children and old people, though tuberculosis was regarded with far more terror. The malnutrition noted by the Schools Medical Officer must have increased the risk of serious disease for some children. Infant mortality, which averaged 77 per thousand births in the province as a whole in the period 1934–8, was 97 in Belfast, high by any comparison; where Belfast had a lower rate than any city in the north of England in 1901, it had the highest in 1938 (Liverpool's was 74, Manchester's 69). The risk to mothers of dying in childbirth actually increased by one-fifth between 1922 and 1938. Though poor housing and poverty itself contributed to this deplorable situation, the main reason for it was the inadequate medical services provided by the Corporation and the Guardians. The author of a detailed examination carried out in 1941, Dr Carnwath, concluded: 'In respect to personal medical services, Belfast falls far short of what might reasonably be expected in a city of its size and importance'. Midwifery services were poor, there was very little education or help for expectant mothers and few health visitors, and many infant deaths could have been avoided by the expenditure of a little more money. The Medical Officer of Health lacked specialist staff and was responsible for things other than personal medical services, such as inspecting food, milk, the abattoir and lodging houses. His advice so far as venereal disease was concerned was that 'people should get a grip of themselves'.[25]

Public Works and Private Pleasures

Aided by government grants and unemployment work schemes, the Corporation was rather more determined about other kinds of municipal improvement. The capacity of the gasworks was further increased and a new electricity generating station was built at the Harbour in 1923 to meet a growing demand. The use of electricity was promoted by the Corporation's Electricity Department, which demonstrated and sold lighting and cooking appliances of all kinds as well as providing the power supply (the first 'all-electric' house was advertised for sale in Balmoral Avenue in 1928). Petrol buses appeared in the city from 1923, at first operated by

The Royal Courts of Justice, opened in 1933. The establishment of a separate administration in Northern Ireland brought Belfast a number of imposing new buildings and gave it something of the appearance of a capital city.

Hogg Collection, Ulster Museum

competing private companies; from 1928, however, the Corporation had a monopoly over all within the boundary. Its Transport Department acquired more land on the slopes of Cave Hill, which it developed as a park in addition to Bellevue (where the Zoo was opened in 1934). And to Hazelwood and Bellevue were added Belfast Castle and its lovely grounds, the parting gift of the earl of Shaftesbury in 1934. Land on the south side, given to the city by Henry Musgrave, was laid out as a park in the early 1920s using unemployed labour. The long-promised Museum and Art Gallery was begun in the Botanic Gardens in 1924 and opened five years later. Under powers obtained in 1924 a lock and weir were constructed on the Lagan below Ormeau Bridge, to control the tidal flow which at low water uncovered evil-smelling mudbanks, and embankments and roadways were built along the river. In 1924 Belfast opened the first municipal aerodrome in the British Isles, at Balmoral; the first flight conveyed the lord mayor, Sir William Turner, to Manchester.[26]

The other civic agencies responsible for maintaining and improving the city were also active. The Water Commissioners in 1933 opened the Silent Valley reservoir in the Mournes, which took ten years to build and increased the daily supply to 21 million gallons. In the same year the Harbour Commissioners opened the Herdman Channel and Pollock Dock on the County Antrim side of the river. Tonnage cleared through the port rose from 3 million in 1923 to over 4.5 in 1937. The reclamation of the sloblands, which had been going on for a long time in a comparatively small way, gathered pace in the early twentieth century. The annual amount excavated in the mid-nineteenth century averaged somewhere between 100,000 and 200,000 tons a year (the formation of the second cut in 1849 produced more than 300,000); the average for the century as a whole was perhaps about 180,000. Except for particular years, notably

The Ritz Cinema at the time of its opening in November 1936. The opening ceremony was performed by Gracie Fields. The Ritz was the largest cinema in Belfast (and Ulster), with seats for more than 2,200 people, a ritzy cafe and a Compton organ which rose up out of the pit. *Hogg Collection, Ulster Museum*

1902 when a million and a half tons were excavated for the Musgrave Channel, the yearly average remained similar up to 1920. Thereafter, however, it rose to nearly 700,000 and in the 1930s it was over 800,000 a year. This increase reflected the purchase of Dutch equipment, namely an elevator dredger which could be used also as a suction dredger. By this means 15 to 20 acres were added to the land at the head of the Lough each year in the 1920s, 35 acres a year in the following decade. Creating land was not the least of the services the Harbour Commissioners performed for Belfast industry. The new harbour site was first used by aircraft in 1933, though Belfast Harbour Airport did not open until 1938.[27]

The replacement of horse transport by cars and lorries was one of the major social changes of these years in Belfast as everywhere else. The number of motor vehicles on the roads of Northern Ireland almost quadrupled, and the number of private cars rose tenfold. By 1937 one family in seven had a car, compared with one in sixty at the end of the First World War. Naturally, much of the increase took place in and around Belfast. The number of motor car agents and hirers listed in the Belfast directory rose from 38 in 1920 to 170 in 1939. In 1928 the flood of imported Fords, Morrises and other makes finally proved too much for the

The opening, in September 1929, of Balmoral Golf Club, one of a number of new suburban courses established between the wars.   *Hogg Collection, Ulster Museum*

one successful native firm of car manufacturers, Chambers Bros, the first of whose beautiful hand-built machines had been produced in 1903. The arrival of branches of Woolworth, Burton the tailors, Austin Reed and other cross-channel shops added to the choice for shoppers in the city centre. Leisure activities too became more varied, for people of all classes. Drinking and drunkenness declined as the first milk bars made their appearance and cinema-going increased. By 1935 Belfast had 31 cinemas capable of seating more than 28,000 people, one seat for every fifteen of the population (the London figure was fourteen). Listening to the wireless became another popular thing after the BBC opened a studio in Belfast in 1924 (Tyrone Guthrie's first post on coming down from Oxford was assistant producer in Belfast). Greyhound racing started in Belfast in 1927, at Celtic Park, the second track to be established in the UK; another was opened in the 1930s at Dunmore Park on the Antrim Road. Sport of all kinds, and for all levels of society, became more widespread. Association football attracted capacity crowds to Linfield's Windsor Park and the ground of their great rivals Belfast Celtic, the 'Catholic' team – the most successful club between the wars. For the middle classes, the Ravenhill ground with its new reinforced concrete grandstand accommodated 30,000 at international rugby matches, and several new golf courses were opened on the outskirts of the city.[28]

In short, despite desperate sectarian tensions and serious economic difficulties, the living standards and social life of the majority of Belfast citizens showed signs of improvement between the wars, in much the same ways as in other British cities.

References

1. Stewart, *Ulster Crisis*, pp. 241–2.
2. D. S. Johnson, 'The Northern Ireland economy', in Kennedy and Ollerenshaw (eds), *Economic History of Ulster*, p. 84.
3. Coe, *Engineering*, p. 122; Johnson, 'Northern Ireland economy', in Kennedy and Ollerenshaw (eds), *Economic History of Ulster*, pp. 184–6.
4. Moss and Hume, *Shipbuilders*, pp. 175–207; Johnson, 'Northern Ireland economy', in Kennedy and Ollerenshaw (eds), *Economic History of Ulster*, pp. 186–8.
5. Patterson, *Class Conflict and Sectarianism*, pp. 92–110.
6. See D. Harkness, *Northern Ireland since 1920*, Helicon Limited, Dublin (1983), pp. 1–21, for an excellent brief account of the establishment of Northern Ireland; also P. Buckland, *A History of Northern Ireland*, Gill & Macmillan, Dublin (1981), pp. 17–21, 31–6.
7. Budge and O'Leary, *Belfast*, pp. 140–3; Boyd, *Holy War*, pp. 181–205.
8. Budge and O'Leary, *Belfast*, pp. 136–40.
9. W. Black, 'Industrial change in the twentieth century', in Beckett and Glasscock (eds), *Belfast*, pp. 161–2, 163.
10. D. S. Johnson, 'The economic history of Ireland between the wars', *Irish Economic and Social History*, 1 (1974), pp. 58–9; and 'Northern Ireland economy', in Kennedy and Ollerenshaw (eds), *Economic History of Ulster*, pp. 194–6.
11. Johnson, 'Northern Ireland economy', in Kennedy and Ollerenshaw (eds), *Economic History of Ulster*, pp. 191–4; Geary and Johnson, 'Shipbuilding in Belfast', *Irish Economic and Social History*, 16 (1989), pp. 53–4; Moss and Hume, *Shipbuilders*, chs 8–10.
12. *Dictionary of Business Biography*, 2, pp. 461–3 (Gallaher); *Ulster Year Books*, HMSO, Belfast, 1926–39; Johnson, 'Northern Ireland economy', in Kennedy and Ollerenshaw (eds), *Economic History of Ulster*, p. 201.
13. Johnson, 'Northern Ireland economy', in Kennedy and Ollerenshaw (eds), *Economic History of Ulster*, p. 202.
14. M. Farrell, *The Poor Law and the Workhouse in Belfast, 1838–1948*, Public Record Office of Northern Ireland, Belfast (1978), pp. 87–104; R. Munck and B. Rolston, *Belfast in the Thirties: An Oral History*, Blackstaff Press, Belfast (1987), pp. 23–7; P. Devlin, *Yes We Have No Bananas: Outdoor Relief in Belfast, 1920–39*, Blackstaff Press, Belfast (1981), pp. 73–137.
15. See A. C. Hepburn, 'The Belfast riots of 1935', *Social History*, XV (1990), pp. 75–96 for an excellent analysis of this 'urban ethnic equivalent of a *jacquerie*'. Budge and O'Leary, *Belfast*, p. 151; Boyd, *Holy War*, pp. 205–18; J. J. Campbell, 'Between the wars', in Beckett and Glasscock (eds), *Belfast*, pp. 153–5.
16. P. Buckland, *James Craig*, Gill & Macmillan, Dublin (1980), p. 107.
17. Budge and O'Leary, *Belfast*, pp. 145–7.
18. Budge and O'Leary, *Belfast*, pp. 147–50.
19. Brett, *Housing a Divided Community*, pp. 21–2.
20. N. McNeilly, *Exactly Fifty Years: The Belfast Education Authority and its Work (1923–73)*, Belfast Education & Library Board, Belfast (1973), pp. 7–13.

21. D. H. Akenson, *Education and Enmity: The Control of Schooling in Northern Ireland, 1920–50*, David & Charles, Newton Abbot, (1973), pp. 72–118; McNeilly, *Exactly Fifty Years*, pp. 25–7.

22. R. Marshall, *Stranmillis College Belfast, 1922–1972*, Belfast (1973), pp. 4–12; Akenson, *Education and Enmity*, pp. 119–33.

23. McNeilly, *Exactly Fifty Years*, pp. 32–5, 42–5.

24. D. H. Craig, *Belfast and its Infirmary: The Growth of a Hospital from 1838–1948*, Brough, Cox & Dunn, Belfast (n.d.), pp. 64, 57–60; Calwell, *A Voluntary Hospital*, pp. 79–80.

25. Johnson, 'Northern Ireland economy', in Kennedy and Ollerenshaw (eds), *Economic History of Ulster*, pp. 210–12; T. Carnwath, 'Report to the Special Committee of the Belfast Corporation on the Municipal Health Services of the City', typescript, Queen's University, Belfast, dated 23 December, 1941.

26. *Belfast Book*, relevant chapters.

27. Loudan, *In Search of Water*, pp. 101–49; E. Jones, 'Land reclamation at the head of Belfast Lough', *Ulster Journal of Archaeology*, third series, 21 (1958), pp. 137–40.

28. Johnson, 'Northern Ireland economy', in Kennedy and Ollerenshaw (eds), *Economic History of Ulster*, pp. 213–4; Belfast street directories, 1920–39; M. Open, *Fading Lights, Silver Screens: A History of Belfast Cinemas*, Greystone Books, Antrim (1985), pp. 5–8.

Chapter 7

The Second World War and After, 1939–72

In the period of thirty years or so that began with the outbreak of war in 1939, Belfast adapted successfully to many economic and social changes – changes which were similar to those experienced by other British industrial cities and which brought similar problems and benefits.

Wartime

The Second World War, like the First, was good for Belfast business. Prewar rearmament had already brought to the city an aircraft industry which by 1939 was employing 10,000 people. The demands of war work, especially in shipbuilding and all kinds of engineering, were to reduce the unemployment of the 1930s to low levels. The shipyard, which employed 9,000 in 1939, had a workforce of more than 21,000 by 1944. Aircraft manufacture in 1943 employed 32,600. Other engineering, which accounted for 14,000 or so before the war, employed over 29,000 in 1943–44. In all, 80,000 or more found work in shipbuilding and engineering, an increase during the period 1939–45 of no less than 138% (the figure for Great Britain was 65.6%). The wartime output of Short & Harland and their sub-contractors (among whom were Harland & Wolff and Mackie's) included 2,381 Stirling bombers and 133 Sunderland flying boats. Harland & Wolff built 170 warships, mostly corvettes, minesweepers and similar small craft but including the aircraft carrier *Formidable*. In addition the firm carried out a large amount of repair and conversion work for the Admiralty, especially the conversion of cargo vessels to aircraft carriers; it also produced large quantities of propelling and auxiliary machinery for ships, not to mention 550 tanks (assembled at Carrickfergus), 10,000 pieces of ordnance, ball bearings, gun mountings and parts for Stirlings and Sunderlands. Lastly, more than sixty merchant ships, with a total tonnage of 421,500, were launched during the period 1941–45. Mackie's and the Falls Foundry made lathes for the production of munitions, and Mackie's organised the manufacture of armour-piercing shells and aircraft parts in redundant linen mills. Sirocco and Musgrave's produced heating and ventilation equipment for war purposes, while smaller firms made motors and generators. The output of the Ropeworks included parachutes and camouflage netting as well as its usual products, for which there was no less demand than in peacetime.[1]

The same could not be said for linen. In the early stages of the hostilities every effort was made to keep the American market supplied and thus earn

153

Wartime aircraft production at Short & Harland: Stirling bombers in the main assembly shop, January 1941. *Photograph courtesy of Short Bros plc*

vital dollars for the war machine, but the German occupation of Belgium cut off the main source of both flax and seed (five-sixths of the former and all of the latter were imported). Ulster farmers were encouraged to grow more, with such success that the acreage rose from 21,000 in 1939 to 124,000 in 1944. The flax that was available was rigidly controlled and directed entirely to approved uses, some for immediate war needs (the Ministries of Supply and Aircraft Production took half of all the cloth made in Northern Ireland), the rest for civilian use such as 'utility' clothing. The military uses included aeroplane fabric – each Wellington bomber took well over a thousand yards of linen – flying suit canvas, parachute harness, gun covers, nurses' uniforms, uniform linings, ground sheets, kit bags, awnings and sail cloth. Most military uses, however, were better met by the coarse dry-spun yarns of Dundee than the fine wet-spun yarns of Belfast. Mills closed or were adapted to produce munitions. Employment fell drastically; the number of insured linen workers out of work in the province, 12,000 in April 1940, was 23,000 by September. Some found work again in textiles as the production of rayons and mixtures was developed, but most had to learn a different trade. The autobiography of William Topping, an overseer in a damask weaving factory, tells how he went to England to be trained to inspect ball-bearings.[2]

The earnings of engineering workers, which had fallen behind those in Britain in the late 1920s and were 10 to 20% lower in the 1930s, caught up with the national average in the early 1940s, largely because of the long hours of overtime worked. Voluntary enlistment in the forces, after an initial rush, was low throughout the war, even after the Belfast blitz of 1941. Conscription was seriously considered by the British government but – despite the advocacy of some leading Unionists – was in the end rejected, partly because any suggestion of it was vehemently opposed by the nationalist population. In practice if not so openly, many Unionists were not enthusiastic about it either, fearing that the jobs of those who went would be filled by immigrants from the south. One strong practical argument against it was that if imposed it might cut off the flow of recruits from Eire, which between 1941 and the end of the war amounted to 18,600, as compared with only 11,500 volunteers from Northern Ireland. Nor was there much compulsion on workers to go wherever they were most needed, though some thousands volunteered to work in England.[3]

Industrial relations were not particularly good in Belfast during the war. Between 1941 and 1945 there were 57 disputes in the shipyard, 20 of which led to stoppages affecting 35,000 workers and losing more than 320,000 working days. In other engineering works stoppages cost 52,000 days, on the docks a further 30,000. The poor performance of Belfast's war industries reflected what English observers saw as a general laxity in Northern Ireland. The strike record of the workers at Short & Harland was described by one official as 'by far the worst of any major military services supplier in Northern Ireland'. In 1943, when it was suddenly taken over by the government, the firm was reckoned to be no more than 65% efficient, and the Ministry of Aircraft Production official who made that assessment also remarked that 'any amount of people are drawing pay for loafing about'. Absenteeism in the shipyard was said to be twice as bad as in the worst British yards, and productivity was low.[4] Mackie's were an honourable exception. Much was later made of the importance of Northern Ireland's contribution to the defeat of Nazi Germany. In truth its greatest contribution was to be still part of the United Kingdom and therefore available – as neutral Eire was not – as a base for the aeroplanes and ships that kept the North Atlantic open, and as a safe training ground for American troops preparing for the invasion of Europe. The presence of a German embassy in Dublin throughout the war, and de Valera's official message of regret to the ambassador at the news of Hitler's death, appeared to underline the difference between north and south. In practice Eire's neutrality was exercised benevolently towards the allies. Aircrew who came down south of the border were usually handed back, while de Valera's ruthless suppression of the IRA in the south made it much easier for the Stormont government to deal with a renewed campaign in Belfast. Six IRA men captured after a policeman was killed in the city in 1942 were sentenced to death; one was executed. Further republican attacks led to a curfew, armoured police patrols and the addition of yet more suspects to those already imprisoned or interned.[5]

Though Belfast did not pay the heavy price in dead and wounded service personnel that it had paid in the First World War, its civilian population this time shared with other British cities the suffering and destruction caused by aerial bombardment. No city was less well prepared for the blitz when it came in 1941, either militarily or psychologically. Few people thought that it would be a target at all, despite the presence of important war industries. In 1941 it had no night fighter cover, no searchlights, no effective balloon barrage and very few heavy anti-aircraft guns. This was scarcely the fault of the Northern Ireland government, which relied on British advice in such matters. The lack of serious planning, on the other hand, and the failure to take adequate precautions in the event of an air attack, were largely due to the government's complacency in the early stages of the war. The fall of France and the Battle of Britain in 1940 led to some action, notably the establishment of a Ministry of Public Security which encouraged the building of air raid shelters and the recruitment of civil defence volunteers and firemen, but by that time other priorities made materials hard to find. When the blitz came in April 1941 most of the people in Belfast had no physical protection. There were no shelters even for 30,000 workers engaged in vital war work, let alone for ten times that number of ordinary citizens who had been promised them at the start of the war. It was no wonder that the Unionists lost a by-election seat to the Labour firebrand Harry Midgley in 1941.[6]

Most of all, perhaps, Belfast Corporation was to blame for a lack of practical preparation that made the effects of the bombing much greater than they need have been. The Fire Brigade in April 1941 consisted of only 230 full-time men, though the Corporation had powers to recruit far more, and the 1,600 auxiliary firemen were scarcely trained at all and were disregarded by the chief fire officer. An official report a month before the blitz indeed recommended that this man should be retired at once. When the bombers came he never left his office and was reported to have hidden under his desk in tears. The sheer incompetence of many Corporation

The lower end of High Street on the morning of 16 April 1941, after the Easter Tuesday blitz on Belfast.   *Photograph courtesy of the* **Belfast Telegraph**

officials, men promoted well beyond their ability, was cruelly revealed. Preparations to deal with dead bodies turned out to be very inadequate. The city's mortuary service could cope with no more than 200, less than a quarter of the number on the worst night. The facilities that might be needed for the homeless were similarly underestimated: the seventy schools and church halls designated as rest centres and equipped with food and bedding could cope with only a tenth of those actually made homeless.[7]

The first raid, on the night of 7–8 April, started before the sirens could be sounded. Considerable damage was inflicted on the shipyard and docks, but only thirteen people were killed and 81 injured. Apart from installing smoke-screen equipment at the docks and getting some searchlights, little could be done to meet the shortcomings revealed that night before the enemy returned in much greater force a week later. The Easter Tuesday raid was a much more serious affair, a five-hour bombardment by over a hundred planes which rained more than 200 tons of high explosive, 76 land mines and some 29,000 incendiary bombs on the almost defenceless city. The peculiar tragedy was that most of the bombs fell not on strategic targets but on densely populated residential streets from which very few people had been evacuated. The very success of the smoke screen over the Queen's Island may have contributed to this by confusing the German aim. At any rate the result was a great many civilian casualties. Estimates vary, but a recent authoritative history of the Belfast blitz puts the number at not less than 900 dead.[8] The official historian of Northern Ireland's part in the war wrote: 'No other city in the United Kingdom, except London, had lost so many of her citizens in a single night's raid. No other, except possibly Liverpool, ever did'.[9] Fearing worse to come, the authorities now set about building more shelters and trying to ensure that fire-watching was taken seriously; they also had all the dangerous wild animals in the Zoo destroyed, lest they escape next time. The bombers returned on the night of 4–5 May, another major raid, when they caused severe damage to the shipyard and aircraft factory, and in smaller force the following night. Only thereafter were defence and civilian services adequately organised to cope with such an emergency, which never came again. One extraordinary feature of the blitz was the appearance on the streets of Belfast of fire crews from neutral Eire, volunteers from Dublin, Drogheda and Dundalk who had come to offer their help.[10]

For several weeks during and after the raids, in the absence of shelters, thousands of people left the city every night by any means they could and slept in the fields and ditches. As many as 10,000 'ditchers' shared a common fear and a rare sense of togetherness. Fortunately the weather stayed fine. Shared suffering in some instances brought Catholics and Protestants together. It did not entirely alter their suspicion of each other, however. Even the fact that Catholic districts of the city suffered much less than Protestant ones, and that large numbers of Protestant churches were destroyed while Catholic ones escaped, could be made to support the belief that the bombers had been guided by Catholic signals, that 'the Pope was in the first aeroplane'. A more likely explanation was that most of the bombers' industrial targets, such as the shipyard, were in Protestant areas. The republican activities and attitudes of some Catholics seemed to give substance to Protestant fears. Quite apart from the antics of the IRA (which included war sabotage), they evinced a lack of enthusiasm for the war effort, a reluctance to undertake civil defence work, and dislike, even hostility, towards the American troops who arrived in 1942. Catholic opposition to any suggestion of conscription was vehemently expressed even before the war began, in a statement by the Ulster bishops read out from the pulpits in April 1939. Their opposition was reiterated, in very much the same words, in 1941 by Cardinal MacRory, to whom at this time of crisis for European civilisation the essence of the question was that 'an ancient land, made one by God, has been partitioned by a foreign power, against the vehement protests of its people' and that conscription would 'seek to compel those who writhe under this grievous wrong to fight on the side of its perpetrators'.[11]

The blitz, especially the Easter Tuesday raid, destroyed or damaged an enormous number of houses. The official estimate was 3,500 totally destroyed and 53,000 damaged, 18,000 of them severely. An existing shortage was thus made much worse. The first comprehensive survey, in 1944, estimated that more than 23,500 new homes were needed. The mass evacuation that followed the blitz revealed to some middle-class people the dreadful condition of the poorest in Belfast – 'the submerged one-tenth of the population' – unhealthy, filthy, verminous, 'inhuman in their habits'. The Moderator of the Presbyterian Church told his congregation:

> After the big Blitz of a few weeks ago I was inexpressibly shocked by the sight of people I saw walking in the streets. I have been working 19 years in Belfast and I never saw the like of them before – wretched people, very undersized and underfed down-and-out-looking men and women …. Is it creditable to us that there should be such people in a Christian country?[12]

In the midst of all this another Corporation scandal was revealed. It began with a dispute between the medical superintendent and some of his staff at the sanatorium in Whiteabbey. The Corporation asked the Minister of Home Affairs for an inquiry into the running of the hospital and two inspectors were appointed. The Council declined to give evidence, however, apart from that furnished by its officials. The inquiry lasted thirty-four days and reported on 15 June 1941. On the immediate point at issue the medical superintendent was censured, but the report went far beyond that to investigate the management of the accounts and the purchasing decisions of the Corporation's TB Committee. The City Treasurer's department was condemned for 'complete laxity' and 'gross neglect' in the management of the accounts, and the Committee was found to have made many 'improvident bargains', including the purchase of totally unsuitable blackout material. The inspectors recommended that the Committee should be dissolved and the Corporation relieved of its powers under the Tuberculosis Prevention Acts. The Corporation immediately set up a special committee of six councillors consisting of the Lord Mayor (Sir Crawford McCullagh), three Unionists, one Labour and one Nationalist, to investigate the affairs of the Council. The six recommended that they should control future appointments. The dud blackout material was traced to a firm in which an interest was held by four councillors, who were asked to resign. At the same time the Town Clerk and Town Solicitor, John Archer, conveniently retired on reaching the age limit. When the Council next met, on 7 August, it voted to dissolve the special committee, a decision rescinded a week later after Sir Crawford had used his considerable personal influence. The committee then appointed a new Town Clerk and got on with preparing its report, which appeared in March 1942. It recommended a special appointments committee, a return to direct employment of unskilled and semi-skilled labour, a stricter definition of what constituted 'interest' and a requirement that anyone tendering for a Corporation contract should disclose the names of helpful councillors. On 2 April the City Council rejected all these recommendations. When it failed to put its house in order within two months the Council was then replaced by three administrators appointed by the Ministry of Home Affairs for a period of three and a half years to make all appointments, purchases and contracts and to fix rates and taxes. A senior civil servant, C. W. Grant, was appointed along with two part-time commissioners, both of them well-known businessmen and former presidents of the Chamber of Commerce. John Dunlop, author of the original report, was brought in as Town Clerk in 1943. Sir Crawford McCullagh, in this instance on the side of the reformers, had given way as lord mayor to one of the opposition, but when this man retired at the end of 1942 Sir Crawford returned and remained in the post until 1946. Ten of the 21 councillors who had voted to dismiss the Big Six sued the *Northern Whig* for libel after it had made derogatory references to them. They won the case but were awarded only nominal damages of £50 each; three of them had already resigned from the Council. The war could scarcely have been less glorious for the Corporation.[13]

Industry: Challenge and Change

The high level of employment in manufacturing industry which had made Belfast prosperous during the war continued for some years after it. Even linen had a period of revival, which lasted until 1952, as the demand for consumer goods after years of austerity gave textile producers a seller's market. Thereafter the decline that had started between the wars resumed and gathered pace. In 1951 the number of Belfast workers employed in linen was 31,000. By July of the following year, however, one-third of them were out of work, by the mid-1960s one-half, and in 1971 only 8,000 or so jobs remained. In Northern Ireland as a whole in the years 1958–64 almost one-third of the linen plants closed and over 45% of the workers lost their jobs. Fortunately the economy was in general buoyant and most of them were able to find other work.[14]

The other great staple industry, shipbuilding and marine engineering, fared much better in the postwar period. Not only was there a great demand for ships but two major competitor countries, Germany and Japan, were for a time in no position to compete. The end of the war, of course, meant an end to new orders for warships, so the workforce had to be reduced to some extent, but the continuing work on three aircraft carriers already started – *Eagle*, *Centaur* and *Bulwark* – provided employment for several years. Indeed *Eagle*, the Navy's largest warship, was called the 'iron lung' of the Queen's Island, as the Admiralty kept on modifying its requirements; some of her compartments were said to have been refitted twenty times. Work on all three ships was resumed in earnest in 1950, after the Korean War had broken out. Payments from the Admiralty enabled Harland & Wolff to repay a £2.5 million government loan and a large bank overdraft; by the middle of 1946 the firm was £1.6 million in the black. Apart from naval work there was a stream of orders for new passenger and cargo vessels – twenty contracts were signed in 1946 alone – and numerous prewar passenger liners such as Union-Castle's *Capetown Castle*, *Warwick Castle* and *Athlone Castle*, which had been used as troopships, were reconverted. New ships ordered in 1947 included several oil tankers, for which there was an increasing world demand, and two more Union-Castle liners were reconverted. The chairman, Sir Frederick Rebbeck, began a programme of improvements at the yard which included a welding shop (costing over £300,000) for prefabricating sections of ships – the development that was soon to supersede riveting. The engine works also thrived in the immediate postwar period, producing not only marine engines but also stationary diesel generating and pumping engines for use in Africa, Malaya and the Middle East; the engine works was in fact extended.

The Korean War raised freight rates and created a demand for more cargo ships. In 1950 Harland & Wolff received orders for eighteen cargo/passenger vessels. Among the launches that year was the whale factory ship *Juan Peron*, ordered by an Argentine firm and named after the dictator. The ceremony was to have been carried out by his wife Eva, but she was prevented from coming to Belfast by the outbreak of the troubles that were to lead to Peron's downfall. Instead, a secretary from the Queen's Island office, chosen for her Latin-American looks, went through the motions. The development of the Cold War in the 1950s brought more orders from the Admiralty. Despite this, in 1952 the shipyard's profits fell by more than half, and those from the engine works by 40%. Such fluctuations could still be seen as normal, however, rather than as symptoms of long-term decline,

Canberra: the last of the great passenger liners built by Harland & Wolff at the Queen's Island, 1960.   *Tourist Board Collection, Ulster Museum*

and in fact the year 1953 was the best since 1946. More orders came in 1954 and results were pretty good for a couple of years. By 1955, however, when the Queen launched Shaw Savill Line's *Southern Cross*, Rebbeck's reluctance to introduce modern methods was resulting in dangerously low levels of productivity compared with those achieved by foreign competitors. Then the Suez crisis and the closure of the canal in 1956 led to the cancellation or postponement of a number of orders. In the yard itself a prolonged wage dispute with riveters, untypical of the good relations between employees and management that usually prevailed, delayed several launches.

1957 was the last good year for orders. The *Canberra*, built for P&O and launched in 1960, was the last great liner to be built by Harland & Wolff. By 1958 all UK shipbuilders were facing changed circumstances with which they were not well equipped to deal. Successive Conservative governments took the view that shipbuilding and marine engineering were old, declining industries and preferred to offer incentives instead to new enterprises in light engineering. In these circumstances Rebbeck's conservative style of management was almost fatal for the Belfast yard. Only after he retired in 1961 were essential changes embarked upon. As the historians of the firm have put it, his retirement

> not only marked the end of the prosperous postwar years, it also symbolised the demise of a whole shipyard culture, the disintegration of a social and technical system based on high standards of personal skill and judgement, and its replacement by an organisation in which skill was built into machines, and judgement passed from the craftsman to the manager.[15]

Much of the social cohesion of the workforce, as reflected in social clubs, sports clubs and choirs, survived for a time, but as the number of employees declined this too would largely disappear.

161

Canberra was the first postwar contract on which Harland & Wolff lost money. From 1964 onward, however, it made a loss every year, the Belfast yard itself losing £887,000 in 1964, £381,000 the following year, over £2 million in 1966 and 1967, and more than £3 million in 1970. Its engine works lost money every year except 1964 and 1968. By 1966 overall losses totalled more than £4 million, by 1969 more than twice that sum. The deepening financial crisis was in contrast to the technical achievement represented by the successful launch in January 1966 of the huge oil rig *Sea Quest*, the first time indeed that such a contraption was launched in one piece (each of its three legs rested on a separate slipway). Unfortunately it did not lead to repeat orders. Another notable achievement was the completion in 1969 of the 190,000 ton oil tanker *Myrina*, the largest launched in Europe that year. The next year, work began on the construction of a great new building dock, 1,825 feet long and 305 feet wide, which would allow even larger ships (up to a million tons deadweight) to be built and floated off instead of launched down a slipway in traditional fashion. The Goliath crane with which the dock was equipped was to become the city's most prominent landmark. The workforce fell from its postwar peak of around 20,000 in 1960 to 9,000 in 1968. The whole period since 1945 was a story of relative decline while maintaining absolute levels of output. Harland & Wolff in fact raised their share of the UK's output, from an average 9.8% in the years 1946–61 to 17.4% in the years 1962–79. The trouble was that the UK share of the world's output, 24% in 1946–61, fell to only 5% in 1962–79. The great days were gone for good.[16]

Aeronautical engineering was a different story, though it too had a chequered history. Short & Harland, which became Short Bros & Harland in 1947 when the works at Rochester were closed down and all activity concentrated in Belfast, reduced its workforce at the end of the war, when production of Stirling bombers ceased. The firm's most successful venture during the next few years was the Sealand flying boat, of which twenty-five were built for sale overseas. There was no long-term future for such craft, however, and by 1950 both the RAF and the airlines had given them up. The firm failed to win production contracts for other aeroplanes it developed, such as the SA-4 Sperrin, a turbo-jet four-engined bomber. The Korean War led to a major rearmament, in which Shorts got useful sub-contract work from other companies, notably for Canberra bombers, of which it produced more than 130 for English Electric. A contract for Bristol Britannias in the later 1950s followed the Bristol Aeroplane Co's acquisition of a share in the Belfast firm. The fluctuations in demand, partly caused by frequent changes in government defence policy, led to labour trouble throughout the 1950s. In the following decade the firm's most successful products were anti-aircraft missiles – the Seacat and Tigercat systems and the shoulder-launched Blowpipe – which were sold in large numbers all over the world. The aeroplane success of the decade was the SC-7 Skyvan. This versatile aircraft, with its ability to take off and land in very little space, was produced in both military and civilian versions and sold particularly well in developing countries where normal landing facilities were in short supply. The firm's research and development work on VTOL (vertical take-off and landing) aircraft, begun in the 1950s with a 'flying bedstead', was an important aspect of its work, if not immediately profitable. More and more in the late 1960s its bread and butter came from 'aerostructures' work undertaken for other companies, such as building the wings for the Dutch Fokker Friendship and the 1968 contract for 'pods' for the Lockheed Tristar's Rolls Royce engines. Finance was a constant problem, however. By August 1966 the accumulated deficit was up to £10.4 million and 550 workers had to be laid off. This still left about 8,000, almost as many as the shipyard employed. The survival of Shorts was all the more important to the local economy as shipbuilding declined, hence the substantial support the company received from the Northern Ireland government.[17]

The engineering firms of Mackie's (textile machinery) and Sirocco (ventilation equipment) not only survived but prospered during the decades after the war, adapting their products to suit a changing market. In the case of Mackie's this meant producing not only machinery for processing flax but also for the new artificial fibres that were replacing it. The old engineering firm of Musgrave's, however, went out of business in 1965, and the famous Ropeworks, which was still employing 2,000 workers in 1951, was forced to reduce to 700 by 1971 (and did not survive the decade). 'Other engineering' (including vehicles) in the census employment returns fell from 13,325 in 1951 to just under 10,000 in 1971, while 'Other manufacturing' fell from 30,189 to 22,828.

Yet the total employed in manufacturing jobs in the Belfast urban area in 1967 – about 100,000 – was only slightly lower than it had been in 1950 (or indeed at the start of the century). This was because, as traditional industries declined, new ones were attracted to green-field sites outside the city boundary. By the late 1960s these were employing more than 20,000 people. Most of the new firms were engaged in light engineering of some sort, producing such things as oil-drilling equipment (Hughes Tool at Castlereagh), computers (ICL, also at Castlereagh) and tape recorders (Grundig at Dunmurry). Other new products included tyres (Michelin at Mallusk). Not only was manufacturing employment maintained, if given a different emphasis and location, but so too was employment in general. By the late 1960s well over a quarter of a million people in the Belfast area had jobs of some kind. This was the result of continuing growth in service trades, distribution, professional services and public administration – which in turn reflected greater prosperity, improved standards in state services such as health and education (there was one teacher to every 34 children in 1961, compared with one to every 58 in 1901) and many more civil service and local government jobs. Unemployment in the Belfast area in the mid-1960s was only about 3%, in retrospect a golden age. As an economist writing in 1967 put it:

163

The years since the Second World War have witnessed the transformation of the industrial structure and the emergence of Belfast as a modern administrative and commercial centre with widely diversified industrial interests.[19]

Trade and Transport

The Harbour Commissioners continued to improve and modernise the facilities of the port after the war, to keep pace with an ever-rising volume of trade. New wharves for foreign trade were completed in 1958, a new deep-water wharf was constructed on the west side of the Victoria Channel, and the channel itself was widened and deepened between 1958 and 1963. A 200-ton cantilever crane was installed in 1959. These and other improvements had by 1966 cost £9 million. By that time work had started on a new dry dock on East Twin. Finished in 1968, it cost over £5 million and was 1,100 feet in length and 165 feet wide at the entrance. Its construction involved the demolition of an earlier harbour improvement – the Inner Lighthouse, erected in 1851. The Musgrave Channel was also widened and deepened in the late 1960s, spoil from the dredging being used to reclaim further areas on both sides of the river mouth. In 1964 BP opened an oil refinery on the Harbour Estate, beyond the shipyard. The changing nature of port business can be seen in the growth of container traffic, which started in the late 1950s; Link Line's service to Liverpool began in 1959, a service to Heysham soon followed, then a weekly service to Preston. Within ten years container tonnage handled by the port amounted to 1.35 million a year, with a hundred sailings a week taking 5,000 containers to Great Britain and the Continent. Roll-on, roll-off facilities were provided to cope with this change in the traditional pattern, which of course had knock-on, knock-off effects on employment at the docks. The bustle of Belfast harbour in the 1960s can be gauged from the fact that as well as daily passenger and cargo sailings to Glasgow, Liverpool and Heysham and container services to Heysham, Liverpool and Preston there were freight services to and from Preston every day, twice a week with Ardrossan, Bristol, Greenock and Manchester, and weekly with Aberdeen, Cardiff, Dundee, London, Leith, Middlesborough, Newcastle, Stornoway and Swansea. The tonnage of imports and exports handled, a little under 5 million in 1956, had risen to 7 million by 1970. By the 1960s a large proportion of the import tonnage was accounted for by oil, which increasingly replaced coal as the fuel used to produce power (the electricity generating stations used it from 1962, and when the BP refinery was opened two years later the Corporation gasworks started using its by-products instead of coal). By 1970 imports of crude petroleum and petroleum products amounted to nearly 2 million tons, coal to 954,000; total imports were 5,826,000. Twenty years earlier, the figure for oil and

Cross-channel passenger ships at Donegall Quay, c.1960. This familiar scene was soon to be transformed, as more and more travellers found it convenient, and financially possible, to go by air.   *Tourist Board Collection, Ulster Museum*

motor spirit was 1.15 million, for coal and coke 1.36. To look at it another way, in terms of value 1968 imports of oil were worth nearly £16.5 million, of coal just over £22 million; twenty years earlier the figures were respectively £2.57 million and £8.4 million.[20]

More and more passengers preferred to travel by air rather than by sea, however. In 1949 only 56,000 did so, but by 1955 the number had risen to 227,000 and it passed the one-million mark in 1966. The Nutt's Corner airport, new in 1948, was replaced by the present, much larger one at Aldergrove in 1963.[21] On the ground, too, public transport underwent a great transformation. In the 1930s the Corporation's Tramways Committee had operated a mixed fleet of trams and motor buses. Early in 1938 it introduced an experimental trolleybus service on the Falls Road route, which was so successful that the decision was taken to replace all the trams with trolleybuses, starting with east Belfast. The cost for the whole city was estimated at £1.25 million, and it was aimed to complete the operation by 1944. The war delayed the process of conversion but after 1945 the trams disappeared rapidly; the last service, on the 'Island' route, ran in February 1954. The trolleybuses were quiet and pollution-free, but they got in the way of the ever-increasing numbers of cars and lorries on the streets, so it was not long before they too began to be superseded. Buses, which had been rejected in 1939 in favour of trolleybuses, had completely replaced them by 1968. These changes not only altered the appearance of the traffic in the streets but the streets themselves, as tramlines and square setts were removed or covered over with asphalt and overhead power lines taken down. Railway lines as well as tramlines were abandoned in favour of road transport, especially after the creation in 1948 of the Ulster Transport Authority, which amalgamated road and rail services outside Belfast. With the closure of many lines the three rail termini in the city became much less important. There was to be no revival until the 1970s, after the break-up of the UTA and the establishment of Northern Ireland Railways, when a new Central Station was built at Maysfield. Underlying all the problems of public transport was the phenomenal growth in the ownership of private cars, from one to every 33 people in 1951 to one to every 8 in 1965.[22] No wonder it was felt that the city's traffic was a problem that could be tackled only by long-term planning.

The period following the Second World War, though on the whole one of decline in the great staple industries of Belfast, was also one of success in adapting to the challenge of such change. Certainly by 1970 there were also signs of growth – of which traffic jams were perhaps a symptom.

References

1. Coe, *Engineering*, pp. 106–9, 122–3; Moss and Hume, *Shipbuilders*, pp. 323–53; J. W. Blake, *Northern Ireland in the Second World War*, HMSO, Belfast (1956), pp. 394–403.
2. Blake, *Northern Ireland*, pp. 383–94; E. O'Connor and T. Parkhill (eds), *A Life in Linenopolis: The Memoirs of William Topping, Belfast Damask Weaver, 1903–56*, Ulster Historical Foundation, Belfast (1992), pp. 57–73.
3. Coe, *Engineering*, p. 179; B. Barton, *The Blitz: Belfast in the War Years*, Blackstaff Press, Belfast (1989), pp. 278–83.
4. Barton, *Blitz*, pp. 283–6; Ulster Year Book, 1947, HMSO, Belfast (1948), p. 168 (Table 8).
5. Barton, *Blitz*, p. 270; Buckland, *Northern Ireland*, p. 84; Harkness, *Northern Ireland*, p. 84.
6. Barton, *Blitz*, pp. 51–63, 47–50.
7. Barton, *Blitz*, pp. 65–7, 135.
8. Barton, *Blitz*, pp. 101–51.
9. Blake, *Northern Ireland*, p. 233.
10. Barton, *Blitz*, pp. 175–208, 136–8.
11. Barton, *Blitz*, pp. 265–72 and 280 (quoting MacRory); P. Arthur, *Government and Politics of Northern Ireland*, Longman Group, Harlow (1980), pp. 42–3 (quoting 1939 statement). The cardinal's reported reaction in 1942 to the arrival of American troops in Northern Ireland – that they were overrunning the country against the will of the nation – drew a severe rebuke from the US envoy in Dublin.
12. Barton, *Blitz*, pp. 222, 256, 166–7; Bardon, *Belfast*, p. 248.
13. Budge and O'Leary, *Belfast*, pp. 153–5.

14. Black, 'Industrial change', in Beckett and Glasscock (eds), *Belfast*, pp. 164–5.
15. Moss and Hume, *Shipbuilders*, pp. 354–99.
16. Moss and Hume, *Shipbuilders*, pp. 400–45; Geary and Johnson, 'Shipbuilding in Belfast', *Irish Economic and Social History*, 16 (1989), pp. 59–62.
17. M. Donne, *Pioneers of the Skies: A History of Short Brothers PLC*, Nicholson & Bass Ltd, Belfast (1987), pp. 113–38.
18. Coe, *Engineering*, pp. 76, 121–2.
19. Black, 'Industrial change', in Beckett and Glasscock (eds), *Belfast*, p. 168.
20. *Belfast Harbour Commissioners, Reports and Accounts, 1956–70.*
21. *Ulster Year Books, 1949–70.*
22. P. E. Greer (ed.), *Road versus Rail: Documents on the history of public transport in Northern Ireland, 1921–48*, Public Record Office of Northern Ireland, Belfast (1982), pp. 63–92; *City of Belfast: Official Industrial Handbook*, E. J. Burrows, Cheltenham, various issues; F. W. Boal, 'Contemporary Belfast', in Beckett and Glasscock (eds), *Belfast*, p. 180.

Chapter 8

Society and Politics, 1945–72

Northern Ireland's contribution to the survival and victory of the United Kingdom was rewarded after the end of the war, when new financial arrangements with Westminster enabled the Stormont government to establish the same kind of welfare state as in Britain. The social history of Belfast in the generation after 1945 was therefore, more closely than ever before, similar to that of urban centres elsewhere in the UK. Social changes, in particular the transformation of secondary and higher education, were not without their effect on politics, but here hopes of a new departure were in the end overwhelmed by the strength of traditional attitudes and enmities.

Housing and Urban Development

By the later 1940s the population of Belfast had reached its greatest extent. The 1951 census figure was 443,671, which represented 32% of the entire population of the province; a further 7% lived in the Belfast urban area outside the boundary. Ten years later, in 1961, the total had actually fallen to 415,856, and by 1971 it was down to 362,082, little more than it had been at the start of the century. This reversal of a trend which had continued without interruption for a century and a half came about through a combination of factors. The most important was the refusal of the government in 1947 to agree to the Corporation's request for a further extension of the city boundary. This refusal was followed by extensive building of new dwellings for Belfast people (and for numbers of new immigrants to the Belfast area) outside the boundary. The process of dispersal was encouraged by the fact that new industries attracted to the region in the postwar period were deliberately established in green-field sites outside the boundary rather than in the city itself, where traditional employment in manufacturing was beginning to decline. The population of the fringe, many of whom enjoyed Corporation bus and other services and looked to Belfast for employment, major shopping facilities and recreation, grew steadily. The built-up areas beyond the boundary – Andersonstown, Dunmurry and Lisburn to the west and south, the towns and villages that became Newtownabbey to the north, Castlereagh and Holywood to the east – had a population of 120,000 in 1951, half as much again ten years later, and 220,000 by the mid-1960s. The fall in Belfast's population was therefore up to a point not so much a decline as a redistribution. At any rate the result was that more and more Belfast city and the Belfast urban area ceased to coincide. By the late 1960s, indeed, geographers could distinguish not one Belfast but three: the Inner City, within the county borough; Greater Belfast, consisting of the inner city and its fringe; and a Regional City, covering an area within a 25-mile radius of the city centre and tied together by road, rail and telephone communications and the ability of its inhabitants to travel to work within it.[1]

The idea of restricting future development went back to a Planning Commission established by the government in the latter part of the war. 'With the unfortunate development of English cities in mind', the Commission in 1945 stressed the importance of 'regulating and limiting the outward growth of Belfast' and strongly recommended that a 'Green Belt' should be established. In 1951 it reiterated the need to distribute population more evenly and to preserve the Green Belt, estimating that some 22,000 houses were needed immediately, with the long-term aim of reducing the population of the Inner City to about 300,000.[2] Nothing much was done in a positive way, however, before the 1960s, by which time the need for a plan was much more obvious. Then in 1962 Sir Robert Matthew produced his Urban Area Plan, which took as its premise the view that Belfast and its fringe were too big and concluded that they should be confined for the future within a Stop Line. The Corporation, faced with the problem of finding houses for large numbers of people from inner-city areas which were in need of redevelopment, accepted the Stop Line with great reluctance, by no means convinced that the municipal impulse towards bigness was such a bad thing as the planners thought. The fact that the Corporation had no planning department of its own until 1965 put it at a disadvantage in the argument. The immediate effect was to stop most of the building already taking place in suburban areas and to slow down the Corporation's not very impressive redevelopment programme.[3]

Most of the 53,000 houses damaged in the 1941 blitz had been repaired by the autumn of 1943. That is not to say that the position at the end of the war was satisfactory; far from it. The Planning Commission's estimated need for 22,000 new homes was if anything a conservative one. What was needed was not only better houses but much less dense housing in many parts of the inner city. Even in 1961 Belfast had the highest density of population per square mile of any city in the United Kingdom with the exception of Glasgow and Liverpool – 16,846 (Glasgow 17,465, Liverpool 17,184), compared with Manchester's 15,517, Birmingham's 13,838, Hull's 13,479, Greater London's 11,323; all the rest were 10,000 or less. The City Council's postwar housing record in fact was not much better than its record between the wars. Between 1945 and 1972 the yearly average of council houses built was only 470, far short of the numbers needed, which was estimated by the city surveyor in 1959 at 2,600 a year for twenty years. A special Housing Committee was set up and modest development plans were made. According to the official handbook for 1950, sites amounting to 525 acres had been acquired at Highfield, Ballymurphy, Clara Park, Mount Vernon and Inverary on which 4,850 houses and flats were to be built, and 800 aluminium bungalows were about to be erected at Glendhu, Inverary, Taughmonagh, Whiterock and Ashfield. By April 1950 over 1,100 houses, 18 flats and 1,000 Arcon prefabs had been erected and occupied. It was noted that the Corporation had been approached by the government to 'try out' blocks of flats in the Parkmount and Skegoniel area on the Shore Road. 'This will be a new departure for Belfast', the handbook noted, 'and since there is a feeling that blocks of flats may not appeal to Belfast people the result of this experiment is awaited with interest.'[4]

Postwar housing at Annadale embankment. This Council scheme was successful, unlike some high-rise developments elsewhere within the city boundary.
Tourist Board Collection, Ulster Museum

The Corporation built on whatever land was available within the boundary – blitzed sites or undeveloped, usually undesirable, areas. The resulting estates were laid out solely with an eye to accommodating as many people as possible, with densities far too high for families with children, in small houses well below the preferred standards for public housing (the Parker-Morris standards). The 1956 Housing Act made the Corporation responsible for slum clearance and thus enabled it to start planning for a programme of inner-city redevelopment, but progress was held up by the discovery that large amounts of land, or ground rents from it, were owned by churches and could not therefore be purchased by compulsory order without first amending the relevant provisions of the 1920 Government of Ireland Act, which had been designed to prevent religious discrimination. In 1965 a joint working party of city and government officials produced a report on redevelopment; three years later the City Council at last adopted a scheme prepared by its planning consultants, Building Design Partnership, for work in three phases. Since its foundation in 1945 the Northern Ireland Housing Trust, funded by the government to supplement the efforts of local authorities, had helped

171

to ease the housing problem in Belfast by building estates outside the boundary. Now its help was enlisted to redevelop the Divis Street and Cullingtree Road areas. As the chairman (and historian) of the Trust's successor, the Housing Executive, puts it, 'The authors of these schemes failed to learn from the bitter experiences of redevelopment in Britain; and it is arguable that the widespread demolition which preceded these sweeping and ill-thought-out schemes contributed largely to the violence of the sectarian strife which marked the Troubles'.[5]

In January 1972, when the Corporation ceased to have any further responsibility for housing, it handed over to the Executive a total of 22,129 dwellings, of which 5,000 were slums acquired for redevelopment and another 1,446 were new ones contracted for. The answer to the question raised in 1950 as to whether the citizens of Belfast would like flats was in most cases an emphatic negative. The Turf Lodge flats on the Falls Road, built in 1966, were detested by people who had known the community life of the little streets of kitchen houses. So too were the 'Weetabix' flats on the Shankill, so called because they looked like cereal packets. Both had to be demolished within a few years. The outbreak of the Troubles in 1969, and especially the massive movements of population and destruction of property that occurred in 1971, made an existing problem much worse. (Whatever else may be said about the Corporation, it made a genuine attempt to have its estates mixed in religion, and most of them stayed so until 1969.) The fact remained that by 1970 there was still a first-class housing crisis in Belfast, not much diminished since 1945. According to the calculations of the Housing Executive no less than 29,750 houses in the Belfast Council area in 1974 (24% of the total) were unfit for occupation. The criteria used were more exacting than those used earlier, but it was nevertheless a sad indictment.[6]

Education

The attempts made to bring education in the city up to standard were much more successful. The 1947 Education Act for Northern Ireland followed similar lines to those laid down by the Butler Act in Britain, with some local variations. The Act was notable not only because it laid the foundations of a vastly improved service but also because for once the Unionist government defied pressure from its more extreme supporters by insisting that teachers in transferred schools should not be obliged to teach Bible instruction and that the capital grant to voluntary (in effect Catholic) schools should be raised from 50% to 65%. The blitz had destroyed eighteen schools in Belfast and damaged another thirty-four, so there was much to be done in any case. Now, on top of this, the 1947 Act completely recast the education system, requiring education authorities to produce plans for a structure of primary (to age 11), secondary and technical schools (to a new leaving age of 15), as well as facilities for further education and ancillary services. The Corporation's Education Committee had in fact decided in 1939 to raise the leaving age to 15 but had had to postpone action because of the war, and during the war it had started providing milk for necessitous children and a general meals service. The first grammar school under its control, Grosvenor High School, had opened in part of an existing primary school in January 1945, while the number of scholarships offered to the voluntary grammar schools had been increased from 50 to 200.[7]

The Committee took two years to produce a scheme for the county schools, as those under public control were now called. Most existing public elementary schools became 5–11 primary schools, but a few were converted into secondary intermediates, the new category for the 80% of pupils who would not transfer to the grammar schools at the age of 11. New purpose-built intermediates were planned, the first of which opened in 1950. By the end of the decade there were sixteen in all, as well as two more county grammar schools. The 1949 development plan was followed by two others, in 1953 and 1957, as population changes and a steadily declining birth rate made revisions necessary. The raising of the leaving age was only achieved finally in 1957.[8]

In the 1960s the main advances were in further education. The Colleges of Domestic Science and Art, both of which were housed in the College of Technology, got separate new premises in 1962 and 1968; the Rupert

The Ashby Institute, Queen's University. New buildings such as this science block were an obvious sign of the expansion of higher education in the 1960s, following the extension of secondary schooling in the years after the Second World War.
Photograph courtesy of the Queen's University

Stanley College of Further Education (named after the city's first director of education) was opened in east Belfast in 1965, replacing an earlier institute, and the College of Business Studies opened in its new building in 1971. A School of Music and Youth Orchestra was started in 1965. The Committee also played a part in the establishment of the new Ulster College at Jordanstown, the Northern Ireland Polytechnic, which opened in 1968; the more advanced diploma courses were transferred to it from the Technical College, while degree-level teaching was transferred to Queen's University.

By 1960 the proportion of the Belfast rate spent on education was 35%, and ten years later it had risen to nearly 43% (health and welfare, the next greatest, accounted for 12%). Another Education Act, in 1968, gave the voluntary schools, which had hitherto remained entirely outside the county system, full grants provided they set up management committees consisting of at least six people, of whom one-third must be nominees of the education authority. Most of the Catholic schools accepted this and became what were known as 'maintained' schools. The grievance felt by Catholics, rightly or wrongly, that the 1947 Act had in effect endowed Protestant control of the county schools while refusing to do the same for the Catholic system, thus came to an end. The outcome, a triumph for sectarianism, was two separate state-funded systems. The Education Committee was faced with increasing financial difficulty in the 1960s. In order to make ends meet it postponed capital projects such as the building of new schools. The result was to lay up trouble for the future. When the Corporation's consultants produced their plans for the city's development at the end of the decade they forecast that by 1986 nearly a hundred new schools would be needed in the Greater Belfast area, 35 of them within the boundary.[9]

Welfare Services

The welfare state created in Great Britain after 1945 was reproduced by similar legislation in Northern Ireland. This was only possible because it was agreed that, provided its citizens paid tax at the same rates as elsewhere in the United Kingdom, the province would get the necessary funds from Westminster. The necessity for a transformation in public health, first demonstrated in Dr Carnwath's report of 1941 and reinforced by the evidence uncovered by the blitz, was further confirmed by a government inquiry in 1944. The figures for deaths from tuberculosis, in fact, were so horrifying that the Stormont government anticipated one of the aims of the national health service by setting up a Tuberculosis Authority as early as 1941. This determination, and the fortunate discovery of effective drugs, brought about a transformation within a few years. By 1954 the death rate had been reduced to the same level as that in Britain, and by 1959 the Authority had worked itself out of a job and was disbanded; the chest hospitals at Whiteabbey and Galwally were converted to other uses. So far as the citizens of Belfast were concerned the elimination of TB was one of the most significant medical advances ever made. The national health service in general, indeed, which came into operation in Northern Ireland in 1948, made a great impact on the lives of Belfast people precisely because things had been so much worse than elsewhere. In medical services the dispensary system and voluntary control of separate hospitals were swept away, to be replaced by a centralised General Health Services Board and a Hospitals Authority. Centralised services for laboratory work, radiotherapy and blood transfusion were set up, along with an Institute of Clinical Science to serve the teaching hospitals and additional chairs of medicine and dentistry at the university. The number of outpatients departments in the city was increased from 46 in 1948 to 85 in 1959. A new 200-bed geriatric unit was opened at the City Hospital (as the old Union Infirmary was renamed when it was made into a general hospital), and work started in 1959 on another, completely new general institution, the Ulster Hospital at Dundonald. By 1954 deaths in childhood, which had been a particular scandal between the wars, had fallen to the same level as in Britain.[10]

The Poor Law system was abolished at last in 1948, when the unlamented Guardians and the two commissioners who had exercised their functions since 1939 were stripped of their powers. First the Infirmary, then the entire premises of the Workhouse, were handed over to the City Hospital. The memory lingered on, however, and it took some time for the hospital to rise in public esteem. The only discordant note in this tale of improvement was a well-publicised and long-lasting dispute over the Mater Hospital. One of the few differences between the British National

Stormont in the 1960s. Built between 1927 and 1932 as a gift of the British government, this fine neo-classical building on the eastern outskirts of Belfast housed both the parliament and the executive of Northern Ireland for forty years. At present it is used mainly as office accommodation for civil servants.

Tourist Board Collection, Ulster Museum

Health Act and the Stormont version was the omission in the latter of a clause allowing hospitals such as the Mater to retain their denominational character. Without such a clause the hospital management refused to enter the national health service. The government then refused to allow the hospital to claim payment for the treatment it offered to the public at large. It was left to finance itself, which it did largely by the proceeds of a football pools scheme – YP Pools, so called because it was devised by the Young Philanthropists' Association, a group of supporters. Not until 1968 was the Mater able to claim for the services it provided free, and the matter was not finally resolved until three years later, when it gained access to government grants and became part of the health service. Not unnaturally Catholics felt a strong sense of grievance, more clearly justifiable in this case than in the matter of their schools since the hospital's services were truly open to all without distinction of creed. In fact Unionists themselves were some-what divided on the question, both at Stormont and in the City Council.[11]

Social Trends

Social change in Belfast in the postwar years followed much the same lines as in other cities of the United Kingdom. Until the mid-1950s radio and the cinema remained extremely popular. As measured by the number of wireless licences issued – no doubt an underestimate of the true figure – radio indeed went on growing: the total for the whole province, 150,000 at the end of the war, was nearly 220,000 ten years later. Thereafter the figure fell steadily as the number of television licences rose. When first noticed in the official statistics in 1953 these numbered only 558. A year later the figure was well over 10,000; ten years later it was 215,700. As television waxed the cinema waned. In the mid-1950s there were three dozen cinemas operating in Belfast. One after another they closed, starting in 1956; by 1972 only seven remained open. In a city as addicted as Belfast had been to the silver screen this was a minor social revolution.[12]

While the cinemas emptied, Belfast retained what was by British stan-dards a very high level of church attendance. Reliable statistics, indeed statistics of any sort, are hard to come by, though the impression recorded by visitors was invariably the same, whether approving or dismayed. One frequently quoted source is a survey conducted among undergraduates of Queen's University in 1959, when the church attendance figures were 94% for Catholics, 64% for Methodists, 59% for Presbyterians and 46% for members of the Church of Ireland. Undergraduates at that date were probably too middle-class a group to constitute a valid sample of the popu-lation at large, an objection which would have had less force in the case of the Catholics. The Protestant average of 50–55% would have been less representative; church attendance in many working-class areas was likely to have been rather lower than that.[13] Many of the new churches built by the Protestant denominations after the war were replacements for

176

buildings destroyed or badly damaged in the blitz. In most cases, however, they were designed for smaller congregations than the original ones. Nevertheless, religion remained a potent force in the lives of most Belfast people and, because it mattered to them, a continuing source of division.

One of the more obvious cultural differences between Catholics and most Protestants was their contrasting attitudes towards Sunday activities. Sabbatarianism of a strict kind was deeply engrained among Protestants, especially those of an evangelical persuasion; unlike Catholics, they did not play or attend organised games on a Sunday. The more extreme disapproved of any use of public facilities on the Sabbath, other than for religious purposes, equating such activities with Catholic practice or the 'Continental Sunday'. Even a proposal, made in wartime, to allow one cinema to open on Sunday for uniformed members of the armed forces met with determined opposition in the City Council; after being turned down several times between 1940 and 1942 it was eventually approved, but only by a small majority. Twenty years later a similar issue – that of 'Sunday swings' – caused a much greater furore, which perhaps showed that public opinion had moved somewhat in the meantime. The question was whether Corporation play centres for children and the swings in the parks should be opened for use on Sundays. A narrow vote in favour in the Education Committee in October 1964 was reversed in the City Council the following month after a campaign by the churches (notably the Rev. Ian Paisley's new church, the Free Presbyterians), backed by the Orange Order. Unionist and Labour councillors were divided among themselves on the matter. In fact the Labour Party was almost destroyed by the refusal of three of its members, all evangelicals and all representing wards in which evangelical Protestantism was strong, to follow the party line. The Council later agreed to open the swings in the parks but not the play centres. Eventually in 1968 all except four of them were opened, after local residents had voted in favour, and the same device of local option was adopted in respect of the swings. The still considerable power of the sabbatarians in local politics was demonstrated in the municipal elections of 1967, when three liberal Unionist councillors who had voted in favour of Sunday opening were not readopted by their local committees and all the Labour councillors who stood were defeated, regardless of how they had voted on the crucial issue.[14]

Belfast Politics

In local politics, throughout this period as before, Unionists retained a huge majority on the City Council. This simple electoral fact conceals a more complex story of three phases – the late 1940s, when Northern Ireland Labour briefly challenged Unionism, only to founder on the constitutional question; a torpid period in the 1950s when little challenge was offered by stricken Labour or feuding Catholic parties to the complacent Unionists; and a restless period in the 1960s which saw a

177

recovery by Northern Ireland Labour, the rise of Republican Labour and the appearance of sharp divisions between liberal and traditional Unionists (to say nothing of municipal scandals over housing and a controversy caused by flying the City Hall flag at half-mast on the death of Pope John XXIII). In the end, despite some hopeful signs of changing attitudes, the basis of local politics for most voters was to remain a matter of religion rather than class.

In the first postwar election, when housing was the main issue, the Northern Ireland Labour Party doubled its representation from four seats to eight and Harry Midgley (ex-NILP, under his own banner of Commonwealth Labour) was elected alderman for Ormeau Ward, though Minister of Labour in the Stormont government at the time. Four Nationalists were successful in Smithfield, but three of the seats in the other Catholic ward, Falls, went to Independent Labour ('Labour with a republican tinge') – a sign that Catholic voters too were changing. Although Labour representatives of various kinds therefore formed a significant section of the Council, the Unionists still dominated it with 43 of the 60 seats.[15]

Under a consolidating Local Government Franchise Act of 1946, councillors had to stand for re-election every third year, aldermen every sixth, and half of the aldermen were to be elected every third year. Unlike Great Britain, however, where the franchise was widened in 1948 to correspond to the parliamentary one, Northern Ireland continued to restrict the vote to householders and their spouses (thus excluding large numbers of lodgers and adult children), while occupiers of property with an annual valuation of £10 or more got an additional vote and could nominate a voter for each extra £10 of valuation, up to a limit of six. The result was that whereas before 1948 the local government franchise in Belfast had compared favourably with that in other British cities, it became in UK terms an anomaly. Furthermore, though the retention of the old link between ownership of property and the right to vote was arguably motivated as much by conservatism as anything else – the system discriminated equally against poorer Protestants and poorer Catholics – the fact that most high-valuation property was owned by Protestants meant that it was the Unionist Party that benefited most from making no change. This departure from the usual postwar policy of keeping in step with Britain was later to provide the civil rights movement of the 1960s with the convenient, if rather misleading, rallying cry of 'One man, one vote' – misleading because the impression was created that large numbers of Catholics were deprived of general political rights. In fact the franchise in Northern Ireland for elections to Westminster was exactly the same as elsewhere in the United Kingdom; for Stormont elections there was also universal adult suffrage, but additional votes for owners of businesses and university graduates – abolished in Britain in 1948 – were retained until 1968. The four MPs elected by Queen's University were chosen by proportional representation.[16]

Both the Stormont and the municipal elections of 1949 were inevitably dominated by the constitutional issue. Early in that year the government of Eire declared the country a republic and left the British Commonwealth. The effect on the Unionists, and on their opponents in Belfast, was profound. The constitution of the southern state, drawn up by de Valera in 1937, claimed the whole island of Ireland as its national territory; and while the claim may in reality never have amounted to anything more than a pious hope of eventual unity, its retention in the constitution of a state now completely separate gave the northern prime minister, Sir Basil Brooke, the chance to go to the polls on the only issue that really mattered to Unionists. Moreover, an Anti-Partition League, supported by funds from the south collected at the gates of Catholic churches, ensured that the same issue dominated the minds of their nationalist opponents. Furthermore the Northern Ireland Labour Party, which up to this point had tried to accommodate both partitionists and anti-partitionists while concentrating on economic issues, was now forced to choose and came down in favour of the constitutional status quo; it promptly split in two and was demolished at the polls, losing all three of the Stormont seats it had won in Belfast in 1945. The party suffered a similar fate in the municipal elections, when six wards went to Unionists without a contest and Labour were reduced to one seat. Most of the Catholic vote went to an anti-partitionist splinter group from the NILP calling itself Irish Labour, which got seven seats; the Nationalists retained only one, that of alderman in Smithfield. The triumphant Unionists increased their numbers from 43 to 48. The constitutional issue – the maintenance or abolition of partition – was to continue thereafter to weaken all attempts to create an Ulster opposition to the dominant Unionists.

In the 1950s there was little sign of Labour groups recovering to challenge the Unionist control of the Council. The last Nationalist was defeated in 1952 by an Irish Labour candidate, but a renewed effort by the NILP in 1955, when it put forward nineteen candidates, brought only one success. Three years later it had an unexpected gain in Court Ward, when a former lord mayor was defeated for the alderman's seat. Among Catholic voters, Irish Labour gave way to Independent Labour, which took all seven seats in Falls and Smithfield. A seat in Dock Ward was taken by Gerry Fitt for his own Dock Eire Labour Party, the start of a political career that was to take him eventually to the House of Lords. Two Protestant Unionists (ultra-Protestant and ultra-Unionist) made their appearance, one of them a convert from official Unionism.[17]

The 1960s were livelier, as Unionists squabbled among themselves and were threatened on the right by the Protestant Unionists and on the left by a revived NILP and a re-formed party led by Fitt. Another municipal scandal rose to the surface to disturb Unionist unity still further. One of the four knighted suspects, Sir Cecil McKee, standing in 1961 as an unofficial candidate after being refused re-selection by his ward committee,

The band of the Royal Ulster Constabulary giving a concert in the grounds of the City Hall in the early 1960s, a time of apparent peace and hope.
Tourist Board Collection, Ulster Museum

defeated the official Unionist candidate for the alderman's seat in St Anne's Ward, Mrs Florence Breakie, who had already been chosen as the next lord mayor. The NILP also gained two seats in Court Ward in this election. The Labour revival reached its height three years later in 1964 when the party won two more seats in Clifton Ward and polled well everywhere – a sign of increasing anxiety among skilled Protestant workers about the decline of traditional industries, and of the willingness of some Catholic voters to vote NILP. Among Catholics in general, however, Fitt's Republican Labour Party, founded in 1962, largely ousted Independent Labour, taking three seats in Dock and two in Falls. At Stormont the Unionist government, led since 1963 by Terence O'Neill, successfully took the steam out of the Labour advance (the NILP had gained four seats in 1958 and kept them with increased majorities in 1962) by giving more prominence to economic issues and state planning. In the 1965 general election two Labour MPs in Belfast were unseated; both had lost credibility with voters for their part in the Sunday Swings controversy a year earlier.

Labour's advance was then further frustrated at the 1967 municipal elections, the last before the present troubles erupted, when the results reflected an increasing instability in politics and a sharpening of traditional tensions. The NILP lost four seats and was left with only two (one of them a new seat in Falls). Fitt's Republican Labour Party won eight, reducing its Independent Labour rivals to two. But even the main Unionist

Party had problems, when the Protestant Unionists improved their support. By the time the next local contest was due, in 1970, the situation in the city had changed dramatically and the future of the Corporation itself was under review.[18]

Sectarian Conflict

Compared with earlier periods in the city's history, the postwar years were pretty quiet so far as sectarian strife was concerned, after the 1949 general election at least. High employment, improving social conditions and changing attitudes created hopes that the outbreaks seen in the past might not be repeated. Belfast was scarcely affected, for example, by the IRA campaign of 1956–62, which was almost entirely a rural affair, though events in the border counties of course encouraged Unionists to go on playing the constitutional card. The failure of the IRA, the lack of support for it among Catholics generally, the emergence of a more confident and forward-looking spirit in the Catholic community combined with the appointment of Terence O'Neill as Unionist leader to usher in a brief era of rapprochement after 1963. In January 1964 O'Neill astonished everyone (including, significantly, most of his own cabinet colleagues) by receiving the prime minister of the Irish Republic, Sean Lemass, for economic talks at Stormont. O'Neill's liberal approach, however, only raised hopes among Catholics which he proved unable to fulfil, since many of his own followers became uneasy about the direction in which he was leading them. In the end, he split the Unionists without gaining the loyalty of nationalists. Inside parliament his position was undermined by ambitious rivals, outside it by a strident, and very effective, 'O'Neill must go' campaign led by Paisley. Disappointed Catholics, and some radical Protestants who made common cause with them, turned to campaigning for civil rights, in the manner of the blacks in the southern states of the USA. By the end of the decade two opposing protest movements were on the streets.[19] The leading Ulster historian shortly afterwards summarised the 1960s as follows:

> Among Ulster Protestants there was a growing body who felt that the union could be maintained without reliance on the old sectarian war-cries. Among Roman Catholics there was a new readiness to accept Northern Ireland as, for all practical purposes, a permanent fact .... It seemed not impossible to believe that at last Northern Ireland was approaching a condition in which all its citizens could feel a common interest in promoting a common prosperity.
>
> Two factors, not unusual in such a situation, brought about the reversal of this hopeful trend – impatience on one side and fear on the other.[20]

In these circumstances the 1960s in Belfast were both an hour of hope and a time of rising tension. In September 1964, during a Westminster election campaign, a serious riot against the police followed the removal of an Irish tricolour flag from the headquarters of the Republican Party in Divis Street in the Falls; thirty people, including several police, were injured. A loyalist march, organised by Paisley, to protest at the flying of the flag (which was illegal under an act of 1952) and the failure of the authorities to remove it sooner, had been turned away from the area to avoid trouble. Two years later in 1966, the fiftieth anniversary of both the Easter Rising and the battle of the Somme, there was more serious trouble. The fire-bombing of the Unionist Party's headquarters in Glengall Street in February was followed by a similar attack two days later on a Catholic primary school on the Crumlin Road. Celebrations in west Belfast of the Rising caused great indignation among Unionists. A woman died when a public house was petrol-bombed early in May, and at the end of that month a Catholic man (the wrong one, in mistake for a known or suspected IRA member) was shot and killed in Clonard Street. There was a short sharp riot early in June, when Paisley led a loyalist march through Cromac Square in the predominantly Catholic Markets area; arrested later in the same day for creating a disturbance outside the Presbyterian General Assembly, he refused to be bound over and was sent to jail for three months. At the end of June the Ulster Volunteer Force, a recently formed secret organisation of Protestants calling itself by the name originally used by Carson's followers, shot three Catholics in Malvern Street off the Shankill Road; one of the victims died of his wounds. The year 1967 was quiet, however, apart from a minor incident in July during a royal visit when a piece of concrete struck the bonnet of the Queen's car.[21]

The present troubles, then, did not erupt without warning. They were, however, immediately more serious in character than anything experienced since the 1930s, beginning with a Protestant invasion of the lower Falls area and Ardoyne on the night of 14–15 August 1969 in which five Catholics and one Protestant were killed and 200 homes burnt, most of them Catholic ones. According to official estimates based on hospital records (certainly a conservative figure), some 450 people were injured, 178 of them Catholic civilians, 199 Protestant civilians, the rest policemen. Over 3,500 families moved house as a direct result of the rioting, to seek safety in areas controlled by their co-religionists. The Stormont government called in the Army to separate the two sides, a move at first welcomed by the beleaguered Catholics. The IRA, which had proved unable to defend them, split in two. The breakaway portion, calling itself the Provisional IRA, was at first organised to defend Catholic areas, but soon developed into a militantly republican guerrilla force with the army as its main target (its first victim among the troops was shot in February 1971). By that time Belfast was in a state approaching civil war. The introduction of internment without trial in August 1971, which was meant to scotch the threat from the IRA, backfired badly and in fact strengthened it; 85% of the 172 people who died violently in 1971 did so after the start of internment. Serious rioting in response to the arrests caused a number

Farringdon Gardens, in the Ardoyne area of north Belfast, 10 August 1969: former residents salvaging their belongings. Forced out by intimidation, the Protestant inhabitants had set fire to their homes as they departed the night before.
Photograph courtesy of the **Belfast Telegraph**

of deaths; on 10 August alone eleven people were killed, one of them a priest administering the last rites. There was massive support thereafter in Catholic areas for a rent and rates strike. More frightened families, over 2,000 of them this time, migrated to safety. It has been estimated that in the first four years of the troubles somewhere between 30,000 and 60,000 people in the Greater Belfast area were driven to leave their homes, at that date possibly the largest enforced movement of population in Europe since the Second World War. In addition to all this, an enormous amount of property was destroyed. By June 1971 criminal injuries claims in the city totalled nearly £9.5 million, a sum that increased rapidly as things became even worse. Early the following year, in March 1972, the Stormont government was suspended and Northern Ireland came under direct rule from Westminster.[22]

Local Government Reform

That was by no means the end of the troubles, but 1972 did see the end of Belfast Corporation as citizens had known it. Among the changes put in train by O'Neill's administration was the reform of local government.

Following the publication of aims and proposals in 1967 and 1969, the Macrory Committee was appointed in January 1970. Its report, published five months later, was even more radical in its recommendations than the Redcliffe-Maud and Wheatley reports for Britain and Scotland. Pointing out that Northern Ireland was smaller than Yorkshire and had a total rateable valuation of only £14 million, compared with nearly £22 million for Leeds alone, Macrory proposed to set up 26 district councils to deal with minor services; major services or functions such as education and libraries, planning, roads, water, main sewerage, gas, electricity, motor taxation, public transport and fire brigades should be transferred to regional authorities. The report did note that Belfast fire brigade was the only one in the United Kingdom to receive no assistance from central government and that Belfast Gas was 'efficient, well-run and up-to-date' and likewise made no call upon the public purse, but such remarks were little consolation. Macrory's proposals were accepted in their entirety and came into effect on 1 October 1973.[23]

The shock of diminution was all the greater because, as one leading civil servant put it, City Hall had always resented interference from 'a parvenu Parliament and Government dating only from 1921', whereas Belfast could trace its origins to the seventeenth century.[24] It was even more galling to be equated with other, much smaller, local authorities. Though retaining its ceremonial dignities and functions, the Corporation would henceforth be directly responsible only for such relatively minor and uncontroversial services as environmental health, cleansing, parks and cemeteries and civic improvement schemes – in crude local parlance 'bins, bogs and burials'. The decision had already been taken to transfer all responsibility for public housing to the Northern Ireland Housing Trust, which was reorganised in 1972 as the Housing Executive. One hundred and thirty years of uninterrupted municipal advance thus came to an abrupt and unhappy end.

In many important respects the history of Belfast during the generation after the Second World War was similar to that of other major cities of the United Kingdom. As elsewhere, traditional heavy industry declined and the jobs thus lost were for the most part replaced by others in light industry and in a growing service sector. Socially, public services such as education, housing and welfare expanded, bringing about a significant improvement in living standards particularly for sections of the population hitherto disadvantaged. In the planning of urban development too, and in such things as entertainment and recreation, the Belfast experience followed national UK trends. It is important to stress these similarities, because in other respects – arising from its deeply ingrained sectarian divisions and its position in a province whose very existence as part of the United Kingdom was a bone of contention between the main political groupings – the history of postwar Belfast was notoriously different and produced by 1970 a very different result. The reform of local government was to the city what the imposition of direct rule was to the province – a judgement that a system which produced the endless rule of one party could no longer be allowed to continue.

References

1. Boal, 'Contemporary Belfast', in Beckett and Glasscock (eds), *Belfast*, pp. 169–72; *Ulster Year Book, 1960–62*, HMSO, Belfast (1962), p. 7. Belfast was ten times the size of the next largest urban area, Londonderry.
2. Boal, 'Contemporary Belfast', in Beckett and Glasscock (eds), *Belfast*, pp. 172–4.
3. Boal, 'Contemporary Belfast', in Beckett and Glasscock (eds), *Belfast*, pp. 174–8.
4. Brett, *Housing a Divided Community*, pp. 25, 32; *City of Belfast Official Handbook*, 12th edition (1950), p.53.
5. Brett, *Housing a Divided Community*, pp. 33–4.
6. Brett, *Housing a Divided Community*, pp. 34–6.
7. McNeilly, *Exactly Fifty Years*, pp. 73–4, 58.
8. McNeilly, *Exactly Fifth Years*, pp. 76–9, 91–3.
9. NcNeilly, *Exactly Fifty Years*, pp. 220–2, 219–20, 158–9.
10. Buckland, *Northern Ireland*, pp. 91–2; Harkness, *Northern Ireland*, pp. 109–10; Bardon, *Belfast*, pp. 251–2.
11. Craig, *Belfast and its Infirmary*, pp. 91–7; Budge and O'Leary, *Belfast*, pp. 159–61; Harkness, *Northern Ireland*, pp. 116–7.
12. Open, *Fading Lights*, pp. 13–15.
13. D. P. Barritt and C. F. Carter, *The Northern Ireland Problem*, University Press, Oxford (1962), p. 21.
14. Budge and O'Leary, *Belfast*, pp. 161–2.
15. Budge and O'Leary, *Belfast*, p. 157.
16. Budge and O'Leary, *Belfast*, pp. 156, 174–8. A later opportunity to modernise the local franchise, in 1961–2, was rejected by the Unionist majority at Stormont; by then, 81,000 people in Belfast could vote in parliamentary elections but not in municipal contests (Harkness, *Northern Ireland*, p. 136).
17. Budge and O'Leary, *Belfast*, pp. 157–8. See Harkness, *Northern Ireland*, pp. 118–23.
18. Budge and O'Leary, *Belfast*, pp. 158–9; Buckland, *Northern Ireland*, pp. 108–9, 114.
19. See Buckland, *Northern Ireland*, pp. 119–23, and Arthur, *Government and Politics of Northern Ireland*, pp. 107–110.
20. J. C. Beckett, 'Northern Ireland', in *The Ulster Debate: Report of a Study Group for the Institute for the Study of Conflict*, Bodley Head, London (1972), p. 23.
21. See Buckland, *Northern Ireland*, pp. 119–22; Harkness, *Northern Ireland*, pp. 139–54.
22. Arthur, *Government and Politics of Northern Ireland*, pp. 111–3.
23. Report of *Review Body on Local Government in Northern Ireland, 1970*, HMSO, Belfast (1970), pp. 24–5, 36, 37.
24. J. A. Oliver, *Working at Stormont*, Institute of Public Administration, Dublin (1978), pp. 79–80.

Chapter 9

Epilogue, 1973–93

During the past twenty years the history of Belfast has been overshadowed by the continuing troubles. In this respect the city is a microcosm of the province as a whole. As by far the largest urban area, however, Belfast has provided the most favourable ground for urban guerilla activity by para-military forces on both sides of the sectarian divide and has therefore suffered a high proportion of the damage inflicted on life, property and prospects. Between 1969 and 1977 over a thousand people were killed in Belfast and 2,280 explosions occurred, not to mention thousands of injuries, forced migrations, lives ruined or disrupted and livelihoods lost. Though the cost in human life has never since reached the level of the worst years in the 1970s, by the late 1980s the number killed had risen to around 1,500. The cost of the damage to property and business life from car bombs, incendiary devices and disruption of trade runs to hundreds of millions of pounds.[1] By no means everything that has occurred during the period has been due to the troubles, however. Contrary to the impression one might gain from the news media, life for many people has been remarkably normal, and much of what has happened in the way of economic and social change would have happened in any case. In its de-industrialisation as in its industrialisation, Belfast has shared the experience of other British cities.

The troubles have, however, made some common problems worse or have given them a peculiar local slant. Population changes are a good example. The decline in the population of the inner city was greatly accelerated in the 1970s and 1980s by the flight of Protestants in particular to safer areas outside the boundary. The total, just over 400,000 in 1971, was down to 330,000 ten years later and the latest available figure (1991) is only 281,000. Not only the inner city but the whole urban area has declined, losing 73,000 between 1971 and 1981, by which date – at 510,000 – it was 90,000 below the limit regarded as desirable by the planners of the early 1960s. The number of households in the inner city fell dramatically, in some wards by more than half between 1971 and 1978 (in Central Ward by 57%, in Crumlin by 64%). The number of people in the average household fell too, from 3.2 in 1971 to 2.8 in 1981, because the Protestants who remained included a disproportionate number of elderly residents; the effect on the enrolment of many state primary schools in the city was quickly apparent. The simultaneous redevelopment of densely-crowded areas of working-class housing contributed to these changes; many of the scenes of urban desolation which formed the backdrop to television reports

Security barrier at the entrance to Donegall Place, shortly after it was put up in 1976. The IRA's bombing campaign led to the erection of permanent gates and check points all around the central shopping area and, incidentally, to its pedestrianisation.

Ulster Museum

of the violence in the 1970s were caused by slum clearance rather than Semtex, while the availability of plenty of accommodation in new Housing Executive estates outside the boundary and well away from the violence encouraged some households to move voluntarily.[2]

The troubles have clearly had some effect too on the city's economic problems in recent years, most obviously on its ability to attract outside investment, but it is difficult to say how much. One estimate, made in 1987, is that 2,000 to 3,000 jobs in manufacturing industry were lost each year in the 1970s. This was all the more serious because, as elsewhere, industry was adversely affected by the oil crisis of 1973. The severe recession in the early 1980s made things worse. The shipyard, which was still employing 9,500 people in 1975, had less than a third of that number by the late 1980s; now, privatised and its debts written off, it employs 2,800. The only area of growth in employment in the 1970s was in services, where successive Westminster governments made increased funds available for social improvements. Manufacturing has continued to decline, and, though governments were less generous in the 1980s, it is now the case that Belfast, like the province as a whole, is dependent to an extraordinary degree on employment in the public sector – jobs in the civil service, government agencies, local government and so on. In Northern Ireland in 1985 there were 346,000 service jobs (nearly 65% of the total);

Attractive new homes built by the Northern Ireland Housing Executive in the Markets area in the 1980s, with St Malachy's Church (1844) in the background.
Photograph courtesy of the Northern Ireland Housing Executive

no fewer than 207,000, or 60%, were in the public sector. Not surprisingly, perhaps, recent commentators have referred to the development of a 'workhouse economy', dependent on public expenditure, in which those not unemployed are chiefly engaged in servicing or controlling each other, few of them in producing tradeable goods.[3]

The paradox is that while unemployment has risen to very high levels, average incomes and living standards have also risen considerably. Personal income per head, always the lowest of any region in the United Kingdom (in part because of larger families, in part because of relatively low earnings), rose from 68% of the UK level in 1960 to 79% in 1979 and 84% in 1984. Average weekly earnings rose from 81% in 1960 to almost 93% in 1979.[4] Those in work have had more money to spend, and they have indeed spent it, as the 1980s boom in retailing showed; the Belfast branch of Marks and Spencer, opened a short time before the present troubles began, became one of the firm's most lucrative outlets despite the attempted

Castle Court shopping complex, 1992. *Photograph courtesy of the* Belfast Telegraph

destruction of the city centre in the 1970s. Following the introduction of urban development grants in 1982, the central business district has been further revitalised in recent years by major investments such as the Castle Court shopping complex, while the decayed docks and riverside area are currently being transformed by the Laganside Corporation, a joint development enterprise by the public and private sectors. Port traffic

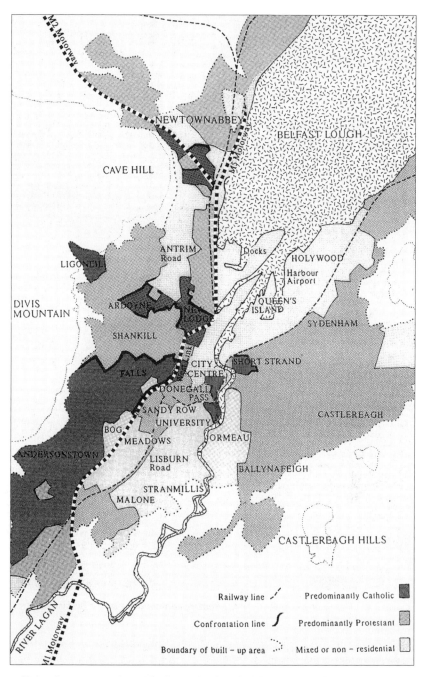

Belfast urban area in the mid-1980s, showing the distribution of population on the basis of religious belief. (Adapted from the map in C. E. B. Brett's *Housing a Divided Community* by kind permission of the author; redrawn by Deirdre Crone, with acknowledgements to Maura Pringle).

A section of the 'Peace Line' which now separates the Protestant and Catholic communities in north Belfast – a photograph taken in April 1993.
Photograph courtesy of the Belfast Telegraph

statistics reflect this remarkable upturn. In 1973 the amount of cargo handled was 7.5 million tons. By 1982 it had sunk to 5.5 million. Five years later, however, it had risen to 7.8 million; and the figure for 1990 was 8.9 million. Nowadays, however, the balance is heavily weighted in favour of imports, which form about 85% of all the cargo handled.[5]

The most successful social enterprise of recent years in Belfast has been the public housing programme carried out by the Northern Ireland Housing Executive. The number of 'unfit' houses in the city in 1974 was nearly 30,000, or 24% of the total housing stock. The troubles created both exceptional needs and exceptional difficulties, which upset all the calculations of the planners and delayed action. A survey of housing conditions in Belfast as compared with other British cities, produced by the Executive's chairman, Charles Brett, in 1980, was startling. In Belfast, 3.7% of households were two or more rooms below the bedroom standard (that is, severely overcrowded), compared with 1.4% in Liverpool and 0.4% in Leeds. 24.2% in Belfast had no inside flushing WC, more than twice as bad as the next worst, Liverpool (11.1%). Those without their own bath or shower were 23% in Belfast, compared with Liverpool's 10.1%, Manchester's 8.4% and Birmingham's 5.7%. By 1985, however, the 1974 proportion of unfit houses had been halved to 12% and in the last available estimate, for 1987, the figure was down to 7.4%. Not only was the long-standing housing problem in Belfast thus substantially solved, but both the quality of the houses built and the planning of the estates laid out were of a very high standard, and far more acceptable to the people who occupied them; this time, lessons were learned from the mistakes of others.[6] The transport plans drawn up in the late 1960s were also considerably changed by community pressures, notably when the intention to build

192

Shankill Road explosion, November 1993.
Photograph courtesy of the Belfast Telegraph

an elevated road joining the M1 and M2 motorways was abandoned in favour of the present West Link.

The City Council, elected since 1973 by proportional representation, has continued to be dominated by Unionists, though they are now quite sharply divided between Official Unionists and Democratic Unionists (Paisleyites). Ranged against them, and representing almost exclusively Catholics, are the Social Democratic and Labour Party (SDLP), Sinn Fein (extreme republicans, who support the Provisional IRA's 'armed struggle') and the Workers' Party, a rival republican group with socialist priorities. The middle ground between the Unionists and their opponents, now very narrow, is occupied by the Alliance Party, which draws support from both Catholic and Protestant voters in the middle classes. Compared with the great days of the municipality, the doings of the Council are now of minor interest, but it has made the most of its limited role by building a large number of leisure facilities and has visibly improved the appearance of the city in recent years by planting trees and flowers. Unfortunately the major functions transferred twenty years ago, which were to have been subject to the political control of the government of Northern Ireland, have in the absence of a Stormont administration been run by Westminster – a paradise for bureaucrats but purgatory (or hell, depending on one's theological stance) for those who believe in local democracy.

The last word must be about community relations. In one respect the experience of the current troubles has been not altogether a negative thing:

there has been far more contact and co-operation between the clergy of the main Protestant denominations and the Catholic church than ever before, and people of both persuasions have shared in a number of joint initiatives, notably the Peace People movement of the mid-1970s, whose two leading figures subsequently shared a Nobel peace prize. In education too there has been a modestly successful attempt to bridge the sectarian divide by establishing integrated schools, the first of which was Lagan College. In politics, however, there has been remarkably little real change. The names of some of the parties may be different, but the main question in dispute remains the same and attitudes have been hardened by the horrors experienced on both sides. Indeed, the segregation in working-class areas which has long marked Belfast as different from other cities has been made still nearer complete by the population movements of recent years – to the extent that a physical barrier in the shape of a high wall or fence, a so-called 'peace line', now literally separates the Protestant and Catholic communities at points where they meet and contend. Divided they stand.

References

1. F. Boal and S. Royle, 'Belfast: boom, blitz and bureaucracy', in G. Gordon (ed.), *Regional Cities in the U.K., 1890–1980*, Harper & Row, London (1986), p. 207; P. Arthur and K. Jeffery, *Northern Ireland since 1968*, Basil Blackwell, Oxford (1988), Appendix 1, p. 98.
2. R. L. Harrison, 'Population change and housing provision in Belfast', in P. A. Compton (ed.), *The Contemporary Population of Northern Ireland and Population-related Issues*, Institute of Irish Studies, Queen's University, Belfast (1981), pp. 40–50; D. A. Singleton, 'Belfast: housing policy and trends', in Buchanan and Walker (eds), *Province, City & People*, pp. 151–2; P. A. Compton, 'Population', in Buchanan and Walker (eds), *Province, City & People*, pp. 246–7; F. W. Boal, 'Residential segregation and mixing in a situation of ethnic and national conflict: Belfast', in Compton (ed.), *Contemporary Population*, p. 74.
3. C. W. Jefferson, 'Economy and employment', in Buchanan and Walker (eds), *Province, City & People*, pp. 206–10; see also B. Rowthorne and N. Wayne, *Northern Ireland: The Political Economy of Conflict*, Polity Press, Cambridge (1988), p. 98.
4. Jefferson, 'Economy and employment', in Buchanan and Walker (eds), *Province, City & People*, pp. 206–7.
5. *Belfast Harbour Commissioners: Reports and Accounts*, 1970–90.
6. Brett, *Housing a Divided Community*, pp. 89–90; *Brick by Brick: A Short History of the Northern Ireland Housing Executive, 1971–1991*, Northern Ireland Housing Executive, Belfast (1991), pp. 57–62.
7. See F. W. Boal, 'Belfast: the physical and social dimensions', in Buchanan and Walker (eds), *Province, City & People*, p. 143.

Further Reading

Arthur, Paul, *Government and Politics of Northern Ireland*, Longman Group, Harlow (1980)

Bardon, Jonathan, *Belfast: An Illustrated History*, Blackstaff Press, Belfast (1982)

Barton, Brian, *The Blitz: Belfast in the War Years*, Blackstaff Press, Belfast (1989)

Beckett, J. C. *et al.*, *Belfast: The Making of the City, 1800–1914*, Appletree Press, Belfast (1983)

Beckett, J. C. and Glasscock, R. E. (eds), *Belfast: The Origins and Growth of an Industrial City*, BBC, London (1967)

Benn, George, *A History of the Town of Belfast, from the Earliest Times to the Close of the Eighteenth Century*, Marcus Ward & Co., London and Belfast (1877)

Blake, J. W., *Northern Ireland in the Second World War*, HMSO, Belfast (1956)

Boyd, Andrew, *Holy War in Belfast*, 3rd edition, Pretani Press, Belfast (1987)

Brett, C. E. B., *Buildings of Belfast, 1700–1914*, revised edition, Friar's Bush Press, Belfast (1985)

—— *Housing a Divided Community*, Institute of Public Administration, Dublin (1986)

Buchanan, R. H. and Walker, B. M., *Province, City and People: Belfast and its Region*, Greystone Books, Antrim (1987)

Buckland, Patrick, *A History of Northern Ireland*, Gill & Macmillan, Dublin (1981)

—— *James Craig*, Gill & Macmillan, Dublin (1980)

Budge, Ian and O'Leary, Cornelius, *Belfast; Approach to Crisis: A Study of Belfast Politics, 1603–1970*, Macmillan, London (1973)

Chambers, George, *Faces of Change: The Belfast and Northern Ireland Chambers of Commerce and Industry, 1783–1983*, Northern Ireland Chamber of Commerce and Industry, Belfast (1983)

Coe, W. E., *The Engineering Industry of the North of Ireland*, David & Charles, Newton Abbot (1969)

Devlin, Paddy, *Yes We Have No Bananas: Outdoor Relief in Belfast, 1920–39*, Blackstaff Press, Belfast (1981)

Donne, Michael, *Pioneers of the Skies: A History of Short Brothers PLC*, Nicolson & Bass Ltd, Belfast (1987)

Farrell, Michael, *The Poor Law and the Workhouse in Belfast, 1838–1948*, Public Record Office of Northern Ireland, Belfast (1978)

Gallagher, Eric, *At Points of Need: The Story of the Belfast Central Mission, Grosvenor Hall, 1889–1989*, Blackstaff Press, Belfast (1989)

Gibbon, Peter, *The Origins of Ulster Unionism*, University Press, Manchester (1975)

Gray, John, *City in Revolt: James Larkin and the Belfast Dock Strike of 1907*, Blackstaff Press, Belfast (1985)

Gribbon, Sybil, *Edwardian Belfast: A Social Profile*, Appletree Press, Belfast (1982)

Harkness, David, *Northern Ireland since 1920*, Helicon Limited, Dublin (1983)

Holmes, R. Finlay, *Henry Cooke*, Christian Journals Limited, Belfast (1981)

Jones, Emrys, *A Social Geography of Belfast*, University Press, Oxford (1960)

Jordan, Alison, *Who Cared? : Charity in Victorian and Edwardian Belfast*, Institute of Irish Studies, Queen's University, Belfast (1992)

Kennedy, Liam and Ollerenshaw, Philip, *An Economic History of Ulster, 1820–1940*, University Press, Manchester (1985)

Larmour, Paul, *Belfast: An Illustrated Architectural Guide*, Friar's Bush Press, Belfast (1987)

Loudan, Jack, *In Search of Water, being a History of the Belfast Water Supply*, Wm Mullan, Belfast (1940)

Macaulay, Ambrose, *Patrick Dorrian, Bishop of Down and Connor 1865–85*, Irish Academic Press, Dublin (1987)

Maguire, W. A., *Living like a Lord: The second Marquis of Donegall, 1769–1844*, Appletree Press, Belfast (1983)

—— *Caught in Time: The Photographs of Alexander Hogg of Belfast, 1870–1939*, Friar's Bush Press, Belfast (1986)

Messenger, Betty, *Picking up the Linen Threads*, Blackstaff Press, Belfast (1980)

Moody, T. W. and Beckett, J. C., *Queen's Belfast, 1845–1949*, 2 vols, Faber & Faber, London (1959)

Moss, Michael and Hume, John R., *Shipbuilders to the World: 125 Years of Harland and Wolff, Belfast, 1861–1983*, Blackstaff Press, Belfast (1986)

Munck, Ronnie and Rolston, Bill, *Belfast in the Thirties: An Oral History*, Blackstaff Press, Belfast (1987)

McCaughan, Michael, *Steel Ships and Iron Men: Shipbuilding in Belfast, 1884–1912*, Friar's Bush Press, Belfast (1989)

McClelland, Aiken, *William Johnston of Ballykilbeg*, Ulster Society Publications, Lurgan (1990)

McNeilly, Norman, *Exactly Fifty Years: The Belfast Education Authority and its Work (1923–73)*, Belfast Education & Library Board, Belfast (1973)

O'Hanlon, W. M., *Walks among the Poor of Belfast, and Suggestions for their Improvement*, Belfast (1853), republished by S. R. Publishers Ltd, Wakefield (1971)

Owen, D. J., *History of Belfast*, W. & G. Baird Ltd, Belfast (1921)

—— *A Short History of the Port of Belfast*, Mayne, Boyd & Son, Belfast (1917)

Patterson, Henry, *Class Conflict and Sectarianism: The Protestant Working Class and the Belfast Labour Movement, 1868–1920*, Blackstaff Press, Belfast (1980)

Stewart, A. T. Q., *The Ulster Crisis*, Faber & Faber, London (1967)

—— *The Narrow Ground: Aspects of Ulster, 1609–1969*, Faber & Faber, London (1977)

Index

198

Montgomery, Rev. Dr Henry, 54
Morgan, J. Pierpoint, 116
Morrison, William Vitruvius, 42
mortuary, 157
Mount Vernon, 171
Mourne Mountains, 76, 148
Mulholland, Andrew, 42, 110
Mulholland, John (Baron Dunleath), 92, 110
Mulholland, Thomas, 31, 32, 33
Municipal Corporations (Ireland) Act, 1840, 41, 45, 46–7, 99
municipal elections, 44–5, 90–5, 125–6, 178–81
  register manipulated, 45–6
  1855, 49
  1868, 92
  1897, 102–3
  1920, 136
  1929, 143
  after Second World War, 178
  1949, 179
  1967, 180–1
Municipal Institute, 115
Murphy, John, 104, 125
Murray Bros, 67
Museum and Art Gallery, 148
Musgrave, Henry, 148
Musgrave Bros, 65
Musgrave Channel, 69, 117, 149, 164
Musgrave's, 139, 153, 163
Myrina, 162

Nance, Andrew, 74
National Amalgamation Union of Labour, 118
National Association of Factory Occupiers, 78
National Schools, 53–4, 80, 111
National Volunteers, 131
nationalism, 43–4, 179
Nationalist party, 99, 102, 103, 121, 128, 133
  influence in Corporation, 123
  and housing improvements, 124
  in Corporation, 125–6, 128
  electoral gains, 1920, 136
  in 1949 elections, 179
Natural History and Philosophical Society, 55
Ne Temere, 120
neolithic period, 11
Nestor, 116
Netherlands, The
  trade with, 15
Newry, 20
Newtownabbey, 169
Newtownards, 22
night watch, 40
North Belfast Mission, 114
Northern Bank, 35
Northern Cycling Club, 101(p)
Northern Ireland Housing Executive, 172, 184, 188, 189, 192
Northern Ireland Housing Trust, 171–2, 184
Northern Ireland Labour Party (NILP), 177, 178, 179, 180
Northern Ireland (NI)
  established, 131, 133–4
  Catholic opposition to, 144
Northern Ireland Parliament. *see* Stormont
Northern Ireland Polytechnic, 174
Northern Ireland Railways, 166

Northern Star, 26
Northern Whig, 40, 90, 94, 159
Northern Whig club, 26
Nutt's Corner airport, 165

oath of supremacy, 17
Oceanic, 62
Oceanic II, 64
Oceanic Steam Navigation Company, 62
O'Connell, Daniel, 45, 50, 51, 89
Official Unionists, 193
O'Hagan, Thomas, 55
O'Hanlon (minister), 40
old age pensions, 113
Olympic, 116, 117(p)
O'Neill, Brian MacPhelim, 12
O'Neill, Hugh, earl of Tyrone, 12, 13
O'Neill, Captain Terence, 181, 183
O'Neills of Clandeboye, 12
onychia, 60, 79
Ophthalmic Hospital, 85
Orange Order, 96, 111, 126
  sectarianism, 52
  parades, 89, 120, 141
  and Town Police, 90
  growth of influence, 92–3
  and politics, 92–3, 94
  and home rule, 95
  temperance, 114
  sabbatarianism, 177
Orient line, 63
Ormeau Avenue, 98
Ormeau Bridge, 74, 148
Ormeau House, 42(p)
Ormeau Park, 99, 101(p), 120(p)
Ormeau Road, 82, 84
Ormeau Ward, 178
Outdoor Relief Workers' Committee, 141

Paisley, Rev. Ian, 177, 181, 182
Parker-Morris housing standards, 171
Parkmount, 171
parks, 99–100, 101(p), 120(p)
parliament, British, 45, 47, 54, 136
  Belfast members, 41
  private Acts, 47–8, 97–9
  constituency boundaries, 92
  and home rule, 95
  House of Lords, 97, 103, 128
  enlarges local franchise, 99
  Nationalist party, 103, 125–6, 133
  franchise for, 178
  direct rule, 183, 193
  funds for social improvements, 188
parliament, Irish, 14, 23, 26, 27
parliament, Northern Ireland. *see* Stormont
Parliament Act, 1911, 128
Parliamentary Gazeteer for Ireland, 33, 35, 56
parlour houses, 72–3
Parnell, Charles Stewart, 93, 94, 95, 103
Party Processions Act, 1850, 89, 92–3, 93
Paul-Dubois, L., 117
pawnbrokers, 113
'peace line', 194
Peace People, 194
Peel, Sir Robert, 45, 54
Pepper Hill Court, 100(p)

204

numbers employed, 116
dockers' and carters' strike, 118–19, 120
First World War, 132
shorter working week demanded, 133
postwar slump, 137, 139
Second World War, 153, 155
after Second World War, 160–2
privatised, 188
shops, 112, 150, 189–90
Shore Road, 73, 74
Short & Harland, 153, 155
Short Bros & Harland, 162–3
Short Brothers, 139
Silent Valley reservoir, 148
Sinn Fein, 133, 135, 193
  poster, 134(p)
  elections, 1920, 136
Sirocco works, 65, 118, 132, 139, 153, 163
Sisters of Charity, 82
Sisters of Mercy, 82, 84
Skegoniel, 171
sleepy sickness, 146
Sligo, 47
Sloan, Thomas, 126
Smiles, Dr Samuel, 65
Smiles, W.H., 65
Smiley, Capt. J.R., 128
Smith, Sir Thomas, 12
Smithfield, 31, 40, 97
Smithfield Ward, 102, 125, 178, 179
social classes, 109–12
  on Corporation, 42–3, 136
Social Democratic and Labour Party (SDLP),
  193
socialism, 125, 133, 141
Society for Promoting the Education of the
Deaf and the Dumb
  and the Blind, 82
Solemn League and Covenant, 127, 128
Somme, battle of the, 131
Southampton, 116
Southern Cross, 161
sovereign (mayor), 14, 15, 16, 46
  and religious test, 17
  abolished, 41
Spain, trade with, 15
Special Constabulary, 135
Spencer dock, 68
spinning mills, 24, 31, 32(p), 33
sports, 150
Springfield, 114
Stormont, 135, 175(p), 178
  outdoor relief, 141
  and local authorities, 142
  Catholics ignore, 144
  and Belfast blitz, 155
  health services, 169, 175–6
  education, 172
  Labour advance in, 180
  calls in British Army, 183
  suspended, 183
Strandtown, 73, 101
Stranmillis College, 145
Stranmillis Road, 98
Strawberry Hill, 145
street improvement, 41, 48, 97–8
street lighting, 40, 47, 48

strikes
  shipyards, 1895, 105
  engineering workers, 118
  dockers and carters, 118–19, 120
  general strike, 1919, 133
  Second World War, 155
suburbs, development of, 74
Suez canal, 161
Sunday School Society, 53
'Sunday swings', 177, 180
Sunnyside Street, 84(p)
Supply, Ministry of, 154
Synod of Ulster, 53, 54

Taughmonagh, 171
Taylor, Sir Robert, 21
TB Committee, 158–9
teacher training, 145
Technical College, 111, 174
technical education, 115
television, 176
Telford, 15
temperance movements, 56, 114
Templemore, Lord, 71
Templeton, John, 55
Templeton, Robert, 55
Teutonic, 63
Thackeray, W.M., 52
theatre, 56, 83
Theatre Royal, 83(p)
Thomas, Arthur Brumwell, 121
Thompson, William, 55
Thompson graving dock, 117
Thomson, Professor James, 99
Throne group, Whitehouse, 85
Titanic, 116, 117(p)
tobacco industry, 15, 67, 139
Toc H, 146
tonic water, 66
Topping, William, 154
Town Book, 15
Town Council. *see* Belfast Corporation
Town Dock, 36
Town Hall, 97, 98(p)
  UVF HQ, 128
Townhall Street, 97
trade, 15, 27, 190
  18th c. growth, 20–1
  value of, 34
  19th c., 34–5, 68–9
  decline in, 137–9
  after Second World War, 164–5
trade unions, 104–5, 111, 118–21, 162
  industrial relations, 118–21, 132–3, 155
Trades Union Congress (TUC), 104
tramways, 74, 122–3, 165
  tracklaying, 124(p)
Tramways Committee, 165
transport. *see* public transport
Transport and General Workers Union, 118
Transport Department, 148
Trinity College, Dublin, 54
trolleybuses, 165
Troubles, 181–3
  effects of, 172, 187–94
tuberculosis, 77, 123, 147
Tuberculosis Authority, 174–5